Beyond Possible

Nirmal ('Nims') Purja MBE was born in Nepal.
He served as a Gurkha and in the elite Special Boat
Service (SBS) before leaving to concentrate on his
passion for mountaineering and exploration.

Beyond Possible

One Soldier, Fourteen Peaks –
My Life in the Death Zone

NIMSDAI PURJA

HODDER

First published in Great Britain in 2022 by Hodder & Stoughton
An Hachette UK company

This paperback edition published in 2022

1

A CIP catalogue record for this title is available from the British Library

Paperback ISBN 9781529312263
eBook ISBN 9781529312270

Typeset in Sabon MT by Hewer Text UK Ltd, Edinburgh
Printed and bound in Great Britain by Clays Ltd, Elcograf S.p.A.

Hodder & Stoughton policy is to use papers that are natural, renewable
and recyclable products and made from wood grown in sustainable
forests. The logging and manufacturing processes are expected to
conform to the environmental regulations of the country of origin.

Hodder & Stoughton Ltd
Carmelite House
50 Victoria Embankment
London EC4Y 0DZ

www.hodder.co.uk

To my mother, Purna Kumari Purja, for working so hard to allow me to live my dreams, and to the climbing community of Nepal, home of the 8000ers.

Your extremes are my normality.

Contents

1

Death or Glory

Dateline: 3 July 2019

The world slipped out from beneath me as I skidded head-first across the side of Nanga Parbat's slushy, snowy face. Ten, twenty, thirty metres seemed to rush by in a blur.

Was I tumbling to my death?

Only seconds earlier I'd felt secure, leaning hard into the steep slope and buffeting winds with a fairly steady footing. Then my grip had sheared away, the teeth of my crampons were unable to chew into the white as I plummeted downwards, slowly at first, then quicker, much quicker, building speed with every second, my brain calculating the moments until I'd sail away from the mountain for ever, my body scattered across the jagged rocks somewhere below, or smashed into a deep crevasse.

Brother, you don't have long to un-fuck this.

If I died, there would be no one else to blame for such a bloody end. *I'd* chosen to climb the world's ninth highest mountain in brutal, whiteout conditions. *I'd* decided to smash all fourteen 'Death Zone' mountains in only seven months during a wild, record-breaking attempt; every climb peaking at over 8,000 metres, an altitude where the air becomes so thin that the

1

brain and body wither and fail. And *I'd* decided to let go of a fixed rope during my descent, in what was a friendly gesture to allow another climber to pass as he made his way nervously down the mountain. But having taken one, two, three steps forwards, the snow had jolted awkwardly, sloughing away, collapsing in on itself and sucking me down with it.

I was out of control and the two rules I'd set previously for myself on expeditions were being tested under extreme pressure. One: *Hope was God*. Two: *The little things counted most on the big mountains*. By stepping away from the rope, I'd already forgotten Rule Two, which was my mistake, my problem.

So now I had only Rule One to fall back on.

Was I scared of dying in those brief seconds? *No way*. I'd have taken death over cowardice any time, especially if it arrived in an attempt to push myself beyond what was considered humanly achievable. Testing the limits of physical endeavour was exactly my hope in 2018 after announcing a plan to crush the previous best time for climbing the fourteen Death Zone peaks, where the benchmark had been set by a Korean mountaineer, Kim Chang-ho, in 2013 – he'd finished the job in seven years, ten months and six days. A Polish climber called Jerzy Kukuczka had done the job in a similarly impressive time of seven years, eleven months and fourteen days.

Aiming to shave away so much time seemed ballsy, even superhuman, but I'd believed in myself enough to quit my position with the British military, where I'd served as a Gurkha soldier for several years before joining the Special Boat Service (SBS) – a wing of the Special Forces and an elite collective of soldiers operating in some of the most lethal battlefields on earth. Walking out on such a prestigious career had felt risky, but I was prepared to gamble everything for my ambition.

Self-belief had shoved me forwards and I treated the challenge like a military mission. During the planning phase, I'd even named my world-record-breaking attempt 'Project Possible' and the title later came to feel like a two-fingered salute towards the people that wouldn't, or couldn't, believe in my dream. There were plenty of them; the doubters appeared from everywhere, though even the more supportive voices sounded a little sceptical at times. In 2019, the Red Bull website claimed my goal was similar to 'swimming to the moon'. I knew differently. I hadn't been delivered into this world for defeat. Quitting wasn't in my blood, even in a near-death crisis. I wasn't a sheep waiting to be prodded by the shepherd; I was a lion and I refused to walk and talk with the rest.

When judged against the expertise of a lot of high-altitude mountaineers, I probably seemed fairly green. I'd started operating above 8,000 metres only a few years previously, but I'd quickly become a beast at high altitude and much of that, I believed, had to do with my freakish physiology. Once I'd started climbing into the Death Zone, I found it relatively easy to move quickly at great heights, taking seventy steps before pausing for breath, whereas other mountaineers were only able to make four or five.

My powers of recovery were also impressive. I often descended from peaks at speed, partying through the night in base camps and moving onto my next expedition the following morning, hangover or no hangover. This was mountaineering, *Nims-style*: the relentless pursuit of excellence under brutal conditions. Nothing could hold me back, no matter the circumstances.

Apart from death or serious injury, that is.

Another thirty or forty metres had raced by. As I fell, I had to find focus. Focus on my movement and increasing velocity;

focus on the people fading into the clouds above me as I slipped further and further away. And focus on the techniques I needed to make an important self-arrest. *Could I use my ice axe, digging it into the mountain to slow my fall?* Yanking my axe underneath me, I held onto the head firmly, jamming the pick into the snow, but the drifts beneath were too soft, so I pushed again. Nothing. *No hold.*

Any confidence I'd briefly felt in my ability to solve the problem was diminishing fast. My descent had increased in pace and I'd lost all control, when . . . *there!* Through the spray I'd spotted the fixed rope we'd been using to descend moments earlier. If I could reach for it with enough aggression, there was every chance I might be able to hang on. This was my last hope, and so I twisted, sticking out my arm and making a grab for the cord . . . *Contact!* Gripping hard, my palms burning, I pulled myself to a stop.

The world seemed to suck in a deep, settling breath. *Was I OK?* By the looks of it, yeah, though my legs were certainly wobbling with the adrenaline. My heart was banging hard, too.

You're good, bro, I thought. *There's no need to stress now.*

Taking a second or two to reset, I rose to my feet and switched into a new rhythm, finding a more cautious stride. 'Bombproof these next few steps and move carefully . . .'

To the guys on the line above, I must have looked unflappable. It was as if I'd already returned to a regular operational setting, working as though nothing out of the ordinary was happening, but the fall had rattled me. My confidence had taken a slight dent, so I gripped the rope tightly and double-checked each and every footfall until my self-belief returned. There was now a different mindset in play. As I planted my boots in the shifting snow, I told myself that death was going to come for me at some point – maybe on a mountain during Project Possible, maybe in old age, decades down the line – but not on Nanga Parbat, and not within the next heartbeat.

Not today.

Not today.

But when?

And would I finish what I'd started?

2

Hope Is God

I'd been inspired to scale all fourteen of the world's biggest peaks at a crazy speed and hoped to top the Nepalese epics of Annapurna, Dhaulagiri, Kanchenjunga, Everest, Lhotse, Makalu and Manaslu; to race up Nanga Parbat, Gasherbrum I and II, K2 and Broad Peak in Pakistan; and finally, to conquer Tibet's intimidating 8,000-ers – Cho Oyu (which was also accessed from Nepal) and Shishapangma. *But why?* These were some of the most inhospitable places on the planet and a challenge of that kind, one with a deadline of only half a year or so, might have sounded like madness to most people. But to me it presented an opportunity to prove to the world that everything, *anything,* was possible if an individual dedicated their heart and mind to a plan.

Who cared how dangerous it was?

The adventure had first started with Mount Everest, the world's tallest peak and an epic Himalayan monument within my homeland. To people outside the small, landlocked country of Nepal, Everest carries a near mythical quality. But as a kid, it had felt like a distant entity. My family was poor; the trek from where we lived to Everest and back was expensive, even for locals, and the journey took around twelve days. It also required a traveller to stay overnight in a series of teahouses – small hotels in the villages that lined the route – and so I never experienced the adventure.

Once I moved to England in 2003, as a young Gurkha soldier serving with the British Armed Forces, people always asked the same question: 'So what's Everest like?' Mates unfamiliar with Nepal's geography imagined that the mountain had probably loomed majestically outside my back garden. They looked unimpressed when I admitted I'd not even seen Base Camp, let alone climbed above it. My strength as a fighter was questioned afterwards.

'It's on your doorstep, mate, and you haven't bothered? *And we thought Gurkhas were tough . . .*'

After ten years, the joking and sniping finally got to me.

OK. I'll start climbing. It's time.

I took my first steps towards the highest place on earth in December 2012, when I made the trek to the foot of Everest's intimidating peak at the age of twenty-nine years old. By that point I had progressed from the Gurkha regiment and into the military elite, and through a mate, I'd been connected with the famous Nepalese mountaineer Dorje Khatri, who offered to guide me to Base Camp on a trek that was set to last several days. Dorje had scaled Everest several times and was a champion for the Sherpa* guide: he defended their rights and campaigned for better pay, but he was also a climate-change activist and tried to alter the way everybody viewed the Himalayas' fragile ecosystem.

I couldn't think of a better person with whom to make the journey. But having stared up at Everest's peak as it loomed

* The name Sherpa means two things: (1) it's an indigenous group from Nepal, but (2) it's also slang or a catch-all term for the Himalayan mountain guide, as used by foreign explorers.

8,848 metres above us, I decided that trekking wasn't enough and I couldn't care less about the risks. It was time to go higher.

After a fair amount of persuasion, I convinced Dorje to teach me some of the skills I'd need to climb an 8,000-er. At first, I begged him to let me attempt Ama Dablam, a nearby peak that towered 6,812 metres above sea level, but Dorje laughed off my idea.

'Nims, that is a very technical mountain,' he said. 'People who have climbed Everest even struggle to get to the top.'

Instead we travelled to the nearby peak, Lobuche East, picking up some rental equipment in a nearby village before trekking to the summit. The work was slow, but steady, and under Dorje's tutelage, I pulled on a pair of crampons for the very first time, walking across a grass slope and feeling the bite of their steel points in the turf. The sensation was weird, but it gave me an idea of what I might experience during a proper mountain ascent and as we slowly worked our way to the top, into the nipping cold and powerful winds, I felt the expedition buzz for the very first time.

Each step caused me to pause and overthink – every now and then I'd experience a surge of fear; sometimes falling to my death seemed like a very real possibility. But having wasted so much energy stressing, I eventually located the confidence to stride forward purposefully, without anxiety.

Once at the summit, I was blown away by the view around me: the jagged Himalayan vista had been shrouded by a blanket of cloud, but here and there, a peak poked through the grey mist. I felt my adrenaline soaring as Dorje pointed to Everest, Lhotse and Makalu. A sense of pride washed over me, but there was a feeling of anticipation as well. I'd already decided to climb those three peaks in the distance, even though I could be considered a late starter in high-altitude mountaineering terms.

I wanted more. Around that time, I'd caught wind of some exciting intel: in 2015, the Brigade of Gurkhas – the collective term for Nepal's Gurkha fighting forces – were marking two centuries of service with the British military in a celebration called the G200. A series of prestigious events were being arranged, among them a memorial service at the Gurkha statue in London, a reception at the Houses of Parliament and a Field of Remembrance at the Royal Albert Hall. But buried within the packed cultural programme was mention of an expedition to Everest.

The Gurkhas had previously built a reputation as being sturdy climbers, but because of the high turnover of war and the regiment's recent deployments in Afghanistan and Iraq, no serving Gurkha soldier had ever made it to the top. (It was also really expensive for Nepalese people to climb Everest, even with some of the discounts afforded to local residents.) That was all set to change when an ambitious plan was announced to take a dozen or so Gurkhas to Everest's peak, via the South Col route, as part of the bi-centennial celebrations.

The mission, called the G200 Expedition (G200E), was set to be both challenging and history-making. Even better, as a serving Gurkha in the UK Special Forces, I was eligible to climb. I was proud of the regiment, I'd do anything to further their standing, and this felt like an honourable cause.

I sharpened my skills and increased my ambition. An advantage of being part of the British military was that I had access to a variety of highly specialised courses. I applied for one which taught soldiers the art of extreme cold-weather warfare until I was able to become a part of that unique cadre of mountain warfare specialists. Then I climbed Denali, the highest peak in the USA and one of the Seven Summits, a group featuring the highest mountain on each continent comprising Denali, plus Everest (Asia), Elbrus (Europe), Kilimanjaro (Africa), Vinson (Antarctica), Aconcagua (South America), and Carstensz Pyramid (Oceania).

A 6,190-metres climb, Denali was no joke. Isolated and brutally cold, the temperatures there sometimes dropped to -50°C, which was a serious problem for the novice climber like me, but Denali was also the perfect training ground. I learned rope skills and put my Special Forces-forged endurance to good use, dragging my sleigh through the thick snow for hours on end, taking care not to fall into one of the many crevasses on the mountain.

Then in 2014, I climbed my first Death Zone peak. Dhaulagiri was a beast. Nicknamed the White Mountain, because of the deep powder smothering its steep and intimidating inclines, it was also regarded as one of the most dangerous expeditions in the world, thanks to a terrifying kill rate. At the time, over eighty climbers had died there and its South Face was yet to be scaled, even though the likes of Reinhold Messner, the first mountaineer to climb Everest solo, had attempted what was an apparently impenetrable route.

Its biggest danger was the risk of avalanches, which erupted from nowhere, sucking everybody and everything away in their path. In 1969, five Americans and two Sherpas were swiped from the mountain. Six years later, six members of a Japanese expedition were killed when a wall of snow buried them alive. Dhaulagiri wasn't an adventure to be taken lightly, especially for a climber with only eighteen months' experience and limited knowledge of the gnarly conditions found on extreme peaks. But eager to improve my climbing skills whenever I was granted leave from fighting in Afghanistan, I decided I was going up.

A brother from the Special Air Service (SAS), a wing of the British Special Forces – let's call him James for the purposes of secrecy – accompanied me for the trip. Neither of us looked the part, having arrived in Base Camp wearing flip-flops, shorts and Ray-Ban sunglasses. Our arrival was also poorly timed. We were joining up with a larger expedition who had been acclimatising to the conditions and thin air for a month. An avalanche in the Khumbu Icefall had curtailed their trip to Everest and so they'd moved across to Dhaulagiri to climb there instead.

The pair of us were behind schedule because of our limited leave with the military, so there was no way for us to enjoy the usual procedures afforded to mountaineers hoping to function at high altitude, such as acclimatisation rotations.* Meanwhile, our climbing buddies looked to be the real deal, having already arrived in the region and settled in, and when we all set off for the trek to Base Camp, we soon fell behind. James was really struggling with the altitude. It took us three days longer than the others to complete the journey.

'What do you guys do?' asked one bloke later. He'd taken an interest in our appearance when we'd first arrived. I knew what he was thinking. Either we were fearless mavericks, or loose cannons to be avoided at all costs during a sketchy summit push.

I shrugged. There was no way either of us was about to reveal our full military roles, especially as we were bound to certain levels of secrecy. Also, both of us liked the idea of being

---

* Mountaineers usually spend a couple of months on 8,000-metre peaks. Over a space of weeks, climbers move from Base Camp to Camp 1 to get used to the debilitating effects of high altitude. They then move between Camps 1, 2 and 3, climbing high in the day and sleeping low, until the symptoms of acute mountain sickness (AMS), such as nausea, breathlessness and banging headaches, have subsided. These climbs are called 'acclimatisation rotations'. Once settled at high altitude, they wait patiently, sometimes for weeks on end, until a suitable summit window opens up, when the weather is considered good enough to climb. Then they'll push on to the peak.

judged on any mountaineering skills we might have possessed, rather than our elite combat expertise.

'Oh, we're in the military,' I said eventually, hoping for an end to the questions.

The climber raised an eyebrow quizzically. Our travelling kit looked fairly piecemeal, although the climbing equipment James and I had brought along was of high quality. Even so, our expedition mates wrote us off as clueless tourists. I suppose the assumption was half-right, but I wasn't going to let anyone pick holes in my weaknesses, and at Base Camp we prepared enthusiastically for our first acclimatisation rotations. Over the coming week, our plan was to climb daily to Camps 1 and 2 of four outposts that lined the route to the peak. We'd then sleep lower down the mountain, until we felt ready for our summit push.

As soon as we'd kitted up and begun our first acclimatisation ascent, it was clear that James didn't possess the same physiology as me. It had first become apparent on our base-camp trek, but once we started the serious business of climbing on our first rotation to Camp 1, he was unable to maintain the pace as I pushed ahead. Altitude sickness was breaking him up and I realised he was struggling once we'd stopped to rest at Camp 1 during our first rotation.

As I surged onwards the next day, James fell behind again, even though a Sherpa was helping him with most of his equipment and I'd been lugging around thirty kilos on my own. Not that I could afford to be cocky. Before too long, I'd also blown myself out. In a rush of madness, I'd wanted to show off my speed, but I pushed too far ahead, and as I rested at Camp 1 for a couple of hours, brewing a cup of hot tea, my small party yet to arrive, a horrible thought struck me.

Was James still alive?

As well as regularly trembling with avalanches, Dhaulagiri

was known for its deep crevasses. Unseen, there was every chance James and his Sherpa might have tumbled into one. If that was the case, it was unlikely they'd be discovered for days, if at all. In a slight panic, I packed up my pot and cup and headed down towards Base Camp to find them. (I'd learned very early on not to leave my kit anywhere on the mountain; it was best to keep everything with me at all times, just in case.)

It didn't take long. Two people were moving slowly below me. It soon turned out to be my climbing party, but James was in a worse state than before.

'This is a big mountain, brother,' I said, having greeted them. 'You're struggling with acclimatisation, let me take that back-pack for you.'

I reached out to lighten his load, but James seemed hesitant. He didn't want to give in to pain, but I was insistent. When fighting through warzones with the Special Forces, an attitude of that kind would have been considered commendable. On a mountain as dangerous as Dhaulagiri, it was an act of suicide.

'Listen, forget your ego,' I said. 'If you want to summit, let me help you.'

James relented. Slowly but steadily, we worked our way back up to Camp 1, but the work had taken its toll on me, too. I'd overreached and the mountains were delivering their first major lesson: *Never burn yourself out unnecessarily*. From then on, I promised not to waste vital energy; I would work hard only when I needed to. When the time arrived to make my first-ever 8,000-metre summit push a few days later, I made sure to hang at the back of the leading group as we snaked our way from Base Camp to the peak of Dhaulagiri, partly out of respect for the several Sherpas leading us to the top, but also because I'd never climbed such a huge mountain before and I didn't want to experience another energy slump.

That's when I noticed the ever-changing work of the guides within an expedition party. Every now and then, the leading Sherpa would take a break from making a path through the waist-high drifts with his footsteps, allowing one of his teammates to take over for a while. He would then fall to the back of the line until it was his turn to head the charge once more, while the rest of us matched his prints in the snow, which made for fairly easy work. This was a technique I would come to know as trailblazing and with his selfless industry, the lead Sherpa was helping the expedition party to follow a much smoother route upwards. I respected the effort that every guide was making.

When it came to trailblazing, there were two techniques to learn.* The first was applicable to shin- to knee-deep snow: in those conditions a climber had to make footfalls by lifting their knee to their chest with every step, then planting their foot firmly. The second was for more extreme conditions when the powder was thigh- or waist-high. In those cases, the leading individual had to push forward with their hips, creating a pocket of space before lifting their leg out and rolling the hip over in order to make the next step.

Suddenly, a bloke in front of me stepped out of the line and started his way to the front of the pack to help.

I shouted up at him. 'Hey, bro! What are you doing? The Sherpas aren't going to get upset, are they?'

---

* I also learned about the different styles of climbing. On Dhaulagiri we worked with a fixing team, who set ropes to the mountain with anchors. The climbers used those lines to pull themselves to the top on steep inclines and sheer faces. Alpine-style climbing involved a team moving quickly over the terrain, while roped together for safety. If one of the group slipped or fell, the others braced hard in order to stop them from tumbling too far. Finally solo climbing, as far as I was concerned, required a mountaineer to work towards a peak alone, while trailblazing and climbing on his own path.

He waved me away. 'No man, I'm doing my bit, helping the Sherpa brothers . . .'

I'd assumed that leading the group in such a way was disrespectful to the expedition guides; it looked as if someone else was trying to play the hero, which I'd previously believed was a dangerous step on such a risky mountain. It turned out I was wrong and another Sherpa soon put my mind at rest.

'Nims, the snow is so deep. If you have the energy and can help out up front too, please do . . .'

Encouraged, I later took the lead and drove forwards. My legs lifted and pushed like pistons as I lifted my feet out of the powder. The work was huge, but by regarding every forward step as a sign of significant progress, and part of some greater team effort, I was able to move steadily. My thighs and calves ached with the endeavour, but my lungs were light. The fatigue that hindered even the most athletic individuals at altitude didn't seem to be striking me down. I was strong. *Boom! Boom! Boom!* Every step arrived with power. When I turned back to see how far I'd come, I was shocked to notice the rest of my climbing party. They were little black dots below.

Wow, this is my *shit,* I thought, admiring the deep footfalls I'd left for the expedition. I'd been working without too much thought, operating in the flow state that athletes mention whenever they break world records, or win championships. *I was in the zone.*

Cautious not to overextend myself like before, I worked my way slowly to the next ridgeline, waiting an hour until the remainder of the group had caught up. When they later gathered around me, the lead Sherpa guide shouted excitedly and slapped me on the back. Other blokes in the expedition, climbers who had looked down on me a few days earlier having written off my chances of summiting, were now shaking my hand.

Everyone seemed relieved that I'd put in some serious legwork and my industry totally changed the attitude of everyone within the team. *I wasn't a tourist any more.* My mindset had shifted, too. By the time I reached the peak, having trailblazed over 70 per cent of the route, I was not only surprised at what I'd achieved, but emboldened.

'Brother,' I thought. 'You're a badass at high altitude.'

* * *

I hadn't been primed genetically for any success in the Death Zone and climbing certainly wasn't a facet of my family life. When I was a kid, I wanted to be one of two things. My first option: to serve as a Gurkha soldier, like my dad, because around the world they were considered to be an utterly fearless military force. As a fighting unit, they had been spread historically between the Nepalese, British and Indian armies, as well as the Singapore police; although everybody within their ranks originated in Nepal, and was considered to be an elite fighter, big on heart and loyalty, with an unswerving belief in Queen and country.

Enough history books have been written about their inception, should you want to go there, but here's the briefest of backstories. During the Anglo–Nepalese War (1814–16) between Nepal, then known as the Gorkha Kingdom, and the British East India Company (or EIC, a private army, which was double the size of the regular British Army), the skills of the Nepali fighters were so admired that any defectors turning to the EIC for work following a treaty agreement were employed as 'irregular forces'.

The Gurkhas later became a highly respected regiment in their own right, and were deployed in the Second World War, as well as Iraq and Afghanistan during the War on Terror. Two of my older brothers, Ganga and Kamal, had followed the same path as Dad, and whenever they returned to Nepal on leave, people looked at them in awe as if they were rock stars. The Gurkha soldier was legendary and their motto, *Better to Die Than to Be a Coward*, conjured up images of heroism. That was only enhanced by stories of successful war missions and against-all-odds adventure.

My second career ambition was to be a government official – but I wanted to be Nepal's version of Robin Hood, stealing from the rich and giving to the poor. The country I grew up in was very small and the man on the street had been disenfranchised for too long; even as a kid I understood that the people around me had very little and the poverty rates were incredibly high there. Many Nepalese citizens were Hindus and despite their lack of wealth they would often give their money to the temple whenever they visited.

Not me. If I ever had money, I was happier emptying my wallet to the person in the street, the homeless, the blind and the disabled outside the temple. I'd do the same on a bus, where buskers would often play, unable to work because a terrible injury or a debilitating illness had left them incapacitated.

Every donation arrived with a contract: *This is for you, brother, but don't spend it on alcohol. Make sure your family gets the food it needs.* I've always been that way. Money never attracted me, but as a kid, I dreamed of taking a job in authority, one with a uniform. Not because I wanted power or status, but because I liked the idea of draining money from Nepal's super-rich, especially those who were corrupt as fuck anyway, before handing the spoils down to the people with nothing.

This attitude probably isn't surprising, seeing as I was broke from the beginning, born on 25 July 1983 in a village called

Dana, in the Myagdi district in western Nepal. The small outpost is positioned around 1,600 metres above sea level, so it wasn't as if I'd been raised with crampons attached to my feet and a physiological connection to high altitude. Dhaulagiri was the biggest mountain in that region, but it was still a long way from my front door and it would have required some serious effort to get there.

There was a gap of around eighteen years between myself and my older brothers, Ganga, Jit and Kamal and was followed by my younger sister, Anita. We were a loving family; we didn't have any money and the thought of running a car was unimaginable, but I was a happy kid. It didn't take a lot to keep me amused.

By all accounts, Mum and Dad had been up against it from long before I was born. Their problems first began after they married from different castes, or classes. It wasn't the done thing in Nepal and their families became resentful of the union. They were soon cut adrift from their parents and siblings, which meant they had to start their new lives together with next to nothing.

Dad was serving with the Indian Gurkha regiment at the time, but his salary alone wasn't enough to support the family, so when Ganga, Jit and Kamal were born, Mum started working on the village farm for money. Most of the time, at least one of the kids was strapped to her back in a cloth. The workload of caring for a young family while bringing money home through hard labour must have been exhausting, but she didn't quit, and a lot of my work ethic came from my mother – she was a huge influence on me, as she was for a lot of people who would go on to meet her.

Mum had not been educated, which must have annoyed her, because she would develop a vision for how to help other women in the area and eventually became an activist in Nepal, where she worked to change the attitudes towards gender and education. This wasn't the norm in Nepal back then, but Mum fought for what she believed in and most weeks she earned barely enough to put food on the table. The family still survived, though. Later, once my brothers were old enough, they were put to work too, and it would be their job to wake at 5 a.m., before walking for two hours to find and cut grass for the family's three buffaloes. They then travelled to school for a full day of classes.

I had it a little easier. Our garden held several orange trees and once the fruit had ripened in autumn, I'd climb into the branches and shake the limbs until they were empty. The ground was soon covered in fruit and I'd eat my way through the lot until I was full. The following day, I'd scoop up more spoils and repeat the feast. But when I was four years old, the family moved to another village in the jungle called Ramnagar, which was located in Chitwan, 227 kilometres away from Dana, and set in the hottest and flattest part of the country. My parents had become worried about the number of landslides that threatened Dana, where several fast-flowing rivers had the tendency to flood and wreak havoc.

Not that I cared about the relocation. With the jungle on our doorstep, Mum would go into the undergrowth to grab wood for the fire, while I had plenty of trouble to find: on the streets, in the woods, by the water – the potential for exploration was huge.

From an early age I'd learned it was fairly easy for me to thrive emotionally on the bare minimum, which might go some way to explaining how I was later able to live most of my life within the chaos of combat, or in a tent pinned to the side of a mountain. My mum was very strict, but on weekends, when I wasn't at school, she was happy for me to explore Ramnagar alone. Most of the time I headed for the nearby river, hanging out on the banks from 10 a.m. to 5 p.m., killing hours by hunting for crabs and prawns. I was happiest in nature; adventure seemed to be everywhere, though Mum often turned her nose up whenever I proudly brought back my catch for her to examine.

'Why have you brought me insects?' she'd complain.

Life would soon improve. When my brothers went off to join the Gurkhas, they explained that it was their hope to help me towards a better life. Every month, a chunk of their wages was sent home, a gift to fund my education at Small Heaven Higher Secondary – an English-speaking boarding school in Chitwan – and once I was around five years old, I was packed away. This was a serious luxury, though it wasn't finite, and Mum often mentioned the temporary nature of my brothers' generosity.

'One day they are going to be married,' she would say. 'They'll have families of their own to look after and they won't be able to support your education any more.'

But even as a young kid, I already had a plan in mind to support the family. 'Look, it's fine,' I told Mum, attempting to shrug off any pressure. 'I'll pass my exams when I'm older and then I'll become a teacher at the school, or even a nursery. Then I'll be able to look after *you*.'

But really, I wanted to be a Gurkha.

I certainly possessed the minerals to cut it in the military. Despite the fact that I was only five years old when I first started at boarding school, the rhythm of a life away from home seemed to suit me. Everybody slept in a hostel, where the older kids held the power and the teachers beat the children if they ever stepped out of line. It was my first challenge, I had to learn how to survive in such a tough environment – and quickly.

As I grew older, negotiating the daily battle in the playground became a tricky experience. Sure, I was tough for my age, but there were plenty of older kids to deal with and if ever Mum came to visit and brought food or supplies with her, one of the senior school bullies often came knocking once she'd returned home. Sometimes my food was snatched away and there was nothing I could do about it.

My first survival instinct was to run off, sprinting into the trees before anyone had the chance to rob me. I was fast; I showed plenty of stamina and enjoyed myself during track and field events in PE. But my second survival instinct when dealing with the school bullies was to fight back. As I developed and matured, I became stronger, much stronger, and once my teens had arrived, I decided to take up kickboxing. I soon learned how to defend myself, breaking down competitors until I made it to the status of regional champ.

By the time I was entered into year nine at school, I'd suffered only one defeat, to Nepal's national champion, and he was several years older than me. Whenever a school bully came for my food supplies, I stood up to the threats, and then smashed him. Very few kids challenged me after that. Kickboxing had been my first step towards becoming a man.

My next was to apply for the Gurkhas.

3

Better to Die Than to Be a Coward

I was the human antibiotic.

Around the age of ten I contracted tuberculosis, which was a serious and worryingly common disease in Nepal, but I fought it off. Later on in life, I was diagnosed with asthma. When the doctor explained some of the long-term impacts it might cause, I thought, *Yeah, no problem*. Nothing was going to stop me from living my life and I was able to shake it away, later running through the woods and over long distances in school races for fun.

From an early age, I believed in the power of positive thinking; I didn't allow myself to become poleaxed by illnesses, or chronic ailments that carried the potential to afflict other individuals for years. I felt like a human antibiotic because I'd taught myself to think that way: I trusted myself to heal. *I believed*. And the same attitude eventually powered me into the British military, where I had next-level resilience under pressure. It surrounded me like a force field and I soon learned that if a warrior had relentless self-belief, anything was possible. I'd need every ounce of it once installed into the Gurkhas.

The Selection process each candidate had to pass in order to join the regiment was notoriously brutal and unforgiving from the very beginning, and I'd heard all the stories from my brothers. Before anyone was even entered into Gurkha training, every applicant between the ages of seventeen and twenty-one years of age was pushed through a thorough physical and mental assessment. For example, any kid with more than four fillings was given the boot. False teeth, or even overly large gaps in the mouth, were grounds for rejection, and brains were equally as important as physical superiority.

I'd needed to pass my Nepalese School Leaving Certificate, which educationally fell somewhere between GCSEs and A-levels in Britain, though I managed that thanks to the schooling provided for me. When my time came to try out for the regiment in 2001, a retired British Gurkha – assessors were then known as Galla Wallahs – looked me over in the village. My entire body was checked; any scars would have seen me rejected, though fortunately I'd avoided picking up any nasty kickboxing injuries. But in the end, I was failed. Why exactly, I'm not sure – I passed all the physical and education assessments – though my hunch is that the assessor had taken a bit of a disliking to me.

While I was one of only eighteen applicants to have passed the physical tests, the Galla Wallah ranked me in twenty-sixth place on the final candidate list. Only twenty-five individuals were accepted into the next phase of Gurkha Selection that year and the rejection was infuriating. Demoralised, I railed against the unfairness of it all and for a little while I considered giving up on my dream of joining the regiment.

In the end, I moved past my disappointment, though I was still grumpy about it, and I was eventually successful on my second attempt a year later, quickly moving on to the next stage, Regional Selection, where I grunted my way through a series of push-ups, sit-ups and heaves before taking an English and Maths test. I was then ushered into the third and final phase, Central Selection, where the work was set to get much harder.

One of the more famous tests in the Gurkha's Central Selection phase was the Doko Race, in which applicants were ordered to carry bamboo baskets on their head. At that time, each one was filled with thirty kilos of sand and every potential Gurkha had to complete an uphill circuit of five kilometres in under forty-eight minutes.

The running part I wasn't so bothered about. My enthusiasm for track and field had developed into something more serious: as a year seven student, I'd helped teachers to organise a series of trials for the older kids who were hoping to represent the boarding school in regional championships. All the athletes involved were much older than me, probably by two or three years, and it was my job to outline the track with a white marker, but when the 400 metres race started, I joined in for fun. At the first turn I was near the front of the pack, but on the second I felt unstoppable and burst ahead of the frontrunners, crossing the line in first place.

My teacher grabbed me by the arm. He imagined that somehow I'd joined in mid-race as a prank.

'Purja, where did you come from? Is this a joke?'

'No, sir,' I said, nervously. 'I started with the others . . . Ask them!'

When it was confirmed that, yeah, I'd raced the other kids, fair and square, the school was left with very little choice. They'd have to thrust a year-seven pupil into a regional competition usually dominated by boys from year ten.

'Despite your age, we're putting you up,' said my teacher.

I was unfazed by the pressure, but completely naive as to

what was expected of me, or how to prepare. Even so, when it came to the inter-boarding-school championships, in which I was running the 4x400 metres relay, 800 metres, 2,400 metres and 5,000 metres races, I felt ready. I'd decided to race barefoot, because I believed that running shoes or spikes might weigh me down, and my only tactical thought was to 'hang back for the first half of the race . . . then go!' But having stuck to that one idea, I took first place in both the 800 metres and 2,400 metres events. I led my school to victory in the 4x400 metres relay, too. What must have felt like a major gamble on my school's part had reaped rewards.

Because I was a more-than-capable athlete, that element of the Doko Race wasn't likely to be a problem, but the bamboo basket loaded up with sand was a challenge to which I'd have to adapt, though I'd experienced some background training at least. For some reason, I'd previously taken an unorthodox approach to race preparation at school and would often sneak away from the hostel at four a.m. to run through the nearby streets, increasing the physical effort by slipping some metal rods I'd found lying around the place into an elasticated support bandage, which I then strapped to my legs. When the sun came up, I crept back to bed before anyone noticed. Hopefully that hard work would now pay off.

I was also helped by the fact that both my brothers had endured the same gruelling exam and knew what to expect. Kamal was on leave shortly before my assessment, which was taking place again in Pokhara, while Ganga, who had retired from the military in 2002, was also there. They joined me for a couple of days and together we formulated a plan.

'OK, Nirmal, we're going to have to intensify your preparation,' said Kamal one afternoon, handing me a bamboo basket. He then dropped a heavy rock into it. My arms buckled a little under the load. 'Now, get used to that weight for a bit and let's run.'

We moved over the rough terrain of Pokhara, along the river and down steep paths, the basket on my head feeling like a ten-ton weight. The pain bit into my neck, back and calves. When we finally came to a stop, Kamal looked down at his watch. A frown creased his brow.

'An hour, Nirmal. You're not going to pass with a performance like that. We'll go again tomorrow.'

The following day, I was faster, bringing my time down to fifty-five minutes. A day later, I sped along the course, completing five kilometres in just under the required time of forty-eight minutes. I was going to be fine. But when I eventually joined a Doko Race that included a large group of teens also hoping to pass through the same Central Selection as me, I looked across the line and worried a little. By all accounts, a number of them had paid a local athletics company to prepare their bodies with an intense training programme. They seemed set for qualification, some of them even had new trainers and fearsome military-style haircuts.

I needn't have stressed. Finishing the race among the leading pack, I knew I had it within me to join the bravest military force in the world.

* * *

All the push-ups during the final physical assessments couldn't break me. The trials involving pull-ups, sit-ups, sprints, cross-country runs or bleep tests were passed with ease – I even came first in a race held over a mile and a half. I was impervious to the mental stresses of an English or Maths test until, finally, I had been accepted as a part of the British Army and soon became a member of the Queen's Gurkha Engineers. Within two weeks of passing Central Selection, I flew to England where I joined with the Gurkha Training Company at the Infantry Training Centre in Catterick, Yorkshire. I had never been abroad, let alone as far away as England, but the thought of integrating into such a different culture was sure to be a relatively straightforward challenge, or so I assumed.

'No *bother,*' I thought. '*I've been to boarding school. My English is the shit. I'll be fine.*'

Upon arriving in January 2003, I was shocked. When our plane landed at Heathrow, it was cold. I assumed that the coach would drive us through central London on a mini sightseeing tour, where I might catch glimpses of all the famous landmarks, such as Big Ben, St Paul's Cathedral and Buckingham Palace. Instead we hit the motorway and having reached the north of England, via a scenic route comprising sheep, hills and the occasional service station, my confidence at settling into the local culture quickly dissipated.

Firstly, the weather was awful, and the wind and rain was so strong, it seemed to be coming down sideways. Secondly, the language barrier proved problematic and entire conversations with the local lads passed me by. Even though my written English had been pretty good at school, I was absolutely lost when it came to accents. Geordies, Mancunians, Cockneys. Every dialect sounded totally alien. The very first person I met in England was from Liverpool and when I shook his hand to say hello, he responded in a thick Scouse accent. I freaked out.

I had no idea what he was saying.

My problem was that in Nepal I'd been educated purely by reading, listening and talking, but nobody had warned me about the different regional dialects. When I was thrown into real-life situations with British lads, I was at a serious disadvantage. In the first few weeks, I often drifted through conversations thinking, *What the hell?*

During my recruit training in Catterick, I also learned how to dress well: one of the many rules we were forced to follow was the need to be suited and booted at all times. On our first trip to the beach, my platoon even walked across the sand in bare feet, with our suit trousers rolled up and our jackets slung over our shoulders. We must have looked ridiculous to anyone passing by.

By the time it came to the business of fighting, I was more than ready, but it took me four years to get there. In a thirty-six-week Gurkha training course, I learned about the core principles of the regiment; we worked through modules on cultural training and infantry battlefield training. Once I passed the recruit training, I joined the Gurkha Engineers and I was instructed to make a trade selection, where I had to learn a skill from a list that included carpentry and plumbing. I opted to work in building and structural finishing, and for nine months I lived in Chatham, Kent, where I was taught how to plaster walls, as well as the finer intricacies of painting and decorating. The effort was dull but worthwhile, and I knew that if life didn't work out for me in the military, I'd have a handy profession to fall back on.

Later, I learned all the skills required of a combat engineer and embarked on a series of field exercises. Having eventually completed the thirteen-week All Arms Commando Course at the Commando Training Centre Royal Marines in Lympstone, Devon, I was deployed in Afghanistan in 2007 as part of Operation Herrick – a twelve-year strategy in place to maintain a military presence within the country, while keeping an eye on any terrorist activities the Taliban might have been orchestrating. Helping the locals to build a new government was also one of our briefs, but the work was hard-core.

At times, it was my role to sweep vast areas of land for improvised explosive devices (IEDs). On operations, the Royal Marines Commandos would often go in first, and having detected a suspected trigger device, my team was then tasked with clearing the area, pinpointing exactly where the bomb had been positioned before dismantling it. Our unit was then able to move forward safely as a whole. The work was always intense, because one misstep might see me blown to pieces, and also there was a speed element to everything we did. There was no time to dawdle in exposed land, as the enemy might strike at any moment.

For the most part I was assigned to work with 40 Commando, the Royal Marines' battalion-sized 'formation'. One of the joint operational tasks was to move from door to door on patrols, checking for ammo and weapons, or Taliban drug stashes. I was a very loyal soldier and proud of the Gurkhas' reputation within the British military – I would have done anything to defend it. I was also incredibly respectful to the Queen and the Crown – they meant everything to me. But I wasn't afraid of speaking my mind.

During one operation, I'd been charged with sweeping an enemy compound for booby-traps and since my unit wasn't standing out in the open at the time, it seemed best to take extra care. I was eager not to miss a spot. But over my shoulder, I sensed a commander watching me. His impatience was building.

'Purja, hurry up,' he said. 'What's the problem?'

'Yeah, I *could* hurry up,' I said. 'Maybe, I could just skip this and say, "Job done!" But the reason I'm doing this properly is because I don't want the Gurkhas to be blamed for missing any IEDs. It's not only about me . . .'

I also hadn't appreciated my commander's suggestion that

something was wrong. *Was he insinuating that I'd been too scared to work quickly?* The reality, having walked around the room, aware a bomb might go off at any second, was that, yeah, I'd been a little edgy – I wasn't crazy. But fear didn't play a role in my world, even in Afghanistan.

'You think I'm fucking frightened of this?' I continued, dropping the Vallon detector we used to locate bombs and mines, and walking around the room, unfazed. 'My life doesn't mean anything here. But reputation does. That's why I'm doing this job properly.'

'Oh . . .,' said my commander. He seemed too taken aback to bollock me for insubordination.

It didn't take me long to develop a respect for the Royal Marine Commandos during my time in Afghanistan. I loved their ethos. They were super-soldiers, but they were humble too, which I appreciated. While I had plenty of self-belief and confidence, I wasn't a fan of the overpowering ego – the Big I Am. Whenever we were caught up in gun battles together, there was a respect between both groups.

Often in those situations it was the Gurkhas' job to provide close combat support and we'd be called in to attach L9 bar mines to the doors of enemy compounds. Originally designed as an anti-tank land mine, these explosive devices were also useful for removing obstacles; they could blow through the thick walls so common in Afghanistan without too much trouble. My job was to creep up to a door, fix the mine, run away and . . . *BOOM!* The unit then pushed into the smoking hole to clear up any enemy fighters engaging us from the other side.

On other occasions, I was deployed with a light machine gun (LMG). I'd rise at 4 a.m., patrolling through open valleys in the desert to make our presence known to anyone watching nearby; my unit would then wander through the towns and villages in the baking heat, checking in with the friendly locals, while taking pot shots from the not-so-friendly. The work was stressful, but rewarding. When the weapons went off, the adrenaline surged through me.

My day-to-day life was about the battle, and the risks were clearly defined. Somebody had to die, which was unfortunate, and at some point that person might be me, but I was ready for it. And I always wanted to go above and beyond. At times I'd hear stories about operations that were going on away from the realms of our deployment: hostage rescue jobs, hard arrests on serious Taliban players and door-kicking raids, all of them performed by the Special Air Service (SAS), or Special Boat Service (SBS). These shadowy regiments made up the UK Special Forces and as far as I was concerned, their work represented a step up, even on the Gurkhas. When I'd first learned about them at Catterick, I was impressed.

Wow. I want to be one of those guys.

I loved being a soldier, but I liked the idea of being top of the league even more, and the Special Forces were very much the elite. So, towards the end of 2008, I sized up my options, learning that the SBS was aligned to the Royal Marines, and the SAS to the British Army. I initially registered my interest in joining the SAS and looked into the squadron's *modus operandi* and application requirements. I was impressed. They operated across land, sea and air. But then a mate gave me a little more intel on the SBS. Apparently, they were even more badass.

'These guys do parachute jumps, they fight on land, and on the water,' he said. 'It's everything the SAS does, but they dive and swim in combat, too.'

Having worked with the Royal Marines in Afghanistan, I knew I'd blend in well, mentally at least, and shortly afterwards I attended an SBS briefing course. My application to join UK Special Forces Selection, the intense, six-month-long test that separated those soldiers with the minerals to join the group from the ones without, was accepted in 2008. After six years with the Gurkhas, I was moving on. My moment to join the military elite had arrived.

4

The Unrelenting Pursuit of Excellence

Nobody believed me when I stated that my mission was to join the Special Boat Service, probably because no Gurkha had made it into their ranks before, though I knew that several brothers had progressed into the SAS. But the SBS was a little harder to crack, because every operator in the squadron had to be able to swim and dive during combat, and Gurkhas come from a landlocked country, so the odds seemed stacked against me from the off, and everybody around me knew it.

Even if I had managed to make it through the Selection programme, I'd then have to pass a series of specialist courses, in order to make it into the SBS. Operating in the water was a whole new experience for me, but I was happy to take on the challenge. Still, the doubting voices came at me from within the Gurkha regiment.

You're joking, man. You're just saying it for the sake of it.

I ignored the comments and worked towards researching my ambition.

I understood that to become a Special Forces operator, it was important to adapt, not only to the increased workload and intense style of fighting behind enemy lines in dangerous warzones, but to the people around me. I was from Nepal.

Nobody else in the Squadron would be like me. So to prepare for the culture shock, I decided to learn a portfolio of British jokes. Dad jokes. Dirty jokes. Jokes from old sitcoms and stand-up shows. The Nepalese sense of humour is very different to the kind found in the SBS, so I memorised any half-decent gags or funny stories.

Why did the blonde stare at the orange juice bottle? Because the label read: 'Juice: concentrate'.

I was that eager to fit in.

There was another important reason for familiarising myself with British culture in that way. When assessing who was capable of cutting it in the Special Forces, the assessors, or Directing Staff (DS), were seeking out the best of the best. Potential recruits also had to be able to fit into a squadron of highly focused soldiers and when fighting within some of the world's sketchiest combat environments, team morale was a vital factor. If a potential SBS operator wasn't able to muck in with the jokes, or didn't understand the gallows humour in play, that was often marked against them.

It was imperative that I slipped comfortably into their world; it wasn't an excuse for me to say, 'Oh, I've come from the Gurkhas, so I don't get it.' Or, 'I wasn't schooled in England, that one went right over my head.' I needed to be fit for purpose on every level.

To prepare myself physically, I put myself through hell in training. While based at the Gurkha barracks in Maidstone, Kent, I'd work through my military commitments during the day, but by the time 5 p.m. came around, I would rush back to the house where I shovelled down a small dinner before heading into the gym for a seventy-mile bike session.

Knowing that combat swimming would play a major part of

my training – and I wasn't the greatest swimmer at that time – I then swam as many kilometres as my body could handle. I blazed through freestyle length after freestyle length in the pool, before blowing out after 2,500 metres. I rarely made it to bed before midnight, where I'd collapse, exhausted, sometimes getting up again at 2 a.m. to perform a seventy-five-pound load carry from Maidstone barracks to Chatham.

On weekends, I'd work on my running, and jogging for hours at a time became a regular part of my daily routine. I'd rise at 8 a.m. to haul my arse around the streets with two or three Gurkha buddies, the group operating in a relay system, where I was the only soldier prevented from taking a break. One guy would accompany me for six miles, dragging me along with him at a strong pace. Once his distance had been completed, another running partner took over and together we'd complete six more miles. This went on for hours and the work was both physically and psychologically rough.

Getting out of bed in the middle of the night with the rain hammering down outside was a demoralising experience, but I pushed through. When the snow swept in, I resisted any temptations to hit the snooze button. Emotional control was only one of the many traits I'd need to possess in order to become an elite soldier.

There was no rest. At other times I'd work alone, cracking on with a backpack loaded down with seventy-five pounds of weight, which made the six-hour sessions tougher still. I understood that when fighting with the Special Forces, there would be no time to rest, so training as hard as I could seemed the best way forward. All the way through I fought against doubt: my teammates and senior officers in the Gurkhas assumed that elite military service was beyond me and the self-inflicted programme of physical hell was the toughest challenge of my life at that point. But none of them grasped how dedicated I'd become, or how my mindset would help me to achieve impossible feats in the years ahead. I had hope. *And hope was God.*

I wasn't a religious person. While my parents were Hindus, I didn't follow one single higher power. Instead, I liked to celebrate everything. Sometimes I went to church, other times I'd visit a Buddhist monastery, but I always wanted to learn new ideas; I was open and human, I respected every religion in the world, but I had faith in myself more than anything. As a kid, becoming a Gurkha was my hope. *It was my God.* Joining the military elite six years later was my next hope. *That had become my God, too.* And I needed to believe in it. Without belief, a challenge the size of passing through Selection was set to fail, so I needed a far higher level of commitment than the mere aim of satisfaction, or bragging rights. Becoming an SBS operator was more like a cause, and I gave everything to it.

When I finally made it on to Selection in 2009, every day was an incredible test of physical and emotional fortitude. Held over six months, Selection began with the Hills Phase, and included a series of timed runs over the Brecon Beacons mountain range in South Wales. Undeterred by the pressure upon me, I focused only on the twenty-four hours ahead, rather than worrying about the succession of tests that were being lined up for my group over the coming weeks.

'Today I will give 100 per cent and survive', I thought at the beginning of each day. 'I'll worry about tomorrow when tomorrow comes'.

Nothing was held back in reserve, because I knew that to give anything less than my full effort would result in failure. I broke myself on the hills every day, regrouping at night, where

I'd summon the will to give the same effort over the following twenty-four hours.

Almost immediately, I seemed to be operating on the back foot. One of the key attributes of anyone operating within the British Special Forces was their ability to become the Grey Man. In a military or surveillance capacity, this process involved blending into the surroundings to avoid detection, or unwanted scrutiny. Sometimes it helped to adopt the Grey Man tactic on Selection, too. Potential operators that continually found themselves at the front of the pack could expect some mental pressure from the DS. Any lads unable to keep up with the heavy physical workload were often verbally thrashed before being kicked off the course and sent back to their regiments.

Because of the colour my skin, I found it impossible to blend in, or to hide in the middle of the group with the other lads. Though everybody screwed up from time to time, my mistakes were usually spotted immediately by the DS, and often from a distance. The yelling and jeering would start shortly after, but I was able to maintain my concentration. Well, for the most part. During one test march, I failed the course's time requirements by barely a minute. Immediately I felt the pressure. Every day in the process became increasingly harder, and by failing one I knew the following twenty four hours would become even more demanding. My ambitions were on the line.

The following morning was set to be a beast too: the penultimate day of the Hills Phase was a speed march over almost thirty kilometres. This was followed by the infamous final march – a test of endurance over more than sixty kilometres to be completed while carrying a heavy Bergen rucksack, weapon, water and supplies. The lot weighed around eighty pounds.

I'd been presented with a death-or-glory situation: finish the time trial and the final march in the required time of twenty hours and I was still in with a shot at making the cut; fail and I was heading home to the Gurkhas. Except there was no way on earth I was returning to my old regiment. I'd decided that if Selection was beyond me, it was time to quit the military for good.

'Either do this, Nims, or go home,' I thought, gathering my kit together the following morning.

My mind was set, but the day caused me to stress a little. Not as a result of the extreme endurance required to complete the course, but because when a spot check was carried out on all the recruits' equipment on the start line, it was clear I'd put myself at a slight disadvantage.

'What's this, Purja?' asked the DS, as he rummaged through the Bergen still strapped to my back.

He was waving my water bottle around. My heart sank. *Fuck, the protective cap was missing.* Even worse, some of the liquid had leaked out.

A key element of making it through Selection was the maintenance of personal equipment – without high standards, an operator would likely fail in conflict. Leaving behind something as small as a water bottle cap might be the difference between a covert mission going well and being detected by the enemy. Fatigue was no excuse either, and feeling tired during the Hills Phase had affected my attention to detail, but I should have had enough in the tank to cope. I was now about to face the consequences.

'Looks like you'll be carrying some extra weight today,' said the DS smugly.

I felt my Bergen being opened. A rock was dropped inside, and my strapping strained under the load, but weirdly, this setback only inspired me even more.

As I set off on yet another leg-buckling yomp, I thought, 'Well, Nims. One way or another, you're going to have to prove you're one of the best here, regardless of whether they can see you or not'.

Settling into the familiar sensation of pain first instilled in me by those heavy training sessions for the Doko Race, I pressed ahead. The required pace over the arduous terrain was unpleasant but within my reach and I adjusted quickly. It hadn't taken me long to realise that the Selection process wasn't about discovering the soldiers that were made of iron; the DS were looking for men that were flexible and able to mould themselves into any situation.

Mentally and physically, I was finding it within my grasp to adapt to the toughest challenges the Hills Phase could drop on me. I felt strong as I yomped up the steep inclines. The flats and downhill stretches were dealt with at running pace, kilometre after kilometre, hour after hour, until after nearly a full day of exertion, I crossed the finishing line, the fastest recruit of the day.

In the face of my toughest challenge yet, I hadn't cracked. I'd bent and flexed. I was malleable.

* * *

At times during my training, as I strived to become an elite operator, my soldiering skills were tested to the limit, none more so than whenever I was asked to operate in the jungle.

In military terms, the remote and top-secret rainforest locations I had to work in were horror shows. The temperatures were incredibly hot and sticky, and so my experience was always gloomy and wet. Everybody stunk. This made the jungle an intense test of military skills. The vegetation was booby-trapped with bugs and snakes, and the tropical conditions were an adversary to be feared.

But whenever I was in there, often for weeks at a time, I always smiled my way through the mud and wet; I was in my element, productive and happy, while a few of the lads around me suffered. Some of the other blokes in the group even thought there was something wrong with me. One morning, while climbing up a huge hill on a navigation check, I noticed the camouflaged faces in my unit staring back at me in disbelief.

'Fucking hell, Nims,' whispered one of the lads. 'I'm hanging out on these patrols, piss-wet through, and you're ... *enjoying it?*'

I laughed it off, explaining that I was functioning in an environment I'd been accustomed to as a kid. *The jungle was home ground*. But I still made the same mistakes as everybody else, as I had done throughout my career so far, but I worked to the theory that the military elite would require me to be resolute and flexible when I got there, and nobody was going to do me any favours, or encourage me to work harder. I had to motivate myself at all times. If I found myself in a bad situation, it was down to me to dig myself out. Often it was hard not to snap under the emotional stress, and everything was a mindfuck.

I also had to bite my lip at any criticism that came my way. One time, a bloke from my patrol screwed up in a reconnaissance exercise, but seeing as so much of the effort in the jungle was based on teamwork, the whole group was given a bollocking afterwards. We'd spent hours crawling through the undergrowth, beneath the noses of a bunch of soldiers living in the jungle with us that were working as a 'dummy' enemy. As we moved closer and closer to their hideout, one of my teammates wanted to push on even further. I tried to dissuade him, but there was no talking him out of it. And while we were able to avoid the attentions of the patrolling soldiers, a member of our assessment team had spotted us while moving back to our camp.

'Oh, have you lads been out for a nice recce?' he said. 'It's probably not the best idea to get spotted here.'

When the patrol called us together, we were dressed down. I was told that I'd achieved the noble position of being the worst soldier in the world.

'What the fuck are you even doing here, Purja?' shouted one of them.

When I tried to answer, he cut me off quickly. 'Speak English,' he said, referring to my strong accent. I wanted to punch him in the face, but I held back, knowing it was all part of the test. I couldn't react to provocation. So I kept my mouth shut and took the criticism on the chin.

I'll just have to hang in here. These bastards might try to break me, but I'm going to last the course no matter what.

It was their job to crush my spirit; mine was to fight on to the very end.

I was soon able to think clearly and work effectively in the tough conditions. My personal maintenance was up to scratch. I dealt with every test the military could chuck at me from live-firing drills to mock casualty evacuation (CASEVAC) operations and my resolve was steady. 'Come and test me, then,' I'd think. 'Try to find a fucking mistake.'

By the end of the jungle training I felt more ready for battle than before; my resolve was unbreakable. And with each new experience, I was even closer to becoming a fully-fledged member of the SBS. *My new God.*

* * *

Having passed a series of additional specialist courses, I was confirmed as a member of the Special Boat Service. On my badging day, I took my first-ever drop of alcohol during an induction ceremony with the other lads from the service. It started with a glass of whisky. This was followed up by a litre and a half of mixed booze: lager, wine, spirits – the lot. I had to down it all in one hit, not that I cared too much at that point. *I had met my God*. I was now a Special Forces operator and part of a unique club, having proved myself to be capable of fighting to the highest standard. *I was one of them*. Growing my hair long seemed like a logical next step – I felt like a rock star.

Almost as soon as my first hangover had calmed down, the pace of life became intense. One minute I was training in a boat, the next I was throwing myself out of a Hercules plane in a parachute as it flew over the sea. My life now was fast paced and demanding but it was never dull.

The work was unforgiving. Having joined with the SBS, each operator undertakes one of several roles to become even more focused on a particular discipline. I opted to become a trauma medic, and it was my responsibility to patch up any wounds or injuries sustained by my teammates during a gun battle; I learned how to deal with bullet wound trauma and any injuries picked up from IED detonations.

Finally, I was thrust into action for real in July 2010, where I operated in a series of warzones, and I worked on hard arrest raids. It was my role to rush through houses and enemy compounds with a unit of men, coming face to face with dangerous enemy forces, or IED booby-traps.

Kicking in doors was exciting, but terrifying, and through-out my work with the Special Forces, I became a seasoned operator. I switched on during a fight; I was able to stay calm under extreme pressure because of my training and experience, but also because the Gurkha spirit kept me motivated during tough times. We had a reputation to upkeep: we were known as being one of the toughest fighting forces in the world and I was determined to maintain that image.

I had a code: bravery over everything else. And there was no other way for me to live.

5

Into the Death Zone

Once entered into war for prolonged periods, life became even tougher. The squadron pushed everybody within it towards the pursuit of excellence, there was no hiding place and the hostile forces we battled against were adaptable and unwilling to surrender. At times the work became emotional.

But I didn't crumble. I wasn't one to express my feelings openly, even to my wife Suchi, and as a soldier I soon learned to mask any grief I might have felt on the job. I believed it was important to hide any emotional pain I might be experiencing while fighting.

During Selection, I didn't want the DS to think I was unable to cope when operating at the edges of my limits; during war, I certainly didn't want the enemy to sense that I'd become weak, tired, or scared – that would only have given them a psychological lift. Disguising my pain and suffering was a skill I practised at all times and I did so by focusing intensely on the job in hand; it helped to shut out the chaos around me.

I was even shot during one mission, but I didn't present fear or vulnerability. The injury happened during a gunfight at a border outpost, when I was asked to provide fire support for a raid that was taking place. We had been pinned down and we'd sustained a handful of casualties. Having taken up a position on a compound roof, firing my weapon while lying flat on my belly, I was struck by something – I wasn't sure by what at first, but it was powerful enough to knock me from the building.

I hit the deck with a thud, and having fallen ten feet or more, my senses took a few seconds to flood back to me. *What the fuck happened?* I tasted the warm, metallic tang of blood in my mouth. A puddle of red was growing around me on the floor. For a split second I worried that half my face had been shredded away by a round, though there wasn't any pain.

Was I in shock?

Was my jaw in one piece?

I pawed nervously at my chin. *Thank fuck. It was still there.* But clearly an enemy bullet had come close to ending me, leaving a nasty wound, slicing across my face, carving my jaw line and lips to ribbons. It was only when I checked my weapon that it became obvious how close to death I'd come. The round had struck my butt extender, the supporting arm that allowed me to rest my rifle into the crook of my shoulder as I fired.

A sniper had taken his shot, I reckoned he was probably aiming for my neck, or head, but the aim was a fraction off. The bullet had ricocheted away from the metal extension and smashed through the rifle's trigger housing mechanism, exiting at an angle that had taken it across my face. Terrifyingly, the energy from that one round had carried enough power to force me off the roof from a prone position. My weapon was now useless, I tossed it aside and rolled into cover. The shooting wasn't over, so I resumed fire with a pistol, calling in to the unit that I'd been hit.

Once our operation was concluded and my wound patched up, I returned to base a few days later, but news of my injury had arrived there in advance. Word spread that I'd been hurt in a gunfight and the squadron's welfare officer had even called Suchi to explain how I'd suffered a bullet wound, though no extra details were passed on. Having become understandably freaked out, she called the base for an update. Not that I had any idea. As I rested up, my sergeant major knocked on the door.

'Fucking hell, you Gurkhas!' he laughed. 'Do you guys not bother telling your family you're OK?'

What do you mean?

'Your wife, she's called, wanting to know you're still in one piece.'

I hit the roof and called Suchi back angrily.

'What the fuck?' I said. 'Why are you calling?'

Suchi explained how she'd feared the worst. The family were also worried that I might have been in trouble. Slowly, I realised my reaction had been excessive – I was a young blood at the time, I hadn't put myself in her position. Calmly, I reassured Suchi that I was fine and that I'd decided not to tell anyone about what had happened until I made it safely home at the end of my military tour. The thought of upsetting my wife or parents while I was away seemed way more stressful than any gunfight.

I explained to Suchi that the only time she truly had to stress was if two uniformed officers wearing black ties from the Royal Marines ever knocked on our front door, and by then it would be too late. Other than that, she was to carry on as if everything was fine. That might sound like a strange attitude to some people, but it was one of the many defence mechanisms I carried with me to manage what was a very chaotic role.

Having survived a succession of gunfights over several years, I focused on the opportunities available within the military's highly specialised climbing courses, and I scaled challenging peaks and abseiled down sheer rock faces, until my place on the forthcoming G200E climb of Everest of 2015 was all but assured. I was then required to train a number of recruits from the Gurkha regiment, hopefuls looking to join the same expedition, and together we climbed around 6,200 metres of Makalu's south-east ridge. Chosen because a lot of technical climbing was required to negotiate its tricky terrain, the expedition team-in-waiting learned how to jumar and belay effectively, while building confidence in their crampon work and climbing skills. They experienced severe exposure on sharp ridges at extreme altitude, and the work was consistently rough.

After a heavy, celebratory drinking session at the expedition's end, I decided to take on Ama Dablam, the mountain I'd fallen in love with during that trek with my friend and climbing mentor, Dorje, in 2012, climbing the near-vertical face of the Yellow Tower. Having taken on the unorthodox route of moving directly from Base Camp to Camp 2 in one hit, rather than resting and acclimatising at Camp 1, I topped out one of the Himalaya's trickiest mountains in around twenty-three hours.

But shortly afterwards, I was struck by a double whammy of tragedies. The first was news that Dorje had been killed on Everest on 18 April 2014, when seracs* from the western spur collapsed, triggering a huge avalanche. A tsunami of snow, rock and ice swept through the Khumbu Icefall, wiping out sixteen Sherpas in what was then regarded as one of the worst disasters on the peak. Everest was to be closed for the rest of

---

* A serac is a pinnacle or block of ice found among crevasses on a glacier, usually on a steep slope. Commonly the size of a house or larger, they are very dangerous to mountaineers, because they are liable to topple without warning and can cause an avalanche.

the season, after guides refused to work as a mark of respect for the deceased. The news, having learned it while away on a military tour, hit me hard, but in a warzone there was very little time to grieve; the enemy rarely afforded us moments of contemplation and I had to get on with my work regardless, acting as if nothing had happened.

Several months later, in what felt like a body blow, it was announced my squadron was being rotated into military action during May, right at the time when the 2015 G200E trip was scheduled to take place. My spot on the team was gone and I felt demoralised. A lot of what I'd been working upon had been leading me towards that one expedition, and by scaling the likes of Dhaulagiri, Ama Dablam, and Denali, my body and mind felt ready, but I had to forget my disappointment. It wasn't my job to be a professional mountaineer. My role was to operate in war and there was no space to grumble, or sulk, though in hindsight, maybe fate had played its part.

When the Gurkha expedition later prepared at Everest Base Camp, an earthquake measuring 8.1 on the Richter scale detonated a huge avalanche, which struck the Base Camp yet again, topping the terrible body count of 2014 by killing twenty-two people, though nobody from the expedition team was seriously injured. Headlines were written around the world, and from my desert base I learned that the G200E was being abandoned, as was every expedition that year. When a date was later set for May 2017, I hoped to make it back on the team.

Not that my position would be 100 per cent assured. Anything could happen in two years, and as I'd previously learned, my commitments to the military overshadowed any personal ambitions I might have carried. I held back from getting overly excited, though I made sure to improve my climbing skills, so that if 2017 went according to plan, I'd be ready for Everest. And then, unexpectedly, an opportunity to climb the world's tallest mountain emerged in the spring of 2016, when my military deployment plans were altered at the very last minute. Having spent the early part of the year training for one top-secret combat environment, I was suddenly asked to operate in another.

'We need your experience out there,' said my sergeant major.

I felt the heft of disappointment. 'Fuck, I was only there six months ago . . .'

But my transfer had already been set in place and there was no getting around it. Luckily, a happy twist was coming.

'Look, Nims, we'll give you four weeks leave rather than the standard three,' said my sergeant major. 'How does that sound?'

This was both good news and bad. The good: I'd previously promised my wife Suchi that we'd take a beach holiday when my next period of leave was granted – I was certainly looking forward to a little rest and recuperation. The bad: there was no way I'd last four weeks sleeping on a beach lounger, reading, listening to music, staring out at sea, *sunbathing*. Boredom would kick in within five minutes. Instead, I spied an opportunity.

Maybe I could climb Everest?

Logistically it was a long shot and the expedition came loaded with risk. Because of the time constraints, I wouldn't have the luxury of a two-month acclimatisation period, as taken by most people when climbing the 8,000-ers. *But fuck it, I'd done the same thing on Dhaulagiri – how would this be any different?* Financially the odds were stacked against me, too. The costs of climbing a mountain of that kind were extortionate and the estimated bill came in at around £50,000 to £60,000. (And Suchi was a little annoyed at first, though she eventually came round when I pointed out my place on the G200E team wasn't guaranteed.) But realising the opportunity might never present itself again, I figured, *so what?* And went to the bank for a personal loan.

'Can I ask what you need the money for, Mr Purja?' asked the clerk.

'Sure, I need to buy a car,' I lied.

Within minutes I'd secured a £15,000 transfer. My personal savings were then drained and I'd booked a flight to Nepal's capital, Kathmandu.

This financial chicanery was only half the battle, however. Having left England, I'd estimated most people climbing Everest that season were already moving towards Camp 3 and were acclimatised in preparation for their summit push via the South Col route – the windy ridge that linked Everest to Lhotse's nearby peak. With Sherpa support I'd be able to make the trek to Base Camp from Lukla Airport, 'The Gateway to Mount Everest', and then move to the higher camps with ease, but I didn't want to take Sherpa support.

I wanted to climb Everest solo.

It was a crazy idea and I knew it, especially as I'd only accumulated a couple of years' worth of experience on the big mountains and was still honing my skills.

Any anxieties I might have felt about my relative inexperience of solo climbing were tempered with a little pep talk regarding my background. If I got into any trouble at high altitude, my medical skills might come in handy, but they alone wouldn't be enough to save me from the dangers of an 8,000-er – my mortality would be decided by the ability to perform quickly at extreme altitude. Thankfully my now extensive military climbing training, and those expeditions to Dhaulagiri, Ama Dablam and Makalu, had given me a fair idea of how to survive.

More importantly, I'd also learned how to control my emotions during combat and so fear barely dinged me, even when I'd been close to getting dropped by the enemy, which was an increasing occupational hazard within my line of work. Climbing a mountain with hundreds of deaths to its name seemed like a risk, but it was one I was qualified to take.

I also realised that if I wanted to be considered an elite climber at some point, then this was exactly the type of challenge I'd have to accept, regardless of my increased workload and the ever-lengthening odds of success. Sure, climbing with a Bergen weighing thirty-five kilos, complete with climbing equipment, a tent and supplies would be no joke, but it was within my skillset. I also intended to use oxygen support above 7,400 metres, which was considered controversial by some climbers who operated at extreme altitudes. The extra kit would only add to the weight, but I reckoned it would be vital, seeing as I was working alone.

Overall, though, the greatest risk was psychological: I was taking a chance with my reputation – *what would people in the military think if I fucked up?* As I flew to Kathmandu and then Lukla airport, I tried not to think too hard about the potential for disaster.

My mission was in place. I was taking on the world's tallest peak.

* * *

'You're fucking bluffing.'

With a rapidly narrowing summit window at the end of May, the majority of people I'd encountered at Lukla didn't expect me to make it to the top of Everest in the space of three weeks. Not least the American camera crew on standby to film a documentary they were loosely calling *Everest Air*. Their aim was to trail a rescue team, in place to conduct any medical evacuations on the mountain. Given the nature of 8,000-ers, *Everest Air* was sure to have plenty of action to edit and while readying my kit, I was bombarded with a series of friendly questions in the kind of conversation that always took place between adrenalised, nervy climbers on the brink of a risky expedition.

'Where are you from, Nims?'

England.

'Oh, right. Long way, dude. What do you do?'

I'm a medic. I work in London.

Following my trip to Dhaulagiri, I'd decided this was the perfect alibi, mainly because there was a pinch of truth to the story. If someone became nosy about my concocted medical career, I'd at least be able to throw him, or her, off the scent with a little talk about my experience in treating trauma injuries. Telling anyone that I worked with the British Special Forces was out of the question.

The main guy in the team was sizing up my kit. 'That's a lot of stuff. Are you here for the trekking? Because you're too late to climb Everest in time.'

No, I'm here for the climb. And I'll make it in time – I have to.

There was a pause. 'What? Where's the rest of your team then?'

I'm doing it solo.

There was a snort of disbelief; someone else laughed. 'You're fucking kidding?'

I shook my head and shrugged it off. The glass-half-empty attitude went against everything I'd been taught in the military, where grumbling or giving up wasn't considered an effective strategy. If ever problems or challenges came my way, I was supposed to find solutions, having been trained to adapt and

...urvive. I picked up the last of my kit and tried my best to ...... the snarky comments, knowing that gloomy thinking was both destructive and contagious.

No. No jokes, brother. I'm fucking doing this.

Besides, I didn't have the time for small talk. My plan for making it to the summit in such a limited window was to do everything more quickly than was recommended, without wasting too much energy. I trekked to Base Camp at speed, making it to the bottom of Everest in only three days. Rather than taking a few acclimatisation climbs through the Khumbu Icefall's notorious valley of toppling seracs to Camp 1, I headed straight for Camp 2 at 6,400 metres, a trip that usually took most people a month, or longer, as they settled into the high altitudes. I was foregoing the luxury of time and rest, trying to adapt and survive, and quickly paid a heavy price for my impatience.

Having passed Camp 1, and stuck midway between the two camps, I noticed the first indicators of an oncoming physical failure. I was exhausted. The lack of acclimatisation had kicked me in the arse, my heavy backpack was now taking its toll, and every step in my crampons along the icy climb felt like a monumental effort. I'd also become seriously dehydrated. The sun had been high; at times it felt as if I was melting under its intensity. Sweat burned my eyes and I could barely see, but there were dangers everywhere.

I was negotiating the Western Cwm and the route was pockmarked with crevasses. Though I was clipped onto a safety rope, I knew that if the ground was to give way beneath me, or if I was to slip from one of the ladders that bridged some of the icy ridges, it might be days before I was discovered. I was close to breaking point with the physical and emotional effort and my eyes brimmed with tears; for the first time in years, self-doubt was leaking into the edges of my thinking.

Fuck, I'm not strong enough to make it to Camp 2. But I really don't want to go back to Camp 1 either.

I knew I had to lose the negative internal chit-chat, and fast. Whenever I'd been in life-or-death events in the past, I had used Suchi to restore my focus and a sense of determination. I'd think of her during gun battles whenever my unit was pinned back by enemy fighters – the emotions were fuel and I was able to reset myself and then concentrate on the job in hand. Now I'd use the thought of her, waiting for me to return home, as the inspiration to push up towards shelter at Camp 2. I rummaged around in my pockets and found my phone, recording a brief video message.

'Look baby, I'm struggling massively, but as always I'm going to make this happen . . .'

I didn't send it; I only wanted to capture the moment. Then I worked on course correcting.

Let's fucking do this.

I attempted to reboot and having sucked in a few deep breaths, my heart felt full again. Before long, my pep talk had jolted me from a fairly doomy headspace and I'd located an extra reserve of strength. The walk along the Western Cwm was ordinarily quite mellow, the route was fairly flat and though there were one or two areas that required a little technical mountaineering, I could spend most of the climb pulling myself along the fixed lines without too much stress, taking a couple of lengthy diversions to avoid the crevasses.*

---

* For those unfamiliar with the details of high-altitude climbing, fixed lines are roped routes set at the start of the season by a designated team. They allow expeditions to move up the steep inclines more easily throughout the same season.

I grabbed my kit together and pressed on to Camp 2, driving my body to safety.

Boom! Boom! Boom! My momentum had returned and every step felt like an achievement. *Boom! Boom! Boom!* Every footfall was a positive push to the Western Cwm's end.

As I'd discovered on Dhaulagiri, it was fairly easy to burn out at high altitudes, but I hadn't yet experienced the full medical consequences when making that kind of mistake first-hand. That moment was soon to arrive. By the time I'd set up my tent at Camp 2, I was feeling good again, so I ate some lunch and hung out with a couple of Sherpa friends, before pushing up another one hundred and fifty metres and back.

By acclimatising a little higher, my hope was to avoid the pounding headaches that sometimes dogged me when sleeping at high altitude. But I overcooked my efforts and by the time I'd lain out in the tent to rest, my lungs were gurgling, a sure sign I was developing a high altitude pulmonary edema (HAPE), an accumulation of fluid in the lungs and a nasty condition where the chest wheezes and heaves, the skin turns blue and the heart pounds like a kick drum. Without treatment there was every chance I might die.

As I recovered in my sleeping bag, listening to the wheeze of my straining lungs, it was impossible not to feel the sting of frustration. I'd been stupid. That extra push of one hundred and fifty metres had broken me. Now every breath was a heavy effort.

Nims, you should have known . . . you're a mountaineer and a fucking medic! You have all the knowledge in the world about altitude sickness. Why couldn't you have taken more care?

When it came to the high peaks, Dhaulagiri had previously taught me that there was a thin line separating success from failure, as there was in battle, but I'd naively believed that my military training, plus the lessons learned elsewhere in the mountains, would guide me through any knife-edge judgement calls on Everest. I'd also wanted to test my limits by pushing up the extra distance.

I'd been wrong. The divide existing between good and bad decisions during war was even narrower in mountaineering, because the extremes of life were so dramatic on 8,000-metre peaks. After only twenty-four hours on Everest, I was learning that to break the line inevitably resulted in disaster. Embarrassed, I returned to Base Camp for a medical check and a period of recuperation in which to rethink my summit push, but no way was I going to allow Everest to defeat me.

Sadly, the first doctor I checked in with had other ideas. 'You can't go back up,' he said, listening to my rattling chest through a stethoscope. 'By the sounds of it, that's a very big pulmonary edema.'

Remembering my childhood success as the human antibiotic, I decided to get a second opinion.

What does he know? I'll find another medic who understands.

But the next mountain doctor was just as pessimistic. 'I'd advise you not to climb any higher,' he said. 'The first assessment was right. In your condition you might get into some serious trouble up there.'

Again, I ignored the diagnosis. *These dudes are erring on the side of caution. That's fine in a civilian hospital, but I'm at Everest Base Camp. Everyone's taking a risk here, one way or another.*

My mind was made up.

Those two fuckers are wrong.

But I wanted to make sure. A doctor friend of mine was also operating somewhere on Base Camp. I tracked him down, hoping for a more casual diagnosis, one where I'd be allowed to return to climbing in twenty-four hours, but instead I was given the third and final warning of the day.

'Nims, man, you've got to get off the mountain. That's a pulmonary edema. You can't mess around.'

Shit. I was going to have to take my recuperation a little more seriously after all. I travelled back to Lukla by helicopter for X-rays and some down time for a few days, discovering that my diagnosis might have some serious implications further in the future. According to every medical journal I skimmed through online, HAPE was a potentially returning condition and the best move was to go home and recover. Without care, my lungs would fail again, so if I was to scale Everest I'd have to ascend with more caution than before, which didn't fill me with confidence, seeing as my leave days from the military were disappearing at a rapid rate and the climbing season was drawing to a close.

Still, I wasn't going to allow a medical concern to derail my plans. I filled my head with positive thoughts as I recovered. I told myself I'd make it to the top, no problem. By focusing only on success, I forced myself to believe.

There was another sobering realisation to deal with. Any opportunity I'd had to summit Everest solo was gone. I now needed a Sherpa to help me out, but there was no way I was taking an easy ride to the top. When it came to selecting assistance, I wanted to employ the least experienced guy I could find. Firstly, because I still hoped for a serious challenge. Secondly, the Nepalese Sherpa was an unappreciated worker and underpaid. Climbers scaling Everest travelled light. Meanwhile their Sherpas and porters generally lugged thirty or forty kilos of rope, kit and provisions, but they received very little pay for their efforts and next to no credit. However, once an inexperienced Sherpa had climbed Everest, his service fees soared, and I wanted to give somebody that same money-making opportunity.

There was another self-imposed restriction. While I had the knowledge and expertise required to climb Everest, it also felt important to be self-sufficient: if I struggled with HAPE again, I wouldn't need to call in a rescue party, because a Sherpa could help me down the mountain. So when I later stumbled across Pasang Sherpa at Everest Base Camp, a young porter from Makalu with zero experience of making it to Everest's peak, I knew he was the perfect candidate for my ballsy adventure. Pasang was so unprepared that he only owned an old summit suit and a beaten up pair of boots.

'This is great, Nims,' he said, pulling on the thermal layers, gloves and other bits of kit I'd given to him. 'If I can get you to the top, I'll be able to charge three times as much for my services.'

Knowing the trip would change both our lives forever, we started our climb, the pair of us hoping for the best, silencing any talk of the worst.

* * *

We moved steadily through the Khumbu Icefall and across the Western Cwm again. The wind had picked up; the conditions were harsh, but our two-man team was able to press ahead from Camp 2 to 3, pitching a tent and sleeping as the weather became increasingly sketchy. My lungs felt good, I was holding up physically and my brush with HAPE felt like a distant memory, not that I was taking any chances. When we eventually pushed for the summit later that night, I made sure to watch the expedition ahead – pressing on blindly through the dark seemed a little sketchy, certainly during my first-ever summit push on Everest. I'd already had one brush with death, I didn't fancy experiencing another.

With the peak in sight, I pulled myself along the fixed line that tethered me to the mountain and by 4 a.m. I had made it past the famous Hillary Step, the technically tricky 12-metre-tall boulder face that every climber on the south east route has to negotiate if they are to reach the world's highest point. (In the 2015 earthquake, the Hillary Step was altered when its largest boulder fell away, but people still refer to it as a landmark.) A rush of excitement pulsed through me. *I was going to do it!* Our timing had been perfect; the sun was about to appear over the Himalayas, but once on the top, 8,848 metres above sea level, as I finally sucked in a reflective moment, Pasang seemed edgy. The strong winds had intensified around us and we were both becoming a little unsteady on our feet.

'Nims, we have to go back,' he said.

'But we've just got here!'

'Yeah, but this is a dangerous time. People die on the way down because they wait too long and get caught out by the weather.'

Despite Pasang's lack of experience on Everest, I knew he was right. There were too many horror stories of people wasting precious time to take selfies or to unveil flags once their mission had been completed, when their job was only fifty-per-cent done. The most important part of any climb was to get back down, quickly and safely. The winds were also known to reach one hundred and sixty kilometres per hour at the peak from time to time.

I checked my oxygen levels. I was in fairly good shape and according to my watch there was plenty of time for a safe descent. I told myself that Pasang had probably become overly panicked because he was unfamiliar with Everest's terrain. Turning around for Base Camp had become his priority.

'Listen, brother, I risked everything to be here, but I'm feeling strong,' I said. 'So I'm not going down until I see the sun rising.'

'No, Nims. *No, no, no!*'

'I can make it down, no problem,' I told Pasang firmly, giving him the permission to leave.

He shrugged his shoulders and turned away sadly, but I was happy to wait alone. As I watched him trudge down the mountain, the sun climbed higher above the Himalayas, melting over the snow-capped peaks in a wash of orange and pink, seemingly burning away the wispy clouds below. The Himalayan prayer flags fluttered behind me. At that moment, I was the highest person on earth; it felt like a life-defining event, and I took off my goggles to feel the cold air against my eyes. The view was every bit as wild as I'd imagined and waiting for the morning light had been the right decision, but I wasn't going to stay around for much longer.

At that altitude, situational awareness, an important facet of elite military life, was a tool every bit as valuable as my summit suit or climbing boots. I took one last look at the epic views around me and trudged down, visualising a celebratory beer at Base Camp. Days earlier, HAPE had kicked my arse and yet I'd still been able to climb the world's tallest mountain. My self-belief was off the scale.

When I saw the stricken climber on the terrain below, abandoned to die by their teammates on an expedition gone wrong, I sensed I'd have to draw on every last ounce of it.

* * *

The mountaineer was incapacitated, or dead, I wasn't sure at first. Leaning in close, I immediately checked for any vital signs.

It was a woman and she was seemingly pinned to the spot, unable to move. Her goggles were gone and when I looked around in the snow there was no sign of them anywhere. Perhaps her mind had become so freaked by altitude sickness that they'd been thrown away in a panic, or dropped in confusion. Physically, the woman was a mess, too. Semi-conscious and barely able to speak, it was a struggle to find her barely-there pulse. I guessed she wasn't going to make it down unless somebody moved her quickly.

Luckily, I was still feeling fairly strong – it was in me to drag her to Camp 4, where she'd hopefully receive the assistance she so badly needed, but time was against us. (I was also hyper-aware of my brush with HAPE, and the fact I hadn't committed to as many acclimatisation rotations as made by most climbers on Everest.) If I couldn't find her a pair of goggles before the sun had risen fully, the woman might suffer snow blindness, a painful burn to the retinas that happened due to the powerful UV rays at high altitude and was comparable to having sand rubbed into the eyes. I cranked up the oxygen in her tank and tried to rouse her.

'Hey, you're going to be OK,' I shouted, shaking her gently. 'What's your name?'

I heard a mumble. She was talking. I leant in closer.

'Seema . . .'

Seema! That was something to work with. If I could keep her chatting, there was a fighting chance I'd save her life.

'Where are you from?'

'India . . .,' she whispered.

'OK, Seema, I'm going to get you home.'

She seemed to nod. I heard her mumbling again, but I couldn't tell if she was showing signs of delirium, or if she was trying to tell me something. I switched into an operational setting and radioed down to Camp 4, where I knew the rescue team working with the *Everest Air* crew were resting, having made a high-altitude mission several hours previously.

'Guys, it's Nims,' I said. 'There's a woman, Seema, stuck here. Can you help her?'

A voice responded straight away. 'Look, Nims, you know us, last night we rescued this climber all the way from the South Summit, and now we're fucked. Can you bring her down to Camp 4 yourself? We can help her from here. If we come up again, one or two of us might die.'

'Sure, no problem,' I said.

Under the circumstances, those guys had made the correct call.

Here's a controversial reality: on an 8,000-metre peak, the attitude *every person for themself* sometimes rings tragically true. People climb, people fail to operate effectively, and people die; badly injured individuals usually go through a moment when their death becomes inevitable to everyone else around them. They might have succumbed to exhaustion, or it could be that HACE* has taken hold and they're unable to think straight. In a confused panic, they sometimes unzip their summit suit in the false belief they're overheating. When the intense cold then sinks its teeth into their flesh, a painful ending becomes unavoidable.

I've also heard of other people wandering away from their group in the belief that they're nearly home. Then they take a nasty tumble off the mountain's edge. At times, high-altitude expeditions can resemble a war zone. A lot of climbers will

---

* HACE stands for high altitude cerebral edema, a severe and potentially fatal medical condition in which the brain swells with fluid, causing confusion, clumsiness and stumbling.

want to stay with a struggling friend as they die. It's a very human reaction to remain close, delivering comfort and reassurance, even though they might be exhausted themselves, or running low on oxygen, but that's actually the worst choice. With every minute wasted on the mountain, the chances of survival shrink for a tired group, and before they know it, one death has become two, three, or even more. Because it's better to have one casualty than two, the best response for a party is to leave. That might sound awful, but if the healthier individuals aren't capable of physically rescuing the injured themselves, it's sensible if they move down the mountain, radioing for help before they do so, in the hope that (a) a stronger climber might be descending somewhere behind them, one that might be in a better position to help, or (b) a rescue team of guides can climb up from a lower camp to assist the casualty.

I guessed that's what had happened on Everest.

Camp 4 was a descent of nearly four hundred and fifty metres in altitude and from there, Seema's condition could be assessed more effectively because the air would be a little thicker at least. The *Everest Air* team would have oxygen, too. If she was able to walk at that point, or even stagger, there was every chance I'd be able to guide her all the way to Base Camp. I'd have to start moving quickly, though. It was important to save Seema from snow blindness and to do so, we had to reach Camp 4 before the sun rose too high.

The alternative was to hand her over to the rescue crew at a tent in Camp 4, while I descended to Base Camp before my oxygen supplies ran out. But moving her down to that point was going to be a challenge, and what I planned on doing wasn't going to be the most comfortable evacuation for an injured climber, or me, but it would certainly be the quickest and most effective.

Pulling a length of old rope dangling from one of the fixed lines on the mountain, I wound it around Seema's waist, securing it tight. I then heaved, edging her slowly down towards Camp 4. With every pull, Seema moaned in pain.

'I know, I know,' I shouted out over my shoulder. 'It feels so bad right now. But take my word, please: this is the best way to get you back safely, and if we don't act now, it's not going to happen.'

The effort took around an hour and having dragged her for two hundred metres, Seema seemed capable of standing. I pulled her up, encouraging her to attempt a few steps, then a few more, until gradually we started making progress. But the effort was painful.

Finally, with around twenty-five metres to go until Camp 4, I realised that Seema didn't have it in her to move any further. She was too weak. I was in a bad way, too, barely able to stand and on the verge of collapse, which was unsurprising given it had only taken me 90 minutes to cover the distance. My climb through the night had finally caught up with me and the adrenaline of scaling Everest had worn off. I fell to my knees and radioed for help. A team of Sherpas rushed from a nearby tent and dragged us both to safety, and once sheltered from the freezing winds, I summoned up enough strength to call Base Camp.

'Guys, this is Nims. I'm at Camp 4 with Seema. She's in a bad way, but the rescue team is looking after her now . . .'

There was a crackle on the other end of the line. One of Seema's expedition buddies was shouting excitedly. In the background, I heard other voices as people gathered around the radio.

'Nims, that's amazing! Thank you.'

There was a pause. 'Are *you* OK?'

I found myself at the tipping point. My oxygen was close to running out and if I hung around for too long there was every chance I might die. Knowing that Seema had enough in her own tank, and that rescuers were with her, I realised my work was done.

'Guys, if I stay here any longer, you may have to rescue me as well. I'm going down now.'

Hours later, I staggered into Base Camp and collapsed, instantly falling asleep in my tent. When I woke the next day, it was to good news: Seema had been successfully extracted and was alive, and as word passed around the tents, people wanted to know more about the unknown climber that had rescued her. There were well-wishers, thankful expedition leaders and even one or two family members trying to figure out who I was.

At one point a media request came through. A journalist had been tipped off and wanted to interview me for a story, but as an elite operator, it was critical I maintained my low profile – I hadn't told anyone back at the SBS HQ about what I planned to do on my holidays. My only chance of escaping any unwanted attention outside of the Himalayas was to apply a little emotional pressure.

'I'm a member of UK Special Forces, I'll lose my job if this story comes out,' I said. 'Please don't say anything.'

My request was passed down the line.

In the aftermath of Seema's solo rescue, I'd learned a serious lesson: by using oxygen during my expedition, it had been possible to save her. Without it, the chances of me summoning up enough energy to conduct a rescue would have been slim to none. For that reason, from now on, I was climbing above the higher camps on an 8,000-er with bottled air, even though it wasn't considered the purest form of high-altitude climbing by some sections of the mountaineering scene. *But who cared?* Nobody was in a position to dictate to me why or how I climbed the mountains, in much the same way that I didn't have the right to dictate to others.

Besides, I hadn't taken on Everest for fame, or an increased reputation among my military brothers, or the climbing community. If anything, I needed to quieten my achievements, because as a former Gurkha I'd jumped the gun: I was now, technically at least, the first serving member in the regiment to have scaled the world's tallest mountain. Had that detail been publicised in a newspaper report, there's every chance the G200E would have been scrapped. I needed anonymity and having returned home, my family and close friends were sworn to secrecy.

Every morning for a week, I scanned the newspapers for any news of my rescue efforts on Everest. From what I could tell, nothing had been written – at least, nothing that mentioned me by name. The mission had been achieved by strength and guile. Shortly after returning from Kathmandu, I flew home to Suchi, happy for the rest, grateful that my secret and job were safe. A few days later, I was back scrapping with the military where I kicked in doors and took down bad dudes, counting off the days until it was time to climb another mountain.

6

Swimming to the Moon

May 2017 came around all too quickly, but my deployment schedule had been kind. I'd been confirmed as a member of the G200E, where I would be working as a team instructor. A second attempt at the world's tallest peak was back on, but this time I wouldn't have to secure a hefty bank loan to finance the trip. I was a member of the British Armed Forces, my expenses would be paid, and I intended to squeeze the experience for every last drop of adventure.

For a while I'd harboured the idea of climbing Everest and the neighbouring peak of Lhotse, before taking on nearby Makalu in a two week period. Though all three mountains were 8,000-ers, I reckoned it was in me to nail them in around a week or so, but the schedule would require me to move quickly after topping out with the G200E – no mistakes, no hold-ups. The celebratory expedition was made up of around twenty climbers and included Gurkhas, one or two faces from the military elite, and a handful of officers, one of whom was the expedition leader.

If I eventually summited, I'd have to break away and descend at speed, reaching the South Col.* From there I could move quickly, climbing Lhotse and heading down to Base Camp. If everything worked out as planned, I'd then party in Kathmandu for a bit with my Gurkha brothers before taking on Makalu.

I was ready for the challenge. The way I'd made it to the tops of Everest and Dhaulagiri had previously reaffirmed my hunch that I was a strong high-altitude mountain climber. But it wasn't simply about physical strength, my mindset felt different, too. I seemed to have a very unusual drive when compared to a lot of the climbers I'd met and I often wondered if I carried a different motivation. Like my work with the military, climbing wasn't about ego, or fame. It was about service.

During operations I constantly reminded myself about the commitment I'd made to the Gurkhas, the British Special Forces and the United Kingdom. I needed to do them proud. The last thing I wanted was to dent their image by failing on a mission and I experienced the same desire on expeditions. I knew that if I could climb Everest, Lhotse and Makalu, the reputations of every institution I'd ever believed in would amplify, as would the efforts of my brothers within them. I also fancied putting my limits to the test, like a runner who sets out to do a five-kilometre run one morning, but ends up doing ten . . . *because they can*. The mountains were there to be climbed. Did I have the minerals to take them on?

Prior to the G200E, I'd even mentioned it to my officer-in-command. 'Look, I want to climb Everest, Lhotse and Makalu while I'm there,' I said. 'It won't need me to take any time off.

* Everest and Lhotse share camps from Base up to Camp 3 on the South Col route. After Camp 3, a climber hoping to top out at the world's tallest mountain travels to the left across the South Col to Everest's Camp 4. An individual hoping to climb Lhotse moves straight up. Makalu was a helicopter ride away from the shared base camp.

I'll do the climbs while the other lads are resting in Kathmandu after the expedition and I'll be on the same flight home.'

'That can't be done, Nims,' he said dismissively. 'It sounds fucking impossible.'

Untroubled by his pessimism, I readied myself for the challenge anyway. *I had to give it my best shot.*

We travelled to Nepal in April and once we'd arrived at Everest, the G200E party was divided into two teams. My first job was to guide one of them through the acclimatisation rotations required to reach the summit. The process, which happened gradually, took the expedition into Camp 1 and then over the Western Cwm to Camps 2 and 3. From there we would return to Base Camp, by which point everyone should have been physically primed for a summit push.

When stacked up against my first attempt at the world's tallest peak, this felt like a tactically wiser operation and I thrived. My confidence had grown so much, but it also helped that some of the group I was leading were both strong and resolute, and able to operate at high altitudes quite comfortably. However, others weren't so well-equipped and, worryingly, a handful of climbers, which included senior leaders, looked exhausted by the time we reached Camp 1 for the first time. They were slow to acclimatise, which led me to wonder how they could lead if they weren't up to speed on what was considered to be a fairly straightforward acclimatisation rotation.*

---

* Previously, people used to organise their acclimatisation rotations very differently. Expeditions would climb to Camp 1, sleep there and then descend to Base Camp. On the next climb, the group would move to Camps 1 and 2, sleep and then climb all the way down again. Finally, for their third rotation, it was considered best to go all the way to Camp 2, rest and then climb up to Camp 3 before returning to Base Camp. For the past few years it has been considered more effective if a climber summits after completing only one acclimatisation rotation, moving quickly through the camps and sleeping at Camps 1 and 2

Because it was clear which climbers were making serious headway and which ones were fading, I decided to take the strongest on to Camp 2 and then 3, while the slower team members rested at Camp 1 for an extra day of acclimatisation. After completing their respective climbs, the two teams took a couple of days to rest in the nearby town of Namche Bazaar, before briefing day arrived in Base Camp – the moment when the groups would be organised into two expedition units.

Team A was set to lead the climb. Team B would start their ascent once the first group had summited. But when the two parties for our historic expedition were revealed, it had been decided that the slower, struggling leaders should go first, which conveniently included the officers in the group. (I found that a bit weird — a lot of the officers I'd served with in the military elite had put the interests of their men before their own). Meanwhile, most of the stronger climbers were set to follow on as Team B – myself included, as well as two Gurkha Special Forces instructors. For some reason, we'd been resigned to the back of the line. I was pissed off. *We'd earned the right.*

'Why are the fastest climbers not on the lead party?' I asked, the meeting having drawn to a close. 'Your mission, the mission of the British Government, is to put the first serving Gurkha on the summit. But the strongest have been put to the back.'

The room fell silent; there wasn't a lot for anyone to say. Their decision had been political and it was painfully transparent. Team A was made up of slower leaders with a handful of Gurkhas chucked in. One of Team A's members tried to end

and moving up to touch Camp 3. This tactic also reduces the threat to a climber's life, because they don't have to move through the very dangerous Khumbu Icefall, over and over. This method applies to those climbers using bottled oxygen.

the dispute by claiming that everybody was now fully acclimatised, and equally strong, but I wasn't convinced.

'I saw you all at Camp 1 during the acclimatisation rotations,' I said. 'You were knackered and struggling to keep up.
How can you lead the strongest members when you are slower
than them? What happens if a rescue situation kicks off?'

I was exasperated. 'OK, if you want to play politics, play
politics. It's not my fight. Good luck.'

Tensions had been running high for days, probably because
the mission was looking increasingly precarious. The weather
conditions on Everest had been horrific. High winds ravaged
everything above Camp 2 and within a week, a series of storms
were due to roll in. Then, twenty-four hours prior to us setting
off for the summit push, it was announced that some of the
fixed lines still weren't in place. The team charged with setting
the last of the rope* had given up around the Balcony, a crest
on the south-eastern ridge, which was positioned 8,400 metres
above sea level.

Apparently, the weather was too bad to climb any higher,
and with the work incomplete, the G200E suddenly seemed in
jeopardy. The mood became bleak, especially as this was our
second attempt at getting the job done, taking into account the
tragedy of 2015. If the decision was made to abandon our
climb, there was a risk we might not get another chance. As a
Gurkha, I knew I wouldn't be able to live with the knowledge
that we had failed to scale Everest, even though it was in our
home country.

* A line-fixing rotation, like acclimatisation, requires a series of climbs in
order to set the ropes for an expedition, sometimes all the way to the top. The
team designated for the job usually features the best climbers on the mountain at that point, but the work is hard going and can take weeks to complete,
depending on the terrain, weather conditions and mountaineers involved.

When I scanned through the climbing order again, I realised I was the only person on the mountain who could take on the responsibility of fixing the lines. A number of more experienced mountaineers, who had planned to climb Everest at that time, were packing up and going home. I was the strongest climber by far; I carried the experience and the capability to function in extreme temperatures, and as an elite operator, I certainly possessed enough resilience to nail the mission. Plus, I trailblazed like a badass.

Who else could they rely on?

'I'll go up and set the ropes,' I announced, as the worrying intel about our fixing team spread through the group.

Most of the lads around me had assumed the mission was effectively over and seemed pleasantly taken aback at my offer, even though everybody on the G200E team had learned first-hand about my mountaineering skills. The fact that I'd scaled two 8,000-ers already, one of which was Everest, was now common knowledge too; as was my rescue of Seema.

Meanwhile, my role on military operations was to get the job done, no questions asked, and personal agendas or politics were always put to one side. I adopted the same attitude with the G200E team. Any negativity was ignored.

'Trust me, I can do it,' I continued.

Eventually, the G200E leaders agreed with my plan – nobody could really argue – and it was decided that I would lead a fixing team, which included two Special Forces operators, both of whom were Gurkhas, and eight Sherpa guides. The expedition schedule was also changed. If our against-the-odds, line-fixing mission ended up being successful, it was decided that the majority of climbers would switch to Team A. While they climbed, Team B would wait at Base Camp, only moving up once the first group had summited.

The pressure was high, but I felt confident enough, climbing steadily by using the trailblazing techniques I'd first learned on Dhaulagiri. We worked comfortably to Camp 2, sleeping overnight before heading to Camp 4. Having rested briefly, we then made our summit push and, keen to lead by example, I burned alone for 450 metres, from Camp 4 to the Balcony. It felt important that my teammates realised I was happy to put in the hard yards, rather than asking a Sherpa guide to do it instead. In situations of that kind, respect and credibility were earned.

The sun was up. As we worked across the South Summit and, later, the Hillary Step, it was impossible not to be overawed by the view of Nepal and Tibet around me. But I had no time to stop and gawp. As the leader of a line-fixing team, I knew that if we were unable to set these last few ropes, the entire expedition would collapse. According to comms, Team A were rapidly closing in on Camp 4 behind us. If we were turned around now, everybody would need to leave for Base, because the expedition's supplies of food and oxygen were about to be used up. The entire mission would need to be resupplied and that would take time and serious effort. Given the season for climbing Everest was about to close and there was no other weather window in sight, the G200E hinged on our progress.

Luckily, my stamina hadn't faded. Around ten metres from the peak, as some of the slower lads in the line-fixing crew caught up, I held back from making the final push alone. 'Brothers,' I thought, 'We're doing Everest as a team.'

Once everybody had joined up, we put our arms around one another's shoulders, making the last steps together.

This was history. We had set the fixed lines and thirteen soldiers from the regiment eventually made it to the top during the G200E. (Our ropes would also provide a route for climbers on Everest at the end of that season). For some of those lads, the climb was a clearly defined endgame, a challenge that couldn't be topped. *Where else would they go next?* But I was a million miles away from closure. When I looked across at the mountain ranges below me, I knew the next phase of my adventure was waiting. A new beginning had been set in motion.

* * *

I was ready. To immediately climb Lhotse and then Everest once more – where I was due to help the second G200E team to the top as the only designated instructor with the stamina to climb the peak, back to back – I'd need support. A Sherpa guide had been called in for each of my summit attempts and several oxygen cylinders* had been distributed across the mountains for me. But everything came crashing down shortly afterwards. As I prepared to leave the South Col for my second peak of the day, word filtered through that the lines on Lhotse were also incomplete. Having experienced the same conditions as the team on Everest, the fixing crew had temporarily halted their work shortly after Camp 4.

Even worse, the Sherpa I was supposed to be climbing Lhotse with had fallen sick and was already descending to Base Camp. I moved from tent to tent trying to convince one of the other guides to join me, but everyone seemed unable to make another summit push in such a short space of time.

My heart sank. Climbing Lhotse solo for the first time was probably beyond me and one fuck-up would have impacted on the hopes of Team B waiting at Everest Base Camp – they

---

* I had placed oxygen in high camps across the mountain. This was done during the acclimatisation rotations and load carry climbs, where equipment, such as oxygen, was dropped off for use later in the mission. Big expedition teams rarely carry all their equipment with them on summit pushes.

needed me to lead them to the summit. I didn't want to let them down. The group had worked so hard to achieve their dreams of scaling Everest with the G200 Expedition. I packed up and headed down, fuming.

By the time I'd reached Camp 2 and rested overnight, it was announced that Team A had reached the top, around eighteen hours after I'd finished my Everest summit. I felt triumphant; our efforts had been worth it, but in a heartbeat the good news was overshadowed by some bad, when it was decided that the expedition was effectively over. Because a number of serving Gurkhas had already summited, the mission had been completed and it had been decided the climbing should stop. The lads still waiting for their shot at Base Camp, blokes who had sacrificed their time and, in some cases, money to fulfil their dream, were going home. It felt like a really selfish move. When I later met up with Team B, the scene was heartbreaking. A few of the lads were in tears.

What had been the point in cutting them down? Some people might argue that, yeah, the job had been nailed, so was there any point in risking more lives on such a dangerous mountain? But those Gurkhas, while not the quickest in the group, were certainly stronger than a lot of climbers that would success-fully top out on Everest at the end of that season. They had also understood the risks associated with high-altitude climb-ing, so there was no harm in sending them up.

But in the fallout, it also dawned on me that had everything gone to plan – if the official fixing team had done their job, and had the original Team A made it to Everest's peak – my role in Team B would have been redundant, too. I'd have been stuck at Base Camp with the others.

I later partied with my Gurkha brothers in Kathmandu a couple of days later, but the buzz of success was offset by a sense of bitterness within the blokes that had been held back. They were pissed off and I couldn't blame them. The expedition had ended on a sour note. And as I knocked back beer after beer, the same question came back to me, over and over. *Yeah, but can you do even more, brother?* My first attempt at Lhotse had been written off, but I was now hearing that the fixed lines had been set all the way to the top. That meant my aim of climbing Everest and then Lhotse and Makalu in the two-week window I'd previously set for myself was back on, though the timing was bloody tight. (And I'd have to climb Everest once again, but I figured, *What the hell?*). I mission-planned my routes along the three peaks, estimating I'd need some luck with the weather to nail the schedule. I'd first work my way up to Everest's Camp 3, climbing across to the summit of Lhotse. I'd then backtrack across to the South Col before scaling Everest. Once that was done, I could then travel over to Makalu's base camp via helicopter.

This was a huge test of endurance, but logistically, I had zero concerns: my oxygen was already in place and I could scoop up the cylinders as I worked my way across the mountains. Plus, the Sherpas I'd booked for the initial attempt were still happy to climb. Yes, I was a little behind schedule, but I'd topped a couple of 8,000ers before and never required anything in the way of recovery time afterwards, so it was within reach for me to move quickly. All I needed was self-belief.

And then disaster struck.

An entire book could be devoted to what happened next, but having arrived at the foot of Everest a day or so later, I noticed a cluster of oxygen cylinders on the ground alongside a pile of other discarded equipment from the G200E. When I looked closely, I realised the bottled air was mine. A Sherpa, having wrongly assumed that I'd decided to pack up and head home, had brought some of my air down from one of the camps. I hit the roof. And then, at the worst possible moment my smart phone vibrated. My brother Kamal was calling. When I answered, he was shouting angrily.

'What the fuck are you still doing up there?' he yelled. 'You've climbed Everest twice already. Last year you saved someone's life. Now this year you saved a whole expedition from being a failure. Your name's already flying around. People know you . . . what are you hoping to prove?'

At first, I tried to explain. I wanted to tell Kamal about what I hoped to do. *Surely he'd understand that this wasn't about me, or my name?* But there was no time and my brother wasn't in the mood to listen. Having been caught in an emotional drama due to my dumped oxygen, it seemed important to avoid any further flashpoints or setbacks. So I hung up. Kamal and his lecture could wait.

I needed time to think. Close to being overloaded with equipment and oxygen bottles for my next climb, I didn't have the space for the extra air I needed, but I consoled myself with the fact that I had air waiting for me at another two camps across the mountain. However, as I ascended to Everest Camp 2 and then Camp 4 at Lhotse, it was clear that nearly all of it had gone. Angrily, I searched the tents and scrabbled around in the freshly dumped snow, as the harsh reality of mountain life dawned upon me.

Someone had stolen it.

I was furious. Climbing without air would go against the principles I'd set for myself following the rescue of Seema. Yes, I had the strength to scale Lhotse, Everest and Makalu anyway, but if I started undervaluing the promises I'd made, the process would become habitual and I'd never hit my targets.

This was an ethos I'd long applied to life: if I ever got up in the morning and told myself that I was going to do three hundred push-ups that day, I made sure to do them, wholeheartedly, because to skip the effort would be to break a commitment, and breaking commitments led to failure. But I also understood that getting angry about the situation wasn't going to help. Military training had taught me it was imperative to remain emotionally strong: flipping a negative event into positive momentum was the only way to remain focused on my primary objective.

Get it together, Nims. Stay tough, bro. You are different – you will *find a solution to this problem.*

Drawing in some settling breaths, I reframed the developing shit show. I visualised my oxygen going to a better place. I forced myself to believe the cylinders had been swiped to save the life of another climber. *Someone has survived because of your oxygen, Nims.* Having emotionally reset, I adapted to the situation, tweaking my schedule and moving across to the South Col again. My plan was now to top Everest first, in what was shaping up to be a stormy event. I'd then climb Lhotse – where I'd arranged for a friend to drop some bottled air for me at Camp 4 – and finally Makalu.

The wind howled around me and for a brief moment, there was a feeling of self-doubt. What I was about to attempt was huge. *But could I make it?*

I steadied myself.

Yeah. You can.

I scaled Everest when the mountain was at its most vicious – hurricane winds swirled at the peak, shards of ice seemed to strike me like bullets, in conditions so severe that a number of other climbers would die that day. But leaning into the blasts, and knowing that my speed would help me, I worked as quickly as I could with my Sherpa; the pair of us fearing for our fingers and toes in the cold as we waited for forty-five minutes at the Hillary Step, a traffic jam of climbers moving up and down its face to the peak. When I eventually topped out, I then dropped to Lhotse with a new Sherpa, pushing on to Camp 4. I looked at my watch at its summit. I'd been climbing for ten hours and fifteen minutes. Now only Makalu remained untested.

Full disclosure: at that point I had no idea I'd broken the world record for climbing Everest and Lhotse in such quick succession. It wasn't my aim, only topping three peaks had been in my sight-lines, but when I was told at Base Camp that the previous best had been twenty hours, I was shocked. I'd accidentally cut nearly ten hours from the fastest registered time.

Another record was in reach. If I could climb Makalu in the next few days, I'd break the world record for the quickest time taken to top Everest, Lhotse and Makalu. I was then informed that nobody had ever climbed Everest twice, plus Lhotse and Makalu in one climbing season. I fancied my chances even though I'd never climbed Makalu at that point and it was the fifth highest mountain in the world. With a helicopter set to take me to the next base camp, piloted by my good mate Nishal, one of the best high-altitude pilots around, I buzzed with excitement at the potential of what was within reach.

'Brother, you've just smashed a world record,' said Nishal, hugging me at the landing zone.

'Yeah, and I can get another one at Makalu.'

I wanted to rush my next steps, but Nishal was keen to put my achievements into perspective. 'Mate, you said you'd do all three mountains in fourteen days,' he said. 'You've got a few days to crack Makalu and still catch your flight home with the G200E guys. Why don't you enjoy the moment? Party for a bit!'

He then pointed out that 29 May was coming up, an event in the Himalayas also known as Everest Day. The celebration marked the first-ever summit of the mountain in 1953 by Tenzing Norgay Sherpa and Sir Edmund Hillary.

'Bro, there's going to be drinking and parades,' said Nishal. 'Everyone's going to be having a lot of fun. You should think about it.'

Realising I could celebrate Everest Day and still have time for the world record, I agreed. I was on holiday after all. Nishal's helicopter swooped into Namche Bazaar and I partied hard, drinking and dancing with some business friends. All the while, though, I remained fixed on Makalu. And Nishal reckoned he had a scheme that would save me even more time.

'Nims, you don't seem tired at all,' he said. 'Why don't you stay here for a bit longer and I'll drop you off at Camp 2 on Makalu rather than Base Camp? No extra charge.'

By my estimate, a chopper ride to Camp 2 usually arrived with an eye-watering price tag of several thousand pounds. What Nishal had proposed was an incredibly generous offer (and he'd stayed sober for my ride the next morning) – but it wasn't for me. To his surprise, I shook my head. By climbing Makalu the next day, from bottom to top, I'd have broken two world records, and learned a lot about the limits of my physical and mental strength. There was no way I wanted to be accused of cutting corners. I needed everything to be legit.

'Thanks, but no way, man,' I said. 'I'm doing this properly.'

Nishal scowled. His friends looked a little annoyed too and I sensed my decision had been mistaken for rudeness, or a lack of gratitude. As the hours passed and the drinking became even sloppier, they couldn't believe I'd passed up such a generous offer. The debate warmed up to the point where a fight looked set to explode. Then Nishal made his final attempt at twisting my arm.

'But no one will know!' he shouted.

'I will! Sure, I *could* lie to the whole world. I *could* make out I've climbed all three mountains from bottom to top, but I won't lie to myself, brother. No way. I'm doing this properly.'

Through the fug of beer, the guys around us gradually came to understand my motives. I explained to everyone that I'd appreciated the gesture, but Makalu was now so much more than the scaling of another peak, or one more achievement on a bucket list of mountains. It was about conquering the last in a hat trick of Himalayan peaks, but in the right way, with integrity, which was important because the effort was a moment of self-discovery on what I could truly achieve if I threw all my physical and psychological resources at a bold expedition idea.

And I smashed it.

Having left Makalu's base camp twenty-four hours later, brutally hungover, I blasted to the peak, all 8,485 metres of it in one hit, leading from the front with my small team and trailblazing through heavy snow, high wind, and disorientating cloud cover until I'd reached the top. This in itself was an achievement. Nobody had climbed Makalu that season, though a number of teams had tried, only to be pushed back by the treacherous conditions.

Once I'd made it back to Base Camp in one piece and discovered our helicopter ride back to Namche Bazaar had been shitcanned thanks to some terrible weather, I then took on one of the hardest treks in Nepal on foot with my Sherpa team, at speed, running all the way to Kathmandu, only stopping to drink beer and whisky, until we'd completed a six-day journey in eighteen hours. Only one dude, Halung Dorchi Sherpa, had lasted the pace with me and I'd felt strong, drawing on my combat training to push through the pain.

I had broken two world records – by climbing Everest and Lhotse in ten hours, fifteen minutes and then topping Everest, Lhotse and Makalu in five days. I was also the first person to climb Everest twice, then Lhotse and Makalu in the same season. And I didn't even feel done.

Having made it to England in one piece, joining my G200E brothers on the flight home, I eventually visited Kamal to see how he was doing. His voice cracked as we spoke. I could tell he was trying not to cry.

'You are my brother,' he said, explaining his anger. 'I was worried about you.'

Any frustration I'd felt for him had faded. 'Listen: it's all good. But when you called me, I was in a moment where I was doubting myself. And then when someone like you, who I respect, tries to put negative energy into my head, it can be hard work to turn it around. I needed positivity. That's why I had to hang up the phone.'

'Why didn't you explain?'

'I had no time! There had been a fuck-up with my oxygen, there was too much going on and I had to focus on that rather than justifying myself to you.'

By the time we'd finished chatting, Kamal understood the whys of what I'd done. It was then my job to figure out the how.

Hanging out with Mum and Dad at Kathmandu International Airport. The three of us were waving off my older brother Ganga who was returning to the UK with the Gurkhas.

With one of my other brothers, Jit. This was taken in the jungle village of Dana.

Getting myself battle-primed for the trials of Gurkha Selection.

All the pull-ups and sit-ups couldn't break me. I was ready for the Gurkhas.

Working hard in the desert. The work was relentless but rewarding.

My first-ever serious climb took place on Lobuche. Just getting used to the feel of the crampons was a new experience.

Once I'd made it to the top of Lobuche, I knew I wanted to climb more and more mountains.

Taking on a fearsome ladder crossing over a crevasse in the Khumbu Icefall during my first expedition on Everest.

Waiting at the South Col on Everest for my summit push to the world's highest point.

Delivering a ladder crossing demonstration to the lads on the G200E in 2017.

Camp One on Everest with the G200E. Politics and pressure would shape an eventful expedition.

When the line-fixing team was unable to set the lines above Everest's high camps, I finished the job with a team of Gurkha and Sherpa brothers.

Job done. Against all odds my line-fixing team made it to the top of Everest.

Making the impossible possible.

Everest in 2017 was no joke. The snow seemed to ricochet off my summit suit like tiny bullets.

The challenging Dutch Rib on Annapurna. Despite the difficulty, this was the safest line to the top.

Emergency Tent

Search and rescue: bringing down Dr Chin from Annapurna.

After five gruelling days on Dhaulagiri we made it to the top, unbroken.

7

The Mission

There were so many questions.

What did I have that many other climbers didn't?

How was it that I'd been able to climb three incredibly challenging peaks in super-quick time without a period of physical recovery in-between?

For some reason I'd felt the desire to run to Kathmandu, when there was time to stroll back at a gentle pace, partying all the way. What was I trying to prove?

Maybe it was because I was constantly trying to push myself, although those qualities weren't exactly unique among the mountaineering community. Meanwhile, I knew of plenty of Special Forces dudes that had climbed Everest, though none that had gone to Lhotse and Makalu, too. But the funny thing was that all of them had been wiped out afterwards, and none of them had possessed the engine to attempt another peak in the immediate aftermath. For some reason, I had the physiology to climb and descend, *climb and descend*, fixing lines and leading expeditions over and over and over, with very little rest. My reserves felt limitless.

Not only was I climbing aggressively, trailblazing through waist-deep snow so easily that I'd left experienced Sherpas in my wake, but I was also able to make highly pressurised decisions at quick speeds thanks to my military training. Assessing risk and reacting accordingly had become second nature; I understood the fine line between being brave and being stupid; negative situations didn't upend me, and I attacked everything with positive thought. Those traits had the potential to turn me into a high-altitude machine.

Of course, there were technically better climbers than me out there, and at sea level I might have found myself on an uneven playing field when my relative strengths and weaknesses were placed against those of some other climbers. But not all of them were able to plan and imagine in the same way as me. Above 8,000 metres, I could locate the self-belief required to take me to the peak of any mountain in the world – whatever the conditions.

I'd also been notified that an honour from the Queen, an MBE, was being arranged as a reward for my outstanding work in high-altitude mountaineering – this included my saving the G200E, rescuing Seema on Everest, and breaking those world records on Everest, Lhotse and Makalu. My achievements hadn't been appreciated by everyone, though. When my records were announced, a number of highly regarded mountaineers were quick to point to the fact I'd used oxygen. But fuck that: my ambitions mainly hinged on pace. I was a trailblazer and I led from the front, fixing my own lines – *that was Nims-style*.

However, it wasn't only about doing everything so much quicker than everyone else. On one hand, Nims-style required me to plan and to lead. On the other, I needed to be self-sufficient on the mountains at all times, and through some hard lessons, I'd come to understand my strengths and limitations; so I worked with them in such a way that I was able to avoid trouble for the most part. I'd rescued somebody at high altitude, but I hated the thought of someone having to leave their own mission to help me. I'd have rather died.

As far as I was concerned, there were no set rules when climbing through the Death Zone. Everyone worked differently and I hadn't complained that some of those same critics had stepped into my footfalls, or used the lines I'd set on their own summit push, hours after my drive to the top, but the snobbery was still annoying, so I worked to make it inspiring. I used it as fuel and in the post-expedition buzz of my climbs through the Himalayas, I decided to up my game. If I could take three of the world's largest mountains in five days, maybe I had it in me to climb the five tallest peaks in an equally impressive time: Everest, K2, Kanchenjunga, Lhotse and Makalu in, say, eighty days? The idea gnawed at me for weeks until I decided to act upon it.

There would be hurdles, I knew that. Having travelled home, I realised my chances of securing the leave needed to take on such an ambitious project were slim, but I was going to take a shot anyway. When the request was made, I tried to be convincing. I reminded the senior officer of my outstanding record, in and out of combat, and my growing climbing expertise. I used my work with the G200E as leverage. *How about the fact I'd advanced the SBS's name even further with those world records?*

My senior officer glanced sceptically at the expedition plan. A negative response was coming, I could tell.

'Climbing K2, Nims? One in four people die there. On Kanchenjunga it's one in seven,' he said. 'This is such a huge project. And it's not as if you're climbing one mountain here. You're running up mountain after mountain in eleven or twelve weeks. *Is this even possible?*'

I tried to appeal to his sense of adventure. 'When I was a Gurkha, I really wanted to join the Special Forces,' I said. 'Not for money, or for the name, but because I wanted to operate among the very best. I fixed lines on the G200E when every-body else had given up. Then I held the flag of the SBS high afterwards. Now I want to attempt this.'

The officer shook his head. There was no way he would authorise so much leave, he explained. It was too risky. Also if it became known that a Special Forces operator was climbing K2, which was located on the border of Pakistan and China, it might invite a terrorist attack. 'It's just not doable, Nims,' he said.

I felt deflated, but I wasn't going to abandon my dream and the toing and froing over my expedition hopes went on for months. On some days, I felt that high command might be relenting. On others, they became increasingly resistant, until eventually, I decided to take matters into my own hands.

'Well, that's it then,' I thought. 'I'm going to quit.'

I felt liberated. I was thirty-five years old at the time and knew that by resigning from my military commitments, I'd give myself the opportunity to think bigger and more boldly in a challenge of my own making. So rather than climbing the five tallest mountains in eighty days, what was stopping me from topping all fourteen Death Zone mountains in the quickest time imaginable? I struggled to think of too many pitfalls. *Only politics or money. Or maybe an avalanche, or a crevasse, if I'm really unlucky.*

It was in the Gurkha blood to be fearless at all times, so while there was every chance an avalanche might sweep me away on Annapurna as it had done for dozens of others, I wasn't going to stress about it too much. Meanwhile, the dangers involved in climbing all fourteen Death Zone peaks were manageable: I'd learned how to work in poor weather and deep snow; I could operate effectively, without fear. Better to die than be a coward, after all. Also, I was comfortable with the idea of going out in my thirties. Hanging on until the age of eighty-something, a time when I'd become unable to look after myself, held very little appeal. I wanted to leave while going out at full tilt.

The political and monetary aspects of the expedition were an entirely different story, though. There would be paperwork and permit requests, particularly from the Chinese and Tibetan authorities, who had closed Shishapangma for the entire climbing season throughout 2019. Then there were the bills. At least £750,000 was required to climb the full portfolio of Death Zone mountains, maybe more, so I'd have to approach a series of sponsors, all the while exploring alternative funding options. But for now the primary mission, in theory, was exciting enough for me to contemplate my departure from the military. If I believed that my goal of climbing all fourteen 8,000-metre peaks in quick succession was achievable, then it was achievable.

Every facet of my training and combat experience had told me so. While serving with the Gurkhas, I'd been constantly forced away from my comfort zones and into moments of extreme pain. Eventually mental strength seemed more important than physical power. Likewise, the British Special Forces, where my training had taught me how to push beyond any psychological limits I'd previously set for myself. The logistics of planning a series of high-altitude expeditions were intimidating, but through my work in the mountains, I'd built up plenty of connections in the climbing community. I possessed the skill and contacts to make it work.

I flipped open my laptop at home one afternoon, hoping to understand how long an expedition of this kind might take. A brief scan online told me that around forty other mountaineers had managed to climb the fourteen 8,000-ers. Of course, there was the current world record holder, Kim Chang-ho, and his time of seven years, ten months and six days during 2013. And Jerzy Kukuczka of Poland wasn't far behind him with a time of seven years, eleven months and fourteen days, as set in 1987, though he was only the second mountaineer to have scaled all the 8,000-ers after the legendary Italian, Reinhold Messner, broke through the glass ceiling of what was considered possible in 1986.

So, the field was fairly small but impressive and, on average, several years seemed to represent the likeliest timeframe. Judging by the way I'd worked through Everest, Lhotse and Makalu in five days – not to mention Dhaulagiri in a fortnight – it was within my reach to go quicker. The only question was by how much.

I worked on a pragmatic estimate. *OK, so there's no funding. It might take some time to get the money together, but if I can stay on home turf in Nepal for the first expeditions, I'll be fine. Plus, I have a ton of contacts there.*

I listed off the mountains I needed to climb: Annapurna, Dhaulagiri, Kanchenjunga, Everest, Lhotse, Makalu and Manaslu . . .

Pakistan will be a different ball game altogether. The treks between mountain base camps is long and the weather is so unpredictable.

Nanga Parbat, Gasherbrum I and II, K2, Broad Peak . . .

But in Tibet, it might take you longer with the paperwork and permits.

Cho Oyu, and Shishapangma . . .

I've only climbed four of these mountains before . . . so how about seven months? That should be enough time to climb all fourteen, give or take a few weeks.

The basic goal of shaving off seven years from the world record was ambitious, but I quickly grew into the idea. The bottom line was to climb as quickly as possible, whatever the weather, *Nims-style*. But there was more than one incentive behind me. Yes, I wanted to push past any physical and emotional limits I might have previously set for myself, but my home country of Nepal had been experiencing the kickbacks of climate change. Alerting the world to the region's floods and disappearing glaciers was a priority too, as was shining a spotlight on the plight of those people living and working within the mountain communities.

Most of all, though, I loved the thought of ripping up the rulebook. If I could show kids and adults alike what was humanly achievable, then my far-fetched ambitions might inspire others to think big; to push themselves in ways that were previously considered unimaginable. It also helped that I might give the world a crazy story to remember.

I gave my grand mission a name – *Project Possible*. Then I prepared a battle plan, steadying myself for the doubters.

* * *

One troubling factor when quitting the SBS was psychological security. That seemed ironic given I'd put my life on the line every time there was a patrol, or a door-kicking operation, but for sixteen years, the British military had been my all. They'd told me where to be and when, and they'd provided me with a house and a daily routine. Yes, the job was dangerous and very high stress, but there were some comforting familiarities to it, even in war, where I had structure, focus and loyalty. Sometimes, while I was planning my exit, I worried whether I'd done enough for Queen and Crown in return.

The other troubling aspect to resigning from the Special Forces was my pension. It was a life-changing chunk of money and to claim it I had to serve for only a few more years. Quitting now meant giving up the lot, which was a worry, and a financial stress I would have to manage down the line.

Putting aside my doubts, on 19 March 2018, having logged onto the Ministry of Defence's website, I submitted my resignation request. My notice period was a year and at first some mates in the squadron tried to change my mind; high command also promoted me to the position of cold-weather warfare instructor, as a subject matter expert (SME), where it became my role to teach other operators how to climb mountains, survive in harsh conditions at altitude, and ski across challenging terrain. This was a prestigious responsibility. It meant that I was considered the best climber within the squadron.

Promotional blackmail wasn't enough, however. I was then asked to consider the logistical pitfalls of my move, and it was argued that by resigning I'd be losing out on the type of financial security that would have excited most people in the Real World. Except, I wasn't most people; I had a different take on the Real World. I'd been raised a poor kid in Nepal. If I really had to, living out of a tent for the rest of my life would have posed no problems at all. The biggest surprise, though, arrived when the SAS learned about my plans to quit and invited me to a meeting at their base. An officer then asked me if I'd ever consider switching regiments.

'Congratulations on the G200E and MBE, Nims,' he said, looking over my records. 'And we know what your strengths are on the mountains. If you were to join the SAS, we'll make sure you'll be looked after, of course. We'll give you better opportunities, which will help you and your family.'

He then offered me some serious bait. I was promised a place on a prestigious, one-year climbing programme in which I'd be able to focus purely on operating at high altitude. Most importantly I'd be provided with a budget for equipment and travel.

It was a dream gig, but as far as I was concerned, jumping between the two wings of the Special Forces felt disloyal, like leaving one football team for a local rival. There was no way I wanted to let the SBS lads down in that way.

'I'm really humbled that you guys have seen something in me,' I said, eventually. 'And it's kind of you to offer me those opportunities . . . but I never joined the Special Forces to be a general, or for money. Going back to financial basics is cool with me and besides, I couldn't switch teams.'

Their response was short and sharp. 'You're loyal, which is to be commended,' said the SAS commander. 'But you're fucking crazy.'

I shrugged my shoulders and thanked him for the meeting, but I was torn. As I drove away from the barracks, it was hard not to wonder if I'd made the wrong decision. *If I did take up this offer, I'd be the first operator to serve in both the SAS and the SBS. There would be some serious kudos.* As I second-guessed myself over the next few days, Suchi even took to searching online for any job opportunities that might suit her in Hereford. In the end I stuck with my original plan: I wanted to climb the big mountains.

My friends and family seemed equally confused. As far as they were concerned, this was the latest in a long line of what they considered to be baffling career developments. My brothers were soon accusing me of being ungrateful. They were arguing that without the money they had sent to Chitwan for my education, I wouldn't have learned English. Without English, it's highly unlikely I'd have made it into the British military. All of this was true, I owed them everything, and Kamal called me in another mood. He couldn't get his head around my plans.

'Brother, *everybody* wants to get into the Special Forces,' he said. 'You're there, but you're turning your back on it. You were ten years in the war and now you are in the driving seat as a cold-weather warfare instructor. You'll get a great pension without losing your fingers, toes, and eyes in battle, but after all that graft, you're going to leave everything behind? *What the fuck?*'

'Kamal, this is not about me,' I said. 'This is not about you either, or the family. We're a small part of a bigger worldwide community and I don't have long to do this – I'm not getting any younger. But if I can make a difference now and show to the world what can be done at high altitude, it's worth it.'

We didn't speak again for two months.

My family life also presented a serious financial commitment. In Nepal, some families insisted that it was down to the youngest son to care for his parents if ever they went broke, or became too old to look after themselves. In Mum and Dad's case, they really needed the money, and Kamal and Ganga had supported them as best they could, but they now had their own families to care for. Since joining the Gurkhas, I'd sent my parents a chunk of wages every month because they were my world, but Mum had recently become very ill.

She was suffering from a heart condition and at one point had to undergo surgery to insert a stent. This was followed by kidney failure and Mum often had to visit hospital for treatment, until eventually she was placed permanently in a Kathmandu facility. (There wasn't a suitable clinic in Chitwan.) My dad, half-paralysed, was unable to visit her in the city and it had become my ultimate goal to bring them together again, in the same house, but with Project Possible now underway, all that was about to be paused, for a little while at least.

The news, when I announced it, upset them at first. Because we had lived so close to Dhaulagiri, it wasn't uncommon for us to talk to climbers trekking through our village as they made their way to and from Base Camp. Sometimes the groups passing through on their way up were visibly reduced in numbers during the return journey, and Mum remembered one occasion when she met two climbers in the local tea house. They were crying. When they told her that some of their friends had been killed on the mountain, she'd found the news disturbing.

A number of years later, having heard about the tragic deaths of so many people on Everest during the avalanches of 2014 and 2015, the thought of me mountaineering filled her with dread. She winced whenever I showed her an expedition video on my phone. The images of me climbing across a crevasse ladder in the Khumbu Icefall seemed to set her off. Mum wanted to know what my new plan entailed.

'So, you know the fourteen biggest mountains in the world, Mum?'

She nodded. 'Some of them.'

Mum listed a few names. *Everest, Dhaulagiri. Oh, and Annapurna.* 'But what has that got to do with you?'

She was fretting. *Was her youngest son losing the plot?*

'Oh, Nirmal,' she said. 'Is it because we're very ill and it's such a burden to look after us? I think you are doing this because you want to kill yourself.'

'It's cool, Mum,' I said. 'I'm going to do this, I'm going to show the world what I am capable of – what we can all do, if we put our minds to something. And I'm going to come back stronger. I'll be a different Nims.'

She smiled. 'You don't listen to what we tell you anyway, so I know you're going to do it whatever we say, but our blessings are with you.'

My family's concerns weren't the only emotional hurdle, however. Friends laughed whenever I talked about Project Possible; fellow operators took the piss. That was fair enough, the goal was supposed to be tough, unrealistic even, but only because nobody had achieved anything quite like it before. But then, space travel and the four-minute mile had both been considered impossible ahead of their realisation, too. At the turn of the twentieth century, the idea that someone might step foot on the moon was the type of fantasy that kids had only read about in Jules Verne novels. If somebody had informed a young Neil Armstrong, then a test pilot on the verge of greatness, that his dream wasn't achievable, would he have listened? No *way*.

Of course, there was a chance I might fail, as there had been during the moon landings. Certainly, the odds I'd be killed along the way were fairly short. In the aftermath of screwing up, people were set to laugh, or to say, 'I warned him.' But at least I wouldn't die wondering, *what if?*

And if I could pull it off . . . *what then?*

8

The Highest Stakes

From the minute my one year's notice was accepted by the Ministry of Defence, I set two plans in motion. The first was to organise my operational detail for Project Possible. I pulled together a team of Nepalese climbers that I knew would be up to the task of supporting me over the fourteen peaks, and for the best part of a year. I figured out which mountains to climb and when, based upon the weather reports of the past five climbing seasons.

Having assessed the topographic conditions of each mountain, I decided to split Project Possible into three phases. The first was to take place in Nepal and it was my plan to crash through Annapurna, Dhaulagiri, Kanchenjunga, Everest, Lhotse and Makalu through April and May. This would be followed by the Pakistani mountains of Nanga Parbat, Gasherbrum I and II, K2 and Broad Peak in July. Finally, it was my aim to return to Nepal for Manaslu in the autumn, before heading to Tibet to top Cho Oyu and Shishapangma. Every mountain required some legal work in order to obtain the necessary climbing permits, but China and Tibet were set to be particularly tricky, because Shishapangma was apparently closed through 2019.

I decided to worry about that particular battle when it arrived.

Prepping for missions was my bag, it had been a part of my military life for so long, but the second part of the organisation process was less transferrable from my career skills: I needed to gather together an operational fund, a daunting task because high-altitude mountain climbing had long been an expensive sport. The cost of climbing Everest alone in 2019 could range between $40,000 and $150,000 and those early financial estimations for completing Project Possible had been intimidating – there was no way I'd be able to drum up a cash reserve of that kind without help.

I'd learned that to fund projects of this nature I would have to rely on a series of sponsorship deals, in which companies financed my trip in return for exposure and branding opportunities whenever I topped one of the fourteen peaks. Some extra cash would arrive from guiding tours,* and I aimed to take experienced mountaineers to the peaks of one mountain from each phase, in this case Annapurna, Nanga Parbat and Manaslu.

The work was relentless. While I planned the fourteen expeditions throughout 2018, a friend worked on securing the financing. Between my military commitments, I knackered myself out with meetings, planning sessions and train journeys when I could, running on fumes for seven days a week. Psychologically, the logistical effort felt as gruelling as my time on Selection. But like those early mornings on the Brecon Beacons, I approached every day with a positive thought: *I can*

---

* I liked the idea of fusing my career to my passion and so I set up Elite Himalayan Adventures in December 2017. In 2018 the group began leading clients – expert climbers who paid to be guided by a team of skilled guides – to the top of 8,000-metre peaks.

do this. I will navigate just about every problem the mission might throw at me. I've already climbed the world's tallest peak. The only thing standing in my way right now is funding. Get out there and smash it.

In the same way that joining the Gurkhas, passing Selection and climbing Everest had represented personal Gods, ambitions to lift myself up for, so raising money became a new and powerful idol. I gave Him everything.

My next detail was to help in the cash-building process and with a business partner – an anonymous accomplice – we contacted a series of contacts for investment. I knew that to present Project Possible as an attractive proposition, it was important to make some bold statement about the mission, something that would generate headlines and get people talking.

Emboldened by my world-record-breaking success, I announced my intention to establish even more benchmarks. The first one, obviously, was the speed at which I intended to climb the fourteen 8,000-ers, and of course I reckoned it was doable to smash my own personal best on Everest, Lhotse and Makalu. (And with it the fastest time from the summit of Everest to the summit of Lhotse.) But I also revealed that I intended to break the world's quickest time for climbing the Pakistan 8,000-ers, as well as the speed taken to climb the top five highest mountains in the world: Kanchenjunga, Everest, Lhotse, Makalu and K2.

My ambitions didn't seem to gather too much attention – maybe people thought I was joking – and after several months spent on a conveyor belt of meetings and phone calls, I was dealt a crushing blow.

'Nims, we've raised barely any money,' said my associate, sadly. 'And it's not looking good.'

He was right, there was nothing in the bank and Phase One already felt like a non-starter. I was in trouble. Or so I thought. I immediately switched up my tactics and decided to front the money-raising drive myself as the daily routine became even more intense. Most mornings I got up at 4 a.m., working on my social media outreach for a few hours before racing to the 7 a.m. train into London from the south coast. Usually I'd take around four or five meetings a day, soaking up the false promises and flat-out rejections. On the rare occasions my work was done before midnight, I'd open up my computer to write a series of follow-up emails, before rounding off the day with another session on Instagram, or Facebook.

I was barely tech savvy at that time. Simply preparing a couple of Project Possible-related posts, while adding the relevant links and hashtags, sometimes took me all of two hours. The work felt like a grind, and at times I voiced my frustration online:

Another day of battle in reference to the fund-raising campaign for Project Possible: 14/7. The journey of fund-raising has been extremely hard for me, and also it's not my expertise. Whoever I approach, they say, 'Nims, why not next year? If we do it next year, we will have enough time to raise the funds.' My answer has always been the same: by saying we will do it next year, we are going for the easier option.

Next to nothing in the way of cash arrived for a couple of months. By the turn of 2019, with my clock ticking, I couldn't seem to convince any potential sponsors of my abilities, and meetings often ended with a thanks-but-no-thanks dismissal. What I intended to do, they argued, wasn't humanly possible and a few people even laughed off my plans. I was in a rough spot. Having departed from the military, my income was slashed, but despite the belt-tightening at home, Suchi remained supportive. She never applied any emotional pressure, even though all my efforts were going into a project that wasn't bringing any money into the household – in the short term at least. I was grateful for the room to breathe.

The implications of my changing role within the financial organisation of Project Possible were problematic, but manageable. The work drained me and it became very hard to switch off from what quickly became a never-ending to-do list. Mentally I felt a little frazzled, but rather than talking to Suchi about the strain I was under, it seemed easier to make out that everything was running smoothly. Passing on any stressed energy to her was the last thing I wanted to do, so I'd creep out of bed at one or two in the morning to work on another email or letter while she slept.

I found it impossible to slow down, because I was carrying so much desire for the mission. Meanwhile, the thought of quitting never entered my mind, as I didn't want to transfer any negative vibes subconsciously to potential investors or sponsors.

To instil faith in others, it was important that I maintained faith in myself. But at times it would prove bloody hard work.

* * *

Every attempt at drumming up substantial finances for Project Possible fell short and I was fast approaching a crossroads where I could either quit the mission, or I could press ahead. Hope arrived shortly afterwards. Through an SBS friend, I was introduced to an interested business partner. He understood my passion and immediately promised to bring £20,000 to the planning kitty; I later spoke at a corporate event and earned another ten grand. It was barely a drop in the ocean, considering I needed to pull together around three quarters of a million quid, but the money represented some progress.

From there, Elite Himalayan Adventures invited private clients to join me on the Annapurna climb during Project Possible and I constructed a GoFundMe page, boosting my followers and donations with daily updates on Instagram and a word-of-mouth buzz. Ant Middleton, another friend from the military, even pitched in a donation of £25,000. He had previously been a keen supporter of the Gurkha Regiment and we'd served together in the same elite squadron.

But it still wasn't enough. To ensure Phase One's inception, I'd need to make a drastic and painful sacrifice: I had to remortgage the house and it was my only way out, seeing that all my personal savings had gone into the mission. While my retired friends from the military had bought two or three houses with their income and savings, and were doing pretty nicely with it too, I'd invested everything else into climbing. It was an expenditure that was bound to pay off in the long run, but in the short term it had proved an expensive trade to develop.

In any event, remortgaging was risky, but I knew that if I were to execute Project Possible, the commercial kickbacks in the afterglow of success would help to repay any loans I might take. I could expect to charge premium guiding fees, and there was a chance I might join the lucrative after-dinner speaker's circuit, like one or two of my buddies from the Special Forces. The consequences of failure were massive, though. If I was unable to climb all fourteen peaks in the time I'd promised, people would write me off as a loudmouth and any expected career boosts in the fallout might take longer to kick in.

While I'd previously joked with friends that, if push came to shove, I'd be able to live in a tent for the rest of my life . . . *I didn't really want to*. A more sobering reality had also struck me. If I couldn't return from my mission in one piece, the entire financial burden of my failure would land on Suchi and the family. I needed her blessing to take this risky next step.

I'd every faith that she had my back. Suchi had always understood the physical and emotional sacrifice I'd made to protect my country at the highest military level. She also knew that Project Possible was a mission for the now, because my recent engagement in combat meant I was physically fit and strong enough to finish the job. Waiting until the following year, or even five years down the line, reduced my chances of survival and success. Psychologically I was also in a very good place following my work in war. I'd seen some horrible things during service, acts of brutality and violence that I sometimes wished I could unsee, but I was mentally steady and for the most part, the horror of conflict had seemingly bounced off me.

I suppose it helped that my retirement from the SBS had been a decision of my own making, and that I had a project to throw myself into. Many lads were forced to leave, either through injury or because they weren't capable of doing a job that required razor-sharp focus any more. A number of operators exited the squadron because they'd been emotionally broken. For those people, finding a new life – one with commitment, unity and excitement – could be a challenge every bit as testing as war. I was lucky. I'd quit the job because I had a new passion and the idea of climbing fourteen peaks gave me something to work for every day. Later, I was able to build a strong camaraderie with the people I'd chosen to join me for the ride.

I also understood the healing power of nature. It felt good to be outside, climbing at altitude across an environment that didn't care about race, religion, colour or gender. Only humans showed bias, the mountains were impartial. *There was no judgement*.

Whenever friends had opened up to me about the serious emotional problems they might have been having, I'd taken them climbing. The mountains were just about the best therapy a person could experience. Life felt so much simpler when you were connected to nature by a climbing rope and a set of crampons.

So I sucked up my pride and asked Suchi.

'I've given everything to this dream,' I said. 'Without this project I wouldn't be the same person. If the worst comes to the worst and I don't complete the fourteen mountains, we can still make a living from the climbing company afterwards. We can survive anything. I believe that if we lose all that we've gained in life so far, and we have to start again, we'll be OK.'

After everything I'd put her through, such as my time fighting in a dangerous job abroad for several years, or my retiring from work early and turning down a huge pension in order to climb mountains, this was a bold ask. But I was all out of options. Using our home as collateral on a massive loan was my only forward step.

She looked at me sternly. 'OK, Nims,' she said. 'But you better be right.'

It was reassuring to know that Suchi still believed in me, and that she had faith in Project Possible. She then told me that there was zero doubt in her mind that I'd succeed in the mission once it was up and running, but she was a little nervous about the financial hit we'd be taking as a consequence. I'd long known that there was a power in her that not a lot of people carried, not only as a wife, but as a woman too, and I was grateful for all of it. She was prepared to risk everything we had for my dream.

In a weird way, the sacrifice wasn't so unsettling for me. I'd spent my military career living at my emotional limits, so the thought of losing our home was another form of mental distress, one that I could manage effectively. My default setting was that if the worst were to happen, I'd find a way to make a living. I wasn't scared to struggle amid uncertainty, but for Suchi it was a very different scenario, and she'd been prepared to gamble all the same.

The relief was huge.

* * *

There was a moment or two where I nearly crumbled during the fund-raising drive.

In February, only a month away from the beginning of Project Possible, and following another chaotic week of endless, fruit-less meetings, train journeys and phone calls, I drove home along the M3 to Poole one afternoon. My mind was a blur of numbers, bills and contracts. The £65,000 equity on the house had been withdrawn, though I'd held back enough cash to pay the domestic bills while I climbed and guided throughout 2019. The rest of it was being ploughed into Project Possible and slowly we were making progress, booking flights, securing permits, and gathering together all the equipment and supplies I needed to start the mission.

But still I stressed. I'd been exhausted by the lack of support outside of my immediate bubble. *Why would nobody back me?* Meanwhile, the weight of Nepalese tradition hung from me like a Bergen loaded with bricks. *What would happen to my parents if I couldn't finish?* For a brief moment, as the brake lights and indicators flickered on the road ahead, I became overwhelmed. My eyes brimmed with tears.

Fucking hell, Nims, why are you doing this to yourself? To everybody you love?

Pulling into a lay-by to compose my thoughts, I recalled the full potential of what might happen if I *was* to achieve the unthinkable.

Point one: Project Possible wasn't just about me. That had always been my truth. Yes, the pressure was all on my shoulders and the ambition and hard work, not to mention any spoils at the end, would be undeniably mine. But I needed to remember my objectives. I was showing humankind what was achievable if an individual put their mind and body to reaching a seemingly insurmountable target – and that was a big deal. Re-establishing the Nepalese climbing community as being the best in the world, as it had been during large chunks of the twentieth century, was important, too. Then there were statements to be made about climate change. Finally, I was a bloody Special Forces soldier. Emphasising the image of the SBS as an elite troop, in and out of combat, was another driving force.

Point two: Project Possible was *never* just about me.

I dried my eyes.

Let's get this fucking done.

As I'd learned in war, every obstacle or enemy was another challenge to be figured out and overcome. I'd needed to adapt and survive in my new environment, as I had while working through Selection, fighting in warzones, and climbing the world's biggest mountain. Rebooted, I pressed ahead for the next few weeks, sucking up the rejections from a string of potential backers, while attempting to convince those individuals that couldn't understand the potential of what I was hoping to achieve.

There were more refusals. *Why should we throw money at a plan that's set to fail?* Others worried that they might be pushing me towards a nasty end. *If we fund the impossible and Nims dies, will we be partially to blame?* It was demoralising, but it made me more determined. I'd prove them all wrong through action rather than presentations, once the mission kicked off.

Luckily, not everyone I spoke to was so pessimistic. I heard that the UK's Nepalese community and a group of retired Gurkhas had organised a Project Possible fund-raising drive. Pensioners and veterans were donating cash sums of £5, £10 and £20, and the gesture was incredibly humbling. As the countdown to my first climb approached, I'd amassed around £115,000 in total from various income streams. The figure was barely enough to cover Phase One of the project, but I expected more interest to arrive with every climb that followed. As sponsors, media and the mountaineering community watched my progress, I figured the sceptics would soon be shocked into action and their money was sure to roll in afterwards.

Relying on self-belief and momentum, I readied myself for the most ambitious operation of my life.

9

Respect Is Earned

There were many reasons *not* to attempt Annapurna as the first expedition on the schedule. For starters, the world's tenth-highest mountain had gathered a fearsome rep as being the deadliest. By the start of 2019, around 60 climbers had died there in total and it carried possibly the scariest survival rate in high-altitude mountaineering, killing 38 per cent of mountaineers brave enough to attempt it. Much of the danger was a result of Annapurna's instability; it was a glacial warzone, prone to avalanches that spewed snow, rock, and shattered ice walls onto anyone unfortunate enough to be standing in the wrong place at the wrong time. Unseen crevasses also crisscrossed the mountain and many people had fallen unknowingly to their deaths after a slip into a hidden crack in the terrain.

Meanwhile, the weather in that part of the Himalayas was temperamental, it changed in a heartbeat, and the conditions could be so extreme that around forty-three people were killed in a snowstorm during 2014, including twenty-one trekkers. It has long been known that when the bad storms rolled in at Annapurna, a fairly inaccessible peak suddenly became impenetrable.

While there was every opportunity to start on one of the less intimidating climbs in the region, Annapurna presented me with the opportunity to assess my expedition team. To climb any 8,000-er an experienced mountaineer required a support crew, and because we'd have to fix a lot of lines ourselves throughout the fourteen peaks, I wanted to work with the right number of climbing buddies per mountain. For example, if I was leading the fixing team to the very top, and we were the only expedition on the mountain, I'd need several guys. However, on some mountains where I was familiar with the terrain and the ropes had been fixed all the way to the top, I'd need only one climbing buddy, such as on Everest.

Discovering exactly how effective my crew could be was critical – and I had to find out quickly. While everyone in the group I'd gathered together throughout 2018 was a seasoned guide with a number of 8,000-metre peaks to their name, executing fourteen climbs in quick succession was a challenge for the ages. My experience in war had taught me that a person's true character always emerged when presented with a life-or-death event, and that reveal often took place in a gun battle. A newly passed-out Gurkha or Royal Marine Commando might have breezed through training, but there was no way to assess their true battle readiness until the bullets and bombs were flying around for real.

In mountaineering terms, Annapurna was a gunfight. We were setting the fixed lines, the work was bound to be heavy going, and potential death awaited us at every stage – it was almost the perfect test scenario for all of us. For the team setting the route, there was no easy path to the top; for the person leading that fixing team, the pressure to execute was huge.

I needed to know which individuals I could trust to keep their head in dangerous flashpoints; I also wanted to discover any weak links or flaws within the group, if there were any at all. Some guides that had joined me were already friends or associates from the mountain, such as Mingma David, Lakpa Dendi Sherpa and Halung Dorchi Sherpa.

Mingma was Dorje Khatri's nephew and I'd first met him in Kathmandu in 2014, shortly after the Khumbu Icefall tragedy of the same year. Through friends I'd heard he was an impressive climber who had scaled Everest, Lhotse, Makalu and K2. He was slight, around fifty-four kilos wet through, but Mingma was built from taut muscle. Whenever I'd bumped into him during expeditions, he always struck me as one of the strongest guides I'd ever seen. And everybody had heard the stories of Mingma's high-altitude rescue missions – he had saved people on Dhaulagiri, Makalu, and Everest.

I knew that Mingma would want to join me, following on from an encounter I'd had with him during my first successful ascent of Everest in 2016. I'd been working my way to the top with Pasang. Meanwhile Mingma was supporting the *Everest Air* team I'd met at Lukla Airport, and he had spotted us as we worked our way steadily to Camp 4. High winds had blasted everybody on Everest that day, and as Pasang and I dug a temporary snow shelter for protection, I noticed Mingma and another Sherpa pitching a tent nearby. Waving, they called us over.

'Nimsdai, what are you doing here?' said Mingma. 'We heard you were sick with HAPE?'

In Nepali, the word *dai* translates to 'brother'.

'Yeah, I was in a bad way, but I've got my shit together,' I said, laughing. 'I just needed to take some time off. I'm going for it now.'

I looked at the faces staring back at me in the fading light.

Mingma seemed to be weighing up whether I was bold, or holding a death wish.

Eventually, he spoke up. 'You know, Nims, our job is to help a climber to the top. We can follow anyone on any mountain.'

He pointed to Pasang. 'Your Sherpa is not experienced, so . . .'

So?

'I'll follow you, Nimsdai. I'll help you.'

I felt torn. My scrape with HAPE meant I'd already blown the goal of making it to the top alone; I needed Pasang to summit Everest. But it was also important that I didn't become a burden to any other expeditions on the mountain, and I was so bothered by the thought of my lungs failing again that the stress of being rescued at high altitude made me feel a little uneasy. Still, Mingma's kind support was something to consider. Feeling humbled, I made myself comfy in their tent, waiting until the winds had died down enough for climbing to resume again. Mingma was a reputable figure; the mountaineering equivalent to an elite operator. *And he wanted to team up with me?*

The gesture had blown me away. While I eventually passed up their assistance and climbed Everest with Pasang, I knew Mingma was exactly the type of individual I would love to work with in the future – he was strong and fearless.

But he was also well connected and wanted to bring Gesman Tamang into the Project Possible family, a strong, but relatively inexperienced climber, in terms of Death Zone peaks at least. Like Mingma he'd been to the peaks of Everest, Lhotse and Makalu, only not as frequently; he was also trained in avalanche rescue and high-altitude mountain rescue.

'He's a good guy, a bull,' promised Mingma, when he first

mentioned Gesman. 'He's done the right courses. You can trust him.'

While hardly being the most watertight of CVs, Mingma's word was as good as any. But physical strength wasn't the only asset possessed by both Mingma and Gesman – they were positive spirits too, and I'd decided that everyone called in to the mission needed to carry an optimistic mindset. I wanted individuals that climbed for passion, not money or glory. (Though they would be getting paid pretty well for the work.) Most importantly, they had to feel a pride for the Nepalese guiding community.

Project Possible was my way of thrusting Sherpa culture into the limelight, because for too long their heroic work had been overlooked within the climbing industry. As far as I was concerned, they had been the driving force behind a lot of successful expeditions above 8,000 metres, and propelling every against-all-odds expedition was a support network of Sherpas that performed all the heavy lifting. Who do you think set the fixed ropes on Everest? And who carried the heavy equipment and supplies over huge distances while their paying clients moved relatively freely?

They executed other, more specialised, roles too. On Everest, for example, a unit of Sherpas called 'Ice Doctors' placed ladders and guide ropes over the hundreds of crevasses that scarred the Khumbu Icefall. Typically, the guys were all paid, but the fees they charged were very low when set against the overall cost of an expedition. Without their work, most ascents would fail; relatively inexperienced climbers would die. The Sherpa guide had been making the impossible possible for years, though for the most part, their work was rarely celebrated.

That attitude – *the politics of the mountain* – annoyed the hell out of me. When I'd first started climbing the 8,000-ers, I watched, impressed, as excellent climbers scaled the Death Zone peaks, and their achievements were always glorified by climbing websites and magazines. Then I looked for the names of the guys supporting that particular climber – *the true heroes*. After all, they were carrying more weight, they were fixing more lines; they were working so much harder than everybody else, but nobody ever mentioned them by name.

The disparity in respect pissed me off, and while it was a paid job, the work required of a Sherpa was incredibly dangerous. With Project Possible I wanted to highlight the skills of Nepal's climbers, but for that to work I needed my team to have the same philosophies as me. I didn't want sheep, or dedicated followers. I wanted a group of thinkers.

There was a hierarchy, though. From the outset, I made it clear that it would be my job to run the team, to make decisions under pressure and to use all the skills I'd learned on the mountain, in the military elite, and while operating as a cold-weather warfare specialist. Some of those skills and processes would be transferred into Project Possible. In the Special Forces, each team was made up of expert warriors. My aim had been to build a climbing group with an identical dynamic. Sure, I was team leader, but the others guys would be operating as specialist climbers; each of them possessed expert skills and were capable of looking after themselves in moments of high drama.

With a superior level of unity, I wanted us to trailblaze through the deepest snow and into the hardest weather towards the fourteen summits. I wanted us to become elite – *to be regarded as the Special Forces of high-altitude mountaineering*. And from there, I wanted that respect to shine favourably upon the entire Sherpa community.

In many ways, I was running a high-altitude equivalent of the UK Special Forces Selection on Annapurna. Project Possible's operators had to be strong, capable and emotionally positive – the lads that were joining me had all proven they had potential to deliver, but our first climb would encompass all the most testing parts of Selection rolled into one.

I was also looking for different things in different people and I intended to split the expedition into two groups. The core team would feature Mingma, Gesman, Geljen Sherpa and Lakpa Dendi Sherpa. Meanwhile a secondary group comprising Sonam Sherpa, Halung Dorchi Sherpa, Ramesh Gurung, and Mingma's brother, Kasang Sherpa would be on hand to provide back-up if necessary. Another colleague, Dawa Sherpa, was in place to double-check all my expedition plans as we went along.

I was happy with the set-up; the team was full of characters. Geljen Sherpa was initially tasked with fixing the lines as part of our team on Annapurna, but had offered to stay on for the duration of Project Possible. I liked the dude; his spirit brimmed with enthusiasm. Geljen danced; he smiled. Nothing seemed to dent or upset him, and as we readied ourselves at Annapurna's base camp, and planned our infrastructure for Dhaulagiri, I noticed a shared mentality was building between us. The team worked hard and played hard and nobody moaned if the effort looked like becoming too rough, as it so often did on the mountains.

Whenever I tweaked our plan for Annapurna, the others said, 'Let's do this!' Every idea was tested and nothing was dismissed out of hand, as if everybody had forgotten how to say no. Plenty of that had to do with our team spirit, but a number of the lads had heard about my previous efforts on Everest, Lhotse and Makalu. I'd earned their respect and they were in the process of earning mine. This was exactly the psychology we needed if Phase One was to be executed.

On the support team, Sonam Sherpa had been installed to look after the logistical side of every summit push, as well as caring for our clients during 'paid-for' expeditions, where expert climbers were guided to the peak, as they would be on Annapurna, and also on Nanga Parbat in July and Manaslu in September. While on the mountain, Sonam would also help us to fix lines and maintain eyes on the whole expedition from the rear, taking our radio calls from higher up while ensuring the expedition was running smoothly at Base Camp and beyond.

If an unexpected weather pattern was pushing in, Sonam acted as our early warning system. If a mission turned ugly, he'd be required to organise any necessary assistance, such as a helicopter rescue. Alongside him on the support team, Lakpa Dendi Sherpa was a climber who had previously helped me to fix the lines on the G200E in 2017. Together, we'd hauled 2400 metres of rope to the top of Everest on summit day. By the looks of things, the dude could lift a mountain on his own.

While the two units were both strong and experienced, managing their skills would be key. Though the guys in place had all climbed several 8,000-ers, some mountains such as Gasherbrum I and II, K2 and Broad Peak were going to be new experiences for all of us – I had topped only four of the 8,000-ers myself at that time. But by climbing them successfully, each individual in the Project Possible crew would expand their experience and reputation; they would become a more sought-after guide for any expedition parties looking to climb the Death Zone peaks in the future.

Heading such a determined group would require all the leadership skills I'd gathered during my time with the military, though I'd also received an education in how *not* to lead, following my experiences with the G200E. There was no way I intended on letting people down at the very last minute. Keeping morale high was going to be key, especially when survival became a major issue.

The work was set to be a balancing act, but I intended on building our operational structure from the heart. When we were climbing unfamiliar mountains, such as Kanchenjunga, the likes of Mingma and Gesman would lack experience, as would I, which had the potential to unsettle everybody's confidence. But at the same time, our work ethic – a desire and ambition; our camaraderie – would drive Project Possible to the top and back. I also understood that to lead with passion, I had to climb more powerfully than the guys around me, but not by too much.

On previous expeditions, I'd worked with strength, trailblazing steadily until the other climbers in the group had been dots in my slipstream. That style of effort had two negative knock-on effects: (1) I often had to wait for an hour or two in the freezing cold while the others caught up with me. (2) My spurts were demoralising to everyone else. Imagine running a marathon with a serious athlete. It's pretty discouraging to watch them sprinting off into the distance. But if that same athlete stays in touch, pushing their colleagues to run a little quicker than they'd previously been used to, their presence can be inspirational. It drags everybody along at a speed they previously hadn't considered possible.

I made it my plan to adopt that same attitude. I would speed up when I thought it might benefit the team, but I would back off when assistance was needed. As a result, we'd hopefully always summit as a group.

If, by the end of 2019, everybody felt proud enough to say

they were an integral part of a successful Project Possible mission, then my work would have been done.

* * *

When I eventually arrived at Annapurna's base camp on 28 March 2019, the doubters were everywhere, and as I readied myself from the small outpost at the foot of the world's most dangerous mountain, there seemed to be a dismissive attitude in almost everybody I spoke to. An expedition of hardcore climbers and seasoned guides had shown up; some of them knew about Project Possible and my plans to conquer the fourteen summits in less than seven months. Those that hadn't heard were given the gossip; they then scanned my posts on social media and laughed. It wasn't hard to imagine what they were thinking. *OK, Mr Big Climber. You've been up and down some pretty impressive mountains, but do you know what it really means to climb all the 8,000-metre peaks?*

I shut out the negative noise and told myself it was nothing more than a distraction.

The climbing community might have misjudged my determination to pull off the impossible in a big way, but at the same time, I understood the surreal mood. Kim Chang-ho had taken nearly eight years to achieve the same feat, so to put my mission into sea level terms, it was as if I'd announced my aim to break Eliud Kipchoge's 2018 marathon world record of two hours, one minute and thirty-nine seconds. But rather than knocking a second or two off an already incredible time, I'd promised to smash all 26.2 miles in around ten minutes.

To a lot of climbers, Project Possible probably sounded like an insane flight of fantasy. A few people had accused me of over-reaching; they wondered why I was shouting about my plans from the rooftops when I could have approached the mission with stealth, without drawing any attention from the outside world.* Thankfully, there were supporters cheering me on too, and every now and then I'd read an encouraging message on Instagram, or chat to someone who'd been enthused by the idea.

I'd need every scrap of their positivity.

A day or so before we began our first rope-fixing climb, the team performed a *Puja*. This was a Nepalese ceremony, conducted with a lama – a spiritual leader – during which the group offered prayers to the mountain gods. Juniper was scorched; rice was thrown and a mast of prayer flags was raised. The hope was that those same gods might grant us a safe passage to the peak, sparing us from the wrath of an avalanche or crevasse fall.

While I wasn't dedicated to one God, I believed in the power of prayer. I also liked to connect with nature alone and once the Puja was completed, I took myself away from the group to stare up at Annapurna's summit. The sky was a bright blue; thick cloud drifted around the higher edges, but I was locked into a one-to-one conversation with the wall of rock and ice ahead. In a way, I wanted to ask the mountain for permission.

OK, can I? Or can I not?

Having watched and waited, I sensed hope.

If anything was troubling me at that point, it was the lack of physical preparation I'd undertaken. Because of my departure from the military and the seemingly endless meetings and fund-raising efforts throughout the past year, I'd been unable to expose my body to the types of pressure I'd once worked

---

* In many ways, executing the work in an off-the-radar style would have suited me nicely. The problem was, I was starting from scratch financially. To get money, I needed sponsorship. To acquire sponsorship, I'd have to put on a show, while working on the mountain and off it.

through in service, although I was still pretty fit. In and out of combat, I was always incentivised to exercise hard as an elite operator and there had been plenty of opportunities for me to gain strength every day, either in battle or through training. But having moved into a civilian setting, where my priorities had shifted to the logistical planning of Project Possible, plus the occasional guiding expedition, I wasn't as sharp as I'd been during previous climbs.

I took any opportunities to ready myself for Project Possible whenever they presented themselves. On the way to Annapurna's base camp, I lifted rocks in strength and conditioning-style training sessions in the village of Dana. I topped that off with a twenty-kilometre run. While this was hardly ideal preparation, and the first session I'd had time to complete in nearly four months, I knew that once we'd started the line-fixing process, I'd become even stronger.

I needed to be. The route we were taking was a monster: a line over Annapurna's north face, an intimidating climb that was first scaled by the French climber, Maurice Herzog in 1950. But once we'd made the decision to commit to the expedition on April 2, as the line-fixing team, I pressed ahead with confidence accompanied by Mingma and Geljen, plus a few other Sherpa guides from other expedition parties; eager to execute the first stage in our mission, which was to set the ropes up to Camps 1 and 2.

The way up was unforgiving. Initially, the path led us through a snow-covered field of rocks that a climber could negotiate without too much bother, but beyond that, the route became sketchy. The landscape was cracked by deep crevasses – some of them were visible, others had been hidden below a carpet of thick snow, and one wrong step would see a climber fall to their death; so it was important that all of us were roped up. If somebody slipped through the snow, the weight of the remaining mountaineers, bracing as a group, would hopefully arrest their fall.

Before long, we were high above Base Camp, but the weather conditions had worsened. As we anchored ropes and fixed lines, a heavy wind seemed to whip around us in a fury. The snow was soon packed into waist-deep drifts and the work became a grind, but as point man, it was my job to drag the other team members along, lifting my legs high and planting my boots firmly, with focus, so that the others could fall in behind, all the while listening out for the tell-tale rumblings of an incoming avalanche. Not that I'd have been able to correct course with any forewarning. With every step, I gave myself a reminder: I was strong; there was no doubt I'd eventually reach the summit, but avalanches were an uncontrollable act of God that nobody could truly prepare for.

I felt the crunch of snow under my boots and the icy burn of oxygen in my lungs and climbed, slowly, but steadily.

10

The Normality of the Extreme

After hours and hours of heavy work, having trailblazed through kilometre after kilometre of knee-deep snow, the Project Possible team walked into Camp 2. We'd tackled steep ribs and buttresses, negotiating a series of crevasses along the way. Bloody hell, the effort had been grinding, but with the fixed lines in place, we were someway closer to being primed for our eventual summit push – *whenever that might happen.* We still had so much to climb, but despite the fatigue, everybody seemed to be in high spirits, mainly because the strong winds had died down and the mountain felt much calmer. The sun was drooping; the group danced and joked, while the smell of fried chicken and rice wafted over the camp.

Then there was a crack, like thunder, from somewhere above us.

Oh no . . .

The all-too-familiar rush of adrenaline kicked in, a sensory call-to-action I'd previously only associated with incoming gunfire, or an exploding IED, but this time the adversary was bigger and potentially more destructive. *Avalanche!* And it was a big one. A large chunk of Annapurna's north face had sheared away and an eruption of white was billowing down the mountain at an unstoppable speed. For a split second I seemed unable to react, paralysed, as the magnitude of what was about to happen shorted my nervous system. Everything in the avalanche's path was in danger of being crushed. *And we were very much in the avalanche's path*. There was no way of escaping it.

Move!

As I looked around for a point of cover, I realised that Mingma and Sonam were rigid too, frozen by fear. The scene wasn't unlike one of those CCTV clips that were sometimes shown in the aftermath of a tsunami, when shocked passers-by stare at the oncoming tidal wave on the horizon, seemingly incapable of running away. By the time their fight-or-flight mechanisms have kicked in, it's usually too late – they're unable to escape. Now an equally terrifying fate was powering towards us.

'Fuck, we're going to go!' I shouted. 'Everybody into the shelters!'

I'd often been told that it was always best to seek some form of protection in the event of an avalanche, even something as flimsy as a tent would do. *Well, it was better than nothing.* Acting on instinct, I ran for the nearest one and dived inside. Sonam and Mingma bundled in behind me, zipping up the door. Readying ourselves for impact, we huddled together, shoulder-to-shoulder, the avalanche's roar growing ever louder as the ground trembled around us. Escaping the chaos seemed unlikely. Sensing we might have to cut our way quickly out of the tent once we'd been smothered, I shouted instructions to the others.

'Mingma, get your knife. Sonam, back yourself against the tent poles and brace.'

But Sonam looked broken. He was mumbling a prayer to

the mountain gods. I felt another shiver of fear. *Fuck, this is bad.*

There was a moment of wishful thinking. *I hope that prayer works, Sonam.* And then god-knows how much snow smashed over us at full force, hammering and tearing at the tent. For several seconds the fabric and fibreglass seemed to buck and wrench without breaking. I expected to be swept down the mountain at any second, all of us tumbling over one another, until suddenly, unexpectedly, everything became still again. There was a silence; then I heard the sound of panicked breathing. We'd survived.

'Sonam, are you cool?' I asked, pulling him closer, shaking him gently.

He nodded, mumbling a thank-you to whichever one of the benevolent deities had spared our lives. Around us, the mountain felt eerily calm and when I left the tent to survey the wreckage of Camp 2, checking on our kit and equipment, it was clear we'd been lucky. Only the tail-end of what was a violent event had caught us and nobody was hurt, nothing had been destroyed, but the mood was very uneasy among the local Sherpas, in place to assist with our line-fixing efforts. As far as they were concerned, our Puja from a few days back hadn't worked and their gods were in a foul mood.

With the last of the daylight fading, they trudged back to Base Camp fearfully and our goal of fixing the lines to Camps 3 and 4 was immediately more daunting than before, but at least we were still alive. Picking apart our options in the darkness, I sensed the usual route, the one first climbed by Herzog, was now too sketchy. Every footfall was an avalanche waiting to happen and the entire team could be sucked to their deaths if one of us slipped, or triggered another collapse.

People are going to blame me if something goes wrong during the summit push up there, or if it later turns out to be unsafe . . . There must be an alternative line.

I stared up at Annapurna's peak and asked the question yet again.

OK, can I? Or can I not?

Then I joined the others for dinner, hoping the mountain might behave more mercifully from then on.

* * *

I woke with the sunrise – and a plan.

As part of the expedition inventory I'd packed a few pieces of camera equipment, and for a long while I'd wanted to film a lot of Project Possible as we moved from mountain to mountain. My aim was to film as much as I could while I was climbing, directing the other guys in my team for the camera, and when that wasn't possible, I'd have one of them film me. Even though I had next to no movie-making experience, I was confident I could capture plenty of exciting material. Eventually, I hoped to show my expeditions to the world by making a documentary, or maybe presenting a live theatre talk or two – but I also wanted to silence any doubters that would inevitably pop up once the operation was done. Whenever somebody executed an effort of the kind we were attempting, it was all too easy for trolls to pick apart the results, unless those results were backed up with an exhaustive collection of footage.

Even then it was tricky. Some people still reckoned the 1969 moon landings were faked; the internet was swamped with all sorts of conspiracy theories and 'evidence', so I certainly wasn't going to expose myself to accusations of exaggeration, or falsifying my achievements. I intended to make it home with as much film as I could and brought along two dudes to help with the editing and social media output – Sagar and Alit Gurung. They had shown so much faith in Project Possible that the pair of them had resigned from their jobs in the UK to join us.

During my fund-raising drive, I'd even approached a number of production companies about buying up the rights to the content. I floated the idea of a camera crew joining us for the entire mission, but nobody seemed that keen and the overwhelming attitude was negative. The general consensus? *This man doesn't have funding for his own project. He's not going to finish. So why should we find a budget for filming him?* Like so many people I encountered in those stressful months prior to reaching Annapurna, there was a reluctance to believe that what I was attempting was humanly possible.

'Well, if they're not interested, I'll do it myself,' I thought.

Before starting our climb from Base Camp on day one, I'd distributed head cams to everyone in the team. There was a handheld digital camera on standby, too. But the most exciting tool in my filming inventory was a drone and having checked it out at home, I'd been struck by its tactical potential. Of course, it would be great for filming aerial shots as we climbed while capturing the impressive scale of our surroundings – we'd look like ants against the vast expanses of rock and ice. But it was also a handy reconnaissance tool and as we planned our best route up Annapurna's avalanche-ravaged terrain, I was struck by an idea.

In the same way that the British military used drones to improve the tactical understanding of a battle space, so I'd be able to fly one across Annapurna, working out the safest route towards Camp 3. With Mingma and Sonam, we hovered the drone over a series of icy ridges, assessing the captured footage on a phone for a new line up. *And there it was!*

A long vertical ridge that ran for a few hundred metres directly above us had come into view. Dusted in snow, from a distance it resembled the bridge of a sharp, angular nose and I recognised it as the notorious Dutch Rib, a knife-edge of powder and ice, so-called because it had originally been scaled in 1977 by a team of climbers from Holland, plus nine Sherpas. Very few people had attempted it since, probably because the line looked so daunting, but by the looks of things, there was just enough width on the nose's bridge to advance upwards.

The work would be challenging, mainly because anyone scaling it was bound to be very exposed, and if a climber slipped on the compacted rock and ice there would be nothing to break their long, and painful, ride to the bottom.

That wasn't the only risk, though. As I scanned the drone footage, I realised that to get across to the Dutch Rib, we'd need to first trailblaze through a no-man's-land of snow – *another avalanche landing zone*. But once we were on the ridge we'd be protected from the fallout to any seracs that might collapse higher up the mountain, and my guess was that the Dutch Rib was so thin and angled that any rushing debris from above would fall away on either side before it reached us. Our only problem was that the climb was set to be a beast.

When I returned to Base Camp later that day and announced my plan to the waiting expeditions, I was told that the Dutch Rib was a no-go zone. One Sherpa, an Annapurna guide with years of experience, instantly knocked back the idea. 'Nobody's climbed that route for years,' he said. 'It's too hard.'

The reaction unsettled me a little bit.

'Fuck, maybe this is going to be a massive risk?' I thought. 'But what other option do I have?'

My military training had instilled a sense of inner positivity, where it was often my job to find creative solutions to sketchy problems without whinging or making bullshit excuses. I assessed the Dutch Rib drone footage once more, and decided to put that theory into practice, figuring, '*What the hell?*' Then I pressed ahead regardless. Besides, I wasn't telling anyone they had to follow my plan. As the leader of the line-fixing team, I was merely giving them an option and it was up to them whether they took it, or not. But days later, having edged my way slowly up the ridge with Geljen – my legs buckling as we dug into the ice, while fixing lines and holding firm – I wondered if my Sherpa friend hadn't been right after all.

After a full day on the Dutch Rib, the work had been rough and with the light fading I found myself caught between Camps 2 and 3. Moving up in the darkness on such a precarious slope seemed risky, but heading all the way down to Camp 2 to reset felt like a cop out – we'd only have to repeat the same process the next day without making any significant progress. In order to push higher, we had to stay put for the night, and so we fixed our tent to the nose's bridge with around thirty anchors, Geljen and myself resting above a sheer drop that would have meant certain death had either one of us rolled over during our sleep.

That wasn't our most pressing issue, though. When we'd decided to set out for Camp 3 that morning, I'd originally expected us to make it all the way there, and back to Camp 2, in one push. At the time it hadn't made sense to pack any overnight equipment, such as sleeping bags, or food; it felt smarter to travel light and so our meals and Jetboil stove were stuck at Camp 2. Worse, a supply run wasn't scheduled to reach us until the following day. Pitched on the Dutch Rib's exposed surface, we soon began to freeze. Both of us were starving hungry and rapidly dehydrating, and Project Possible was now at risk.

I realised that by not being able to make my way up to Camp 3, there was every chance the mission could be abandoned.

Without immediate progress, we'd find ourselves stuck in a perpetual loop for days, where returning to Camp 2 and climbing to the Dutch Rib's midway point, over and over, would eventually force us to give up. I was also pinned to my position by pride – for both the Gurkhas and the British military elite. – and I had no right to dent either reputation by turning back and losing face.

I radioed everybody on the mountain for assistance.

'Hey guys, we can't go any further than this,' I explained. 'If we come back down to Camp 2 now, we cannot progress, and we won't be able to summit at all, so I'm going to stay here and commit. But . . . we don't have food. Can someone bring up a stove and some noodles.'

My calls went unanswered. But I still wasn't in the mood for retreating. Besides, I was used to periods of discomfort in war, where I'd had to function in conflict with nothing in the way of food and very little water.

'We'll hold tight here,' I told Geljen, defiantly.

But as we settled into our uncomfortable surroundings, fearful that a strong blast of wind might rip us away from the ridgeline, the radio crackled. A voice then cut through the static.

'Nimsdai, if nobody brings food and water from Camp 2, I'll bring you some from Base Camp.'

Who's this?

'It's Gesman.'

Gesman?

Geljen smiled. Gesman had arrived on Mingma's recommendation as the least qualified mountaineer of the team. Despite having climbed only a few Death Zone peaks, he was now offering to scale the Dutch Rib with supplies, when other considerably more experienced Annapurna guides and climbers had ignored my calls for assistance. That was a huge response.

'No, brother,' I said. 'We're good, but thank you. We can hang on.'

I felt happy. Gesman's offer was both reassuring and inspiring. I instantly understood that if the least qualified climber on Project Possible could be as fearless and as dedicated in the face of adversity as the most experienced, then I'd found my new Special Forces. *We were already the extreme altitude elite.*

As far as I was concerned, Selection was done.

* * *

Having eventually progressed along the Dutch Rib and set the fixed lines to Camp 3, we returned to Base, readying the expedition team and accompanying Sherpas for our summit push. A plan was set: I would lead the way with Mingma, climbing a full day ahead of our paying clients, who would be steered through the camps by Sonam, all of them following our deep footfalls in the snow. The fixing team intended to push to Camp 2 and sleep overnight. A day later, we'd scale the Dutch Rib, resting at Camp 3 before setting the lines to Camp 4, from where we could expect to spend a full day trailblazing through the deep snow while anchoring lines to the mountain.

If everything went according to plan, our expedition team, plus the other parties climbing Annapurna that day, would probably meet us at Camp 4 shortly after the last of the lines had been set. Then we'd be able to climb to the very top as a group.

This was the first summit push of the mission; I was ready for the effort, but fixing lines meant that I had to travel with a lot of weight on my back. I generally carried around twenty or thirty kilos in my rucksack, though a lot of this weight was rope. I'd also be trailblazing through deep snow, so the exertion was set to be huge, but as we moved upwards and fixed the lines, the load became lighter, until I was usually left with around ten kilos. I also carried very little in the way of food or water.

I never took energy gels, supplements or snacks; everything I ate on the mountain depended on my mood and I often worked off egg-fried rice and dried chicken. I couldn't be dealing with pre-packed meals – it was too awkward. When it came to hydration, I didn't need a lot to get me through a summit push and I often conserved my water for other climbers. As a soldier, my body had become accustomed to working with very little, but on the mountain I always kept a one-litre Thermos with me. My trick was to pack a cup with snow, melting it down with a small splash of hot water from my flask. That was usually enough to get me through a summit push.

All of this kit had the potential to slow me down, but not by much, and after two days of solid work, we were able to rest at Camp 4 for a few hours as the other parties caught up to our position. I was tired, but there was plenty of energy left in the tank and as I kicked back in my tent, I was suddenly struck with an idea. *I wanted to climb without oxygen.* To scale the 8,000-ers without gas had long been considered the purest form of mountaineering.

When Reinhold Messner and his climbing partner, Peter Habeler, topped the world's highest peak in 1978 without oxygen, it was rightly hailed as an incredible achievement, so much so that a number of people made claims that it hadn't happened at all. In their opinion there was no way a climber could have topped the world's highest peak without oxygen. To silence the doubters, Messner repeated the feat, this time climbing from the Tibetan side of Everest, alone. By all accounts, his ascent was agonising, but at least he managed it.

In 2016, I had made a promise to myself: that I was going to climb the 8,000-ers with oxygen, without fail. That first trip to

Everest had shown me how essential a supplemental air supply was when helping a stricken individual on the mountain, and there was every chance I might encounter at least one other incapacitated mountaineer while working through Project Possible. I'd never be able to forgive myself if I couldn't then administer assistance. But there were other responsibilities to consider, namely the fact I was about to help lead a team of clients to the top. Had one of them fallen seriously ill, or been injured, my chances of getting that climber back to Base Camp alive would have been severely reduced without oxygen.

And yet, despite all of this, I felt tempted to take the personal risk. (I still had oxygen with me should anyone else require it). With hindsight, I reckon the high altitude had fucked with my mind. I wasn't thinking straight and the lack of oxygen in my blood had caused me to lean into my competitive spirit. The same drive that had once inspired me to take those middle-of-the-night training runs as a teenager in Chitwan, or those gruelling load carries to Maidstone while I prepared for UK Special Forces Selection, was now goading me into taking a risk on Annapurna, and all because my reputation had been challenged by one other climber.

It had started a week or so earlier. As I rested between line-fixing efforts, Stephen – a European mountaineer from another expedition team – had made a comment or two about my use of air on the 8,000-metre peaks. He was a seriously fit guy, an ultra-marathon runner, and proud of it. 'With this body I can climb the big mountains without oxygen,' he announced when we were first introduced.

'That's cool, brother,' I said. 'We all have our own reasons for climbing the way we do.'

I soon forgot the comment, but it quickly became apparent that Stephen wasn't a team player. He hadn't offered to help with the line-fixing work like the Sherpa guides from his expedition. Resting, drinking tea and chatting was more his vibe. A few days later, as I partied with Mingma, Sonam, Geljen and Gesman, Stephen walked by once more. Trying to unify the different groups on the mountain, I shouted out to him, offering him a bottle of beer. But Stephen turned it down.

'Nah, man, I'm climbing a mountain,' he said, stiffly.

'Yeah, we're all climbing the mountain.'

'But you're using oxygen.'

There it was – *the challenge*. A big deal was being made by the mountain-climbing community about the Project Possible team's use of air at high altitude and it had annoyed me a little bit.

'Yeah, but not until after Camp 4,' I said. 'And you haven't had to trailblaze up to Camp 3 like us, so calm your ego down.'

Nothing more was said about it, but once the summit push began, my competitive streak took over. There had been a brief catch-up period when all the mountaineers had congregated at Camp 3. My team was about to spend the day fixing lines to Camp 4. Everybody else was taking a rest and by the looks of it, a lot of them were in dire need of it, especially Stephen. Hours earlier, I'd watched as his expedition team, small dots on the landscape below, fought hard to scale the Dutch Rib and when they eventually staggered towards our shelters, Stephen had vomited blood. His body was blowing out; I felt sorry for him.

Had he been a client of mine, one of us would have been forced to take him down for medical treatment. There's every chance we'd have used oxygen to maximise Stephen's chances of a swift recovery. But the dude wasn't quitting; he announced he was still fit enough to climb.

Twenty-four hours later, at Camp 4, I was struck with my idea. One climb, no oxygen: *the critics silenced*.

The odds were certainly in my favour. This was our first expedition on the schedule. I was feeling strong and because Annapurna's promontory was only just in the Death Zone at 8,091 metres, the thought of climbing without air was very appealing. But when I mentioned my plan to Mingma in our tent, he shook his head. He worried the mission might lose its momentum if I wasn't able to power forward at my usual speed.

'We need your aggression, Nimsdai,' he said.

I tried using reason. 'I've been leading from the front the whole expedition. I know I can climb any mountain without oxygen.'

The chances of him backing down, I knew, were slim, but I pressed ahead anyway. 'Mate, just for the sake of these fucking people and their opinions, let me climb without air.'

He laughed. 'No, Nimsdai!'

Mingma's opinion was important to me. His uncle, Dorje, was regarded as a totemic figure in Nepalese climbing and had shared his knowledge with the mountaineers in his family. Mingma had since become a hugely knowledgeable guide in his own right and a Sherpa of the Year in-the-making – the highest accolade anyone could expect to receive in what was a very noble profession.

I knew Mingma was right, too, and his strong opinion forced me to recall an ideal I'd once held as a kid hoping to make it into the Gurkhas: *You don't have to prove anything to anyone.* Then there was the promise I'd made to myself about always carrying gas on the 8,000-ers. Breaking it might lead to bad habits. Bad habits might result in failure.

And so I backed down.

I didn't have the time to lose focus. In order to function effectively during combat, it was important to shut out any pain such as the heat, discomfort, hunger, dehydration and emotional upset, and I applied the same attitude to Annapurna. I understood the final push to the top would be brutally hard, even with air. There was around 1,000 metres to go and some of the route required me to trailblaze through another blanket of waist-high snow, though the slope was gentle enough for us not to need fixed lines. I'd also have to scale a steep climb through an ice cliff before negotiating a final section of tricky, slippery rock shortly before the peak. Once the team had departed from Camp 4 at 9 p.m., I realised that most of my route fixing team were now guiding their private clients, one-on-one, and that the work to come would be hard going and intense. By the looks of things, only Mingma and myself were available to power through the snow. Realising that we didn't have enough manpower, I pulled my guides in close.

'Guys, everyone does ten minutes of trailblazing,' I said. 'Twenty minutes if you can. Whatever you have in the tank, use it. When the person leading the team gets too tired, he should stop and move to the side, waiting to join the end of the line. The second guy then becomes point man for his ten minutes or so. This will keep our momentum going.'

With a clear operational brief in place, we set the rope and trailblazed most of the route, each of us taking turns to lead the way, one by one, until Annapurna's peak was finally in sight. We understood there were other expeditions following up behind and they were relying on us to lead them to the top, but I was confident of nailing the job.

Since Dhaulagiri, I'd come to realise that my comfort zone generally opened up at around 8,000 metres – *where other people began to fail, I came alive*. I owned the ground; the self-doubt and fear that sometimes dragged an individual down tended to pass me by. I rarely asked, 'Can I really do this?' And if ever the tiniest sliver of doubt seeped into my self-belief, I remembered my new God: proving to the world that imagination was the greatest power of all.

During previous expeditions, the buzz of achievement usually kicked in a few metres before the peak, in those minutes when every climber sensed that the hardest yards were done, and the final steps were within reach. But at the top of Annapurna, weirdly, there was no rush, no feeling of overwhelming emotion. Well, apart from the realisation I was fortunate to be alive – our close call with that powerful avalanche had been a little *too* close. But any mountaineer taking on a climb as high-risk as Annapurna needed a heavy slice of luck to match the other attributes required above 8,000 metres – strength, resilience, a sense of team and an optimistic mindset. The environment had been uncontrollable and savage, but at 3.30 p.m., we were perched above it.

I took a little while to soak in the view below, the jagged teeth of the Himalayas, swaddled in cloud, laid out ahead of us. From my position, Dhaulagiri was clearly visible. Dana was somewhere in its shadow – I'd succeeded on home ground.

Maybe the charge of euphoria I'd previously experienced on other expeditions was being dampened by the massive challenges that seemed scattered around me on the landscape. I knew my workload was going to be huge.

And how the hell was I going to get all that money?

But the first peak on the list was done, and I remained unbroken. I recorded a quick thank-you message to my sponsors at home and made another appeal for funding. There was no harm in asking – and I was bloody desperate.

The date was 23 April 2019. A clock was ticking and the world was watching. *My race was on.*

11

Rescue!

Nims! *Nimsdai!*
         I woke in Camp 4 on Annapurna to the sound of shouting. Shrinking into my sleeping bag, the events of the day rushed back to me. For the past few weeks I had barely slept and having summited Annapurna, my strength was dwindling away. I was in agony; my legs and back ached, and shortly after topping out, Mingma, Gesman and I had trudged towards Camp 4 before collapsing into our tents, exhausted. But around us a new drama had unravelled. A Sherpa was moving from group to group in the camp. He was panicked.

'Nims, I've left my client,' he said, frantically. 'He's still up there. His oxygen ran out and mine was low, so I gave him my cylinder to keep him going until I managed to get him some help, but I don't know if it's too late. I don't even know where he is . . .'

I remembered the man he was talking about – a 48-year-old Malaysian doctor called Chin Wui Kin and a fairly experienced climber. When my team had performed our Puja, Dr Chin had joined us for a while. We'd shared a drink and I remember him watching us and smiling as we conducted the ceremony. We'd even danced and taken selfies. I'd also seen them both on the summit and they seemed to be a little tired, but in fairly good shape, though I had warned them to leave quite quickly.

'Guys, let's get down as soon as we can,' I'd said as they hung around to take photographs. 'Then we can celebrate.' Had we known that they were running low on air, I'd have handed over a cylinder, no problem. Maybe the guide hadn't anticipated that Dr Chin might struggle at the peak. Perhaps he'd overestimated his client's abilities. Either way, those calculations had been wide of the mark.

'I think he might be dead,' said the Sherpa. 'He's very tired. Nims, can you help?'

I nodded. The idea of leaving Dr Chin behind was too upsetting to consider, but seeing as I had experience of such a situation after my first climb of Everest, I was probably the strongest and most qualified on the mountain to conduct a search and rescue operation at that point. Saving Dr Chin was a huge risk, but I was up for it on one condition: I'd need extra oxygen. My team was running low and it would require all three of us to find and then extract the casualty from his position, wherever that might be.

'I'm happy to go up there and conduct a search and rescue mission,' I said. 'But we're going to need the insurance company to pay for some oxygen cylinders to be flown up here so we can get to him.'

The Sherpa looked at me blankly.

'Listen,' I said. 'One: I don't know if the man is alive. Two: I'm not going to wander up the mountain searching for Dr Chin without air. It puts my whole team at risk, which is a chance I'm not prepared to take, especially as he might be dead already.'

A call was made to Base Camp, but by 6 a.m. our requests for a drop to us had gone unanswered. I knew any attempts at that stage were now out of the question, because we simply didn't have the oxygen to conduct a search, but I wasn't going to give up on Dr Chin just yet. *Maybe there was an alternative way to find him?* I reached for the drone again, and having warmed it up in the morning sun, I attempted to lift it into the air, hoping that we might catch sight of the casualty by flying it across the terrain above – that's if he hadn't walked off a cliff edge. But the motor wouldn't start. I tried again – *no luck*. Our plan was in tatters.

After making one last call to confirm that the insurance company hadn't changed their position, I descended to Base Camp sadly, believing Annapurna had claimed another victim, eager to escape in one piece myself. It was around 10 p.m. by the time we made it to the bottom. I was knackered, physically and mentally, though not so fatigued that I couldn't drink whisky until three in the morning. I was trying to shake away the heavy emotions I'd been feeling: I hated the thought that one guy had been left behind. The impact upon his family would be devastating, but it was also a reminder that I might end up in the same position one day.

I eventually fell asleep to the sound of other returning climbers, while a man was probably dead, or dying alone, above us on the mountain. But several hours later, as I slowly woke up, the drama was starting again. Mingma was calling my name.

What the fuck?

'Nimsdai! Dr Chin, they've seen him . . . he's alive!'

I heard the *whomp-whomp-whomp* of helicopter rotary blades. A chopper had been called in to conduct a search and rescue operation.

'Are you sure?'

Mingma nodded. *Yes, brother.*

'Right, let's get eyes on him. We'll take that helicopter to his position and I'll ready a rescue team.'

I quickly pulled on my clothes and started planning for the

mission. I even sent out a call for help on social media, outlining the situation to anyone following our expedition that might be able to come to our aid:

> *Chin Wui Kin is still alive on Annapurna (HELP)*
> *Action required: His insurance company to authorise the rescue.*
> *Request: Can someone with media power help us please?*
> *Current Situation: My team is waiting at the base camp for heli support (to bring six oxygen cylinders), but this can only be achieved if the rescue company authorise the rescue.*
> *Let's save a life.*

I gathered my kit together and clambered into the chopper, later circling above Dr Chin's last known location. *There!* A man, stranded on the ice in a bright red summit suit, his body buffeted by the winds, was waving up to us.

'Yeah, that's Chin!' I shouted to the pilot. 'We have to get down there.'

I had no other choice but to help. If I had been in his position, the emotional turbulence would have been too intense and I imagined his thoughts and feelings as we approached from above. *I'm seeing a helicopter – I think. I'm waving at them and they're waving back . . . I'm saved!* Then to be forced into a feeling of false hope, waiting for a rescue that might never come, seemed like a cruel end.

Even though I'd been physically thrashed by the summit push on Annapurna and my second team were waiting for me in Dhaulagiri, having set the lines to Camp 2 already, there was no other option. The biggest downer was that Project Possible now hung in the balance. Our weather window on Dhaulagiri was closing rapidly; a huge storm was rolling in and if I couldn't make it to the top within a couple of days or so, my whole schedule could be thrown into disarray. With only one mountain checked off the list, any chances of completing Phase One in the required time would be severely reduced.

When we circled back to the camp to brief Gesman, Mingma and Geljen, I outlined our mission plan. Dr Chin's wife, by all accounts, had self-financed a rescue mission and oxygen was en route to us. (The Project Possible team did not charge anything for our manpower.)

'We can't leave him there,' I said. 'This is a tough mountain, but I think, together, we have the strength to save him. I've never left anyone behind in war. I'm not going to do it on the mountain either.'

Descending directly onto Dr Chin's position was too risky. Instead we strapped into harnesses and individually attached ourselves to the helicopter, with a length of rope called a 'long line'. The effort was intimidating, and it required a rescuer to hold their nerve as they were lifted off the ground, feeling the tension in the rope. As I was sucked up into the sky by the chopper, the sensation was intense. The wind blasted my face. Even though I was wearing goggles and a facemask, the cold seemed to sear my flesh and my peripheral vision became blurred as the helicopter's speed and the whirring rotary blades above distorted the view of the mountains around me.

I couldn't let the fear factor knock me off course; it was important to enjoy the ride. For five minutes I dangled precariously, suspended several hundred feet above an expanse of snow and rock, as the pilot located a suitable drop zone.

As part of my elite military service, I was often called up to fast rope in on boats moving at speed or enemy compounds in order to execute missions. The process became routine during combat, but dropping onto the world's deadliest mountain was a totally new experience, though I could reassure myself that nobody was shooting at me this time. Once all of us had arrived on the ground, one by one, we moved quickly and the route to Dr Chin's position was arduous.

A few days earlier, as we'd trailblazed forwards and fixed lines between camps, it had taken us around eighteen hours to get from our drop zone to where Dr Chin was lying stricken. But charged up with adrenaline, we moved at far higher speeds, a team of mountain-climbing Usain Bolts, our lungs fighting for air until the form of Dr Chin, lying prostrate on the white snow, came into view. We had covered that same distance in four hours, but I feared our efforts might have been for nothing. Dr Chin was in a bad way. As we gathered around him there was no visible reaction, although he seemed to be alive. His eyes were moving, so I gave his shoulders a shake. I needed to communicate with him if we were to extract him to safety.

'Hey, Dr Chin!' I shouted. 'You're going to be OK.'

I checked him over. He looked close to death. The man had been stranded for around thirty-six hours and was in a physically distressed state. One hand was completely frostbitten; Dr Chin's face had been ravaged by the cold too, as were both legs below the boot. I knew that if we were able to get him to a hospital, the injuries would be life-changing. Still, there was something about his movements that told me he hadn't given up. Dr Chin was trying to talk and seemed to be fighting hard for his life as I tested his levels of consciousness.

'Hey, Dr Chin, how many people are here?' I shouted, pressing my ear to his mouth so I could hear any mumbled responses.

'Four.'

Four! Dr Chin was hanging on.

'You're doing great, brother. Can you drink?'

'Water . . .'

I pressed a canteen carefully to his lips as the others carefully packed him into a rescue sleigh.

There was no time to lose. The light was dipping behind the mountain peaks and given the rescue helicopter was unable to lift us away in the dark, it was critical that we moved Dr Chin into a suitable shelter as quickly as possible, where we could at least attempt to keep him alive and warm until the chopper arrived the following morning.

We pushed on down the mountain, clambering into our tent at Camp 4, where we worked to keep the casualty conscious for as long as possible. We rubbed his body in an attempt to increase his circulation. At one point, I even tried to remove one of his boots to assess the damage to his feet and warm his toes, but it was impossible to free either shoe. The intense cold had caused the fabric to freeze to Dr Chin's flesh and removing his footwear was impossible, even with a knife. His body would have to thaw first.

At times I was confident of saving him. Every now and then, if I felt Dr Chin was drifting into unconsciousness, I'd try to rouse him. 'You've got to stay strong now, man. You can stay alive.' He'd respond with a groan.

But there were other moments when he seemed to be fading from view and I doubted our decision to conduct the rescue.

'Fuck, have we done the right thing coming here?' I said to Mingma. 'He might die and we'd have risked our lives for nothing.'

Just by checking in with Dr Chin, I could tell he was in pain. His lungs rattled with every breath and any reserves of resilience seemed to be fading away. This was a signal I recognised from my experience of patching up wounded soldiers. An individual, having clung on to life alone for so long, was often offered a window of psychological rest when the CASEVAC team showed up. Rather than thinking solely of self-preservation, the casualty was able to put his or her life into the rescuer's hands. The responsibility had shifted; survival became dependant on the efforts of others.

In this case our arrival and shelter had presented Dr Chin with some respite, but it was a dangerous time. For the briefest of moments, Dr Chin relaxed, which was all it took to kill a climber in such a precarious position.

But we were exhausted, too. All of us had paid the price for climbing Annapurna's summit twenty-four hours earlier. We had then raced towards Dr Chin's location at high speeds the following day and now, in the early hours of the morning, while working to keep Dr Chin warm, I nodded off to sleep, until . . .

WHACK! I felt the sharp sting of an open hand. Mingma had given me a slap on the legs.

'Wake up, Nimsdai!' he shouted. 'Wake up!'

I jolted. Aware that fatigue would smother me again, I energised myself even more by giving myself a smack around the chops, and then another. Gesman and Geljen did the same. It was all we could do to stay awake, until someone had the idea that we should shout and scream at one another instead. It might have looked like madness, all of us packed into a tent, yelling loudly, crowded around a stricken man in the hope that our body heat might keep him alive. But seeing we were in desperate times, we understandably resorted to desperate measures. Falling asleep would surely be the end for Dr Chin.

There were other factors the team had to consider, though: the helicopter was picking us up from Camp 3 at 6 a.m. and it was vitally important we left on time if we were to meet it. If we arrived too early, Dr Chin would have to hang around, his body exposed to the wind and cold; get there too late and our ride to the hospital would probably be delayed, which might prove costly in a situation where every minute counted.

Glancing at my watch, I realised we had only another couple of hours to wait until the sun rose, and when the time came we pushed down the mountain, dragging Dr Chin with us. A helicopter was soon hovering above our position. We clipped Dr Chin to the rope and he was lifted away to Kathmandu for treatment.

In Nepal, CASEVACs of that kind take place all the time, but there was sometimes a game to play. Because of finances, search and rescue teams were usually left to make their own way down, because it was costly to lift climbers, one by one on a long line, during a series of trips up and down the mountain. Turning the chopper around for the rescuers in what would be four flights could add tens of thousands to the bill. But on this occasion, I was offered the next ride back down the mountain.

'Not yet,' I said. 'Please take all of my team first. Then come for me. I'll be the last man.'

I understood that if I was winched away by the helicopter, straight off, it was unlikely that it would return for the others – the rides were too costly an expense. But if I remained on the mountain, having rescued the primary casualty, there was no way they could abandon me, not after the hard graft I'd put in to saving Dr Chin. My reputation and connections in Nepal also lent me a certain level of power. They couldn't mess with me. So, to make sure they wouldn't be able to play games with my expedition team, Mingma, Geljen and Gesman were transported to Base Camp shortly after the casualty.

By the time I was eventually flown into the helipad at the hospital in Kathmandu where Dr Chin was being treated, word of his rescue had spread. His wife had arrived to see him, as had a mob of cameramen and journalists who surrounded me once I'd left the chopper. When I met Mrs Chin at the intensive care unit, she was relieved, but emotional.

'Thank you so much, I don't know what to say,' she said. 'The doctors aren't sure if he'll survive.'

'He wants to live so much,' I said. 'He's been fighting up there for the past thirty-six hours. We did everything we could to help.'

I was pleased to have brought them back together, but the rescue forced me to consider briefly the truths of high-altitude climbing and mortality. It was yet another reminder that life above 8,000 metres could be both savage and unpredictable, though whenever somebody signed up for an expedition like the one Dr Chin had undertaken, they generally understood the dangers of mountain adventure. Falling to altitude sickness, or suffering from a serious injury, rarely came as too much of a shock whenever it happened – and it happened all too often on Annapurna.

But presented with the choice between dying slowly and uncomfortably through age, or passing away during an expedition or mission, my feelings were clear: I would definitely take the latter. I wasn't afraid to die on the mountain; I'd rather burn out in style than drift away quietly.

I wondered if Dr Chin shared the same belief.

* * *

While we finished up in Kathmandu and made plans to head to Dhaulagiri's base camp, I fumed. I was angry at the way Dr Chin had been treated on the mountain. But there was also a brewing frustration with those Project Possible team members waiting for me on Dhaulagiri: Lakpa Dendi, Ramesh Gurung and Kasang Tenzi.

Our delay in arriving on the mountain meant we'd missed our best window for climbing and a nasty weather system had now blown in with devastating results. A heavy snow dump was burying our fixed lines and by the sounds of it we weren't going to find them. Meanwhile, our tents on the mountain's higher camps had been beaten down by the powerful winds. By all accounts some of the shelters were in ribbons. Once I'd arrived by helicopter, accompanied by Gesman, Mingma and Geljen, the morale of my team at Base Camp was in equally bad shape. Our supplies had run out, too. We were screwed.

Though I understood the importance of climbing Dhaulagiri quickly, the growing unity within Project Possible's team members was also important. I'd learned that organising an expedition party was no different to organising a group of soldiers in war: they needed purpose and incentive, but food and downtime was vital, too. Without periods of rest and recovery, there was every chance that an individual, or the whole team, might fail in the heat of a battle. So I told the guys we were withdrawing from the mountain in order to regroup together. A little drinking and dancing was in order, and we rode into Pokhara for a week of partying; we even hired some motorbikes and cut about the fields at high speed for an afternoon.

The mood was lifted and our brief period of rest and recuperation paid off. On 12 May, we summited Dhaulagiri at 5.30 p.m., battling through 70 kmph winds and heavy clouds for twenty hours non-stop, digging our way across deep hills of snow to climb a few metres at a time. Much of the work was done alpine-style, where we operated for the most part without fixed lines, making exceptions for a particularly technical ridge, or rock face. The effort was exhausting. It certainly wasn't safe, but I knew I had it in me to lead what was proving to be a brave and highly skilled team through the extreme weather. Whenever the wind seemed to die down for the briefest of moments, the team exploded forward at speed, climbing as quickly as possible before the next squall arrived. We would then lean into the storm, bracing ourselves until it was time to move up again.

There was no room for complaints. I knew that wallowing in misery, or inviting fear into our thinking, wasn't going to help. Whenever the team rested, I only ever allowed them to sit for five minutes, and when the time was up, I made sure to be the first one to stand, and then to trailblaze. I figured it was best to lead by example. But while I was eager to move quickly, I wasn't about to risk the lives of my teammates. When Ramesh started to feel unwell with altitude sickness, I told him to get down to safety.

But Kasang had struggled, too. While he'd gained some experience of climbing the 8,000-ers, he wasn't as physically agile as his older brother, Mingma, and he seemed to wilt under the intense workload. An intense toothache was also bothering him and he seemed to deteriorate as we edged into the Death Zone. At times, Mingma had to prop him up as we struggled to the top. I was worried.

Kasang is not as strong as his brother. Is he going to make it?

Then an awful realisation struck me: if the two siblings were taken by an avalanche or fell into a crevasse together, the family's bread earners would have been wiped off the face of the earth in one cruel stroke. Weirdly, Kasang seemed to have imagined a similar ending. When we finally made it to the summit, he patted me on the back.

'Maybe it's wrong to have both brothers on the mountain at the same time,' he said. 'If something goes wrong, who will look after the family?'

I pulled Kasang close. 'I promise we'll make it home together, brother.'

Then I led the team down quickly.

At times, the conditions threatened to overwhelm us all during our descent; the mountain was in an increasingly hostile mood and the winds were so powerful that, at times, it was impossible to see. My eyes burned even though I was wearing protective goggles, but as we worked our way to Base Camp, I sensed a shift had taken place: Gesman had shown me on Annapurna that we were an elite unit. But the Project Possible team had now discovered a unique bond, too – intense loyalties had developed between us because the stakes we were facing were so huge.

I knew the likes of Mingma and Geljen could be trusted during the pressure of a search and rescue operation. Lakpa Dendi had already proven himself to be tough during his work on the G200E. Surviving the treacherous conditions on Dhaulagiri had also brought us all a little bit closer. The group had my back and I had theirs. As in the SBS, we were working towards the unrelenting pursuit of excellence.

We'd need every connection in that bond to hold firm if we were to survive Kanchenjunga.

12

Into the Dark

Kanchenjunga is the third tallest mountain in the world at 8,586 metres above sea level, but it was also potentially the toughest expedition within Phase One. That might sound weird considering the intimidating kill rate of Annapurna, but Kanchenjunga was renowned for being brutally tough to climb; few people had the resilience, luck, or strength to reach its peak because the ascent to the summit from Camp 4 – which was pitched 7,750 metres above sea level – was a soul-breaking grind. Despite there being only around a thousand metres in altitude remaining to scale, the distance left to travel was long, while deep snow often smothered the ascent up to the shoulder that ran towards Kanchenjunga's peak.

Having made it to the final ridge, a mountaineer was then exposed to awful winds and biting cold. The oxygen levels dropped to 33 per cent and the terrain was a head fuck – a bewildering minefield of loose rock, ice-covered boulders and blinding spindrift. Psychologically the route felt never-ending, the summit seemed forever out of reach, and many people turned back for home long before making it to the top. On average around three hundred people climbed Everest successfully every season; at Kanchenjunga that number came in at around twenty-five.

I didn't feel overwhelmed by the challenge. We had blitzed the first two mountains in double-quick time under incredibly gnarly circumstances, so I knew we had it in us to charge up Kanchenjunga too, but there was little doubt that everyone within the team was feeling frazzled. Having spent five days on Dhaulagiri, fixing lines and digging up the rope that had been buried by a heavy snowfall, while carrying thirty kilos of gear on our backs, we were battle bruised. When we arrived at Kanchenjunga's base camp on 14 May, the team fell into a short period of relative luxury, stuffing our faces with some fried chicken bought in a nearby village while we readied our tactics for the next twenty-four hours.

We were to move fast, pushing immediately to the top in one hit, rather than resting for a day at Camps 1, 2, 3 and 4, like normal expeditions usually did. *No fucking around.* Our intense work rate was born out of necessity, though: we were already acclimatised to high altitude and because of our fading energy levels, to stop and rest would have caused us to fail. I'd have fallen asleep on the spot; Gesman and Mingma were joining me for the push and were tiring as well.

We set out in high spirits, switching into a powerful gear and climbing quickly through the valley to Camp 1, spiking our heart rates and shocking our bodies into action. Beneath us, the snow-covered terrain was booby-trapped with hidden crevasses. Above, the lower slopes were notorious for drop-ping heavy avalanche payloads and rock fall onto unsuspect-ing climbers, though the weather had created further dangers.

A number of boulders around us had been frozen together, but because the sun was high during the day, any thawing ice had the potential to trigger a mini avalanche. Taking it in turns to work as sentries, one of us would scan the ridges above for potential bombardments, while the other two sprinted to the nearest point of shelter. If ever anybody shouted, 'Rock!' the group dived for cover.

At first, our rapid tactics worked well; our energy levels were high.

'We'll fucking climb this mountain as fast as we can, brothers!' I shouted, excitedly. 'When you're panting, you can't sleep!'

By 5 p.m., we were zipping up our summit suits at Camp 1. The expedition parties already on the mountain were into the thick of their respective summit pushes and at 7 p.m. a lot of them were already leaving Camp 4. (On Everest, which has the longest climb in terms of altitude from Camp 4 to peak, mountaineers generally leave at around 9 p.m.) In the fading light, I noticed their headlamps flickering high above us, which worried me a little. The distance between the high camp and the peak looked challenging.

I knew we'd have to move fast if we were to make the summit in good time, but my optimism later began to fade when I noticed Gesman lagging behind. He had long been struggling to keep up with the momentum set by Mingma and myself as we pulled ourselves along the fixed lines, and while I was feeling strong as we moved towards the peak, the thought of waiting for Gesman as he caught up with us was a little unsettling.

There was always a risk in carrying a passenger. Our chances of making it away from a mountain as deadly as Kanchenjunga in one piece would be very low if we were to be held back from making the summit window – the time in which it's safe to scale the mountain and turn around safely for home. It's highly likely we'd be stranded during the descent, unable to move up or down in the dark if the weather conditions deteriorated and we were stuck between camps, though we hadn't intended on an overnight stay.

By mission planning to climb and descend the mountain in one hit, we were only carrying our essential equipment such as oxygen, emergency rope, food and a few personal items. The brief was to bomb on, fighting to stay awake whenever we paused for a breather, knowing that death might catch us if we eased our foot from the pedal.

'Guys, whenever we're partying in Kathmandu, we're happy to dance until six o'clock in the morning,' I said. 'That's for fun, and we manage it no problem. But climbing Kanchenjunga is for something rare, we will all get rewarded, and this might change our lives if we succeed. We don't need to rest.'

The trick was to present a psychological reframing of what was set to be a painful encounter. The emotional switch soon helped us to eat up the metres, but physically we were suffering.

At times during my then relatively modest portfolio of high-altitude expeditions, it was possible to sense a disaster unfolding on the mountain, in much the same way that I could often sniff approaching trouble while working in war. For the most part on military tours, the work was familiar; a soldier could remain fairly alert and functional without being fully focused, just as somebody could drive their car on the motorway while engaging in a conversation at the same time. If trouble loomed on the road ahead, it was still possible to maintain enough alertness to react and slow down, or even swerve.

In much the same way, a soldier was able to understand that life was about to get ugly simply by observing the behaviour of some of the human traffic bustling around them. In some desert outposts, if the locals suddenly disappeared into the nearby doorways and alleys – it was time to switch on: a battle was coming.

As we moved up to Camp 3 and beyond on Kanchenjunga, I experienced that familiar rush of anxiety and excitement. Trouble was brewing. I first sensed it having spotted a climber directly above us as we worked our way along a steep, icy slope; it took every ounce of strength to manoeuvre up the line, but we were moving steadily, even though Gesman had long faded away in the distance.

The bloke ahead, a Chilean, was struggling. He was moving very slowly and we'd have to overtake him quickly if we wanted to reach the summit in good enough time to turn around and descend safely. I also recognised that he was in no fit shape to finish the expedition – from a distance he looked exhausted. The rational option was for him to turn around, but he was pressing ahead regardless.

I felt a lot of sympathy. Everyone has a goal when climbing an 8,000-er – *a cause*. Some people are experienced alpinists that enjoy bettering themselves for kicks. Others have more personal ambitions: maybe they're raising money for charity; many people use an expedition to overcome mental health issues like PTSD, or to celebrate their recovery from a nasty condition such as cancer; others are determined to set a personal record or some wider-reaching benchmark.

I'd learned in Base Camp that the Chilean climber – a man

named Rodrigo Vivanco – fell very much into the latter category. Apparently, nobody from his country had ever made it to the top of Kanchenjunga and yet there were two Chilean mountaineers attempting the feat that same day. Rodrigo was working without oxygen; his fellow countryman had gas and was now a speck above him in the clouds. The realisation he was set to be the second climber from his country must have been psychologically tricky, even though he wasn't using bottled air.

When we finally met on the line, I noticed Rodrigo's laboured movements and tired breathing. He was knackered; the safest option was for him to head down.

'Brother, look, it's very late now,' I said. 'The summit is quite far away, so you need to be very, very cautious about this.'

He nodded, but seemed determined to push on. 'No, I climb. I climb!'

'It's your decision,' I said. 'But what I'm saying is your pace is very slow, and the summit is still fucking miles away.'

It wasn't my place to force Rodrigo. Had he been a member of my expedition party, I'd have ordered him down to safety, or if he'd been a paying client I'd have forced him to Base Camp with a guide. But I could only advise him and Rodrigo had brushed off my help. I sensed a moment of looming disaster; my focus sharpened. For a split second, I assessed the smaller details around us.

Physically, Rodrigo was in a bad way. *At what point would he collapse: on the way up, or the way down?*

Were we strong enough to rescue Rodrigo if that happened? *Probably. Gesman's flagging, but between the three of us we can manage it.*

Could we make it to the top of Kanchenjunga first and grab

Rodrigo on the way back if necessary? *I'm feeling strong, the summit is in reach, so . . . yeah.*

I was fast learning that the biggest challenge for any climber was self-awareness; it's impossible for anyone to run or hide from themselves, *their truth*, on the mountain. My primary instinct at that point was to turn Rodrigo around, but once he'd announced his decision to press ahead, I switched to my secondary instinct: to concentrate on the mission.

I have to climb fourteen mountains in seven months. This is the next one on the list.

My immediate step was to figure out how.

Luckily, I understood myself as a person and a mountain climber, *my* truths. I knew it wasn't in me to wait around for Rodrigo, hoping he might revive himself and hurry up. Walking behind somebody as I worked towards my objective, in the hope they might move aside, had never been my *modus operandi*, and the chances that Rodrigo would briefly detach from his rope to let us pass were slim. He was burnt out. Instead, both Mingma and I unclipped from the line. We advanced past the Chilean as quickly as possible, continuing our rapid ascent in the first light of the morning; but swerving Rodrigo was only the first in what became a series of high-altitude manoeuvres.

The mountain was log-jammed with people moving up and down the rope. Those moving towards the peak seemed to vibrate with urgency, but the mountaineers descending to the lower camps carried a different energy. Many of them were exhausted; others looked stressed. Some climbers even seemed to be teetering on the tipping point between death and survival, having blown themselves out on the way to the summit. The worst of them was an Indian climber who had slumped beside a rock with his Sherpa, seemingly unable to move either up or down, while facing a terrifying reality. Their truths had been exposed by Kanchenjunga.

* * *

We summited at noon on 15 May. Hugging Mingma, I shouted into the clouds excitedly and reached into my rucksack – there were photos to take and flags to unpack. The first one carried the Project Possible logo; another had the Special Boat Service badge printed across it.

'This is it,' I shouted, repeating the regiment's motto. 'By strength and guile, the only one, SBS!'

From our position, the peaks of Everest, Makalu and Lhotse were in full view, the final three destinations of Phase One. Somewhere in the distance were the contours that separated Nepal's border from China and India, too. This was the banner day I'd long dreamt of and bright blue skies arced overhead, but time was fading fast. When I looked at my watch there were only a few hours of daylight left, though an exhausted Gesman had finally, thankfully, joined us. But who knew about the shit show awaiting us on the lines below? It was time to begin the long walk home. I was already switched on and ready for trouble, half expecting to carry a broken Rodrigo to safety.

Drama struck us almost immediately. The Indian mountaineer we'd seen earlier, and his guide, were still stranded fifty metres below us, unable to move and locked into the type of death spiral that sometimes happened at high altitude: a familiar story featuring the incapacitated climber and his or her stronger teammate, where the sick were desperately coaxed and cajoled to safety, but having hung around for too long, the healthy then found themselves in an equally perilous state. With no energy to escape, they all died. Here it was again, and now both climber and guide were stuck to Kanchenjunga.

I tried to rouse them. 'What's the problem?' I asked. Some horrible attack of altitude sickness appeared to be overwhelming the mountaineer.

The Sherpa shook his head. 'It's his oxygen – it's run out. My air has run out as well. Now this guy can't move down and obviously I can't leave him here, so I'm trying to convince him to come with me, but he's not even moving. He thinks the next step will be his last.'

A slow-moving car crash was unfolding in front of my eyes.

'We met you here before we got to the summit and you haven't made any progress?'

'No, brother. This man cannot make one step.'

I looked down at the climber. 'What's your name, buddy?'

'He's called Biplab,' mumbled the guide. 'He's stopped talking.'

When I checked him over, Biplab was thankfully conscious, but it was hard to tell whether he was suffering from HAPE or HACE. His Sherpa seemed to be in a bad way too, though he could at least stand and place one foot in front of the other, albeit very slowly.

I wasn't going to leave either of them in such a precarious state. They were unable to save themselves, so it was on Mingma, Gesman and myself to get them both down. Operating quickly was imperative, though. Some oxygen might be enough to get Biplab on the move, though all of us knew that if he was unable to descend, at least to Camp 4, he was probably going to die. Worryingly, our biggest hurdle looked to be psychological rather than physical. Biplab was paralysed by fear.

'We're going to get you home,' I shouted, helping him to his feet.

We immediately moved into a CASEVAC setting. Mingma volunteered his oxygen cylinder to Biplab. Because the air was dangerously thin, the shock to his system would prove debilitating over a number of hours, but for now Mingma was tough enough to support the slightly more stable Sherpa, who was getting to his feet.

'Let's use our speed,' I suggested. 'The only way these people get better is if they get down. Oxygen is the biggest medicine for all of us.'

I radioed down to Base Camp for assistance. 'Guys, it's Nims,' I said. 'We've got two stranded climbers up here and we've given them our gas. We're going to conduct a rescue, but we need some more air. Can somebody from Camp 4 help us?'

My comms crackled. 'Yes, we'll help,' shouted a voice. 'Three Sherpas are coming to you with oxygen.'

I moved closer to check on Biplab, asking if he'd like to speak to anyone on the satellite phone. Although time was against us, I knew that a shot of positivity would stand him in good stead during what was bound to be a long, tough descent.

'My wife,' he said.

Shortly afterwards, the distanced couple were connected. By the sounds of things, his entire family had gathered around one mobile and Biplab was laughing. He'd located the inspiration and sense of positivity that was so important when making it off the mountain in one piece. There was a feeling of relief and hope. For a brief moment, I believed we were going to be OK.

But I was wrong.

Mingma and I grabbed Biplab's arms, Gesman held his feet, and we attached him to our safety rope. Together we started the heavy, painful slog towards Camp 4, but because this was an unexpected rescue operation, and we were without our usual kit, we had to improvise. On a rescue of this kind, the casualty would normally have been moved on a stretcher with one person at the front, while the people lifting the back of the stretcher worked as brakes. Any other available bodies chipped in by balancing the casualty and guiding the carriers.

This CASEVAC was very different, though. The terrain was a challenging mix of rock, snow and ice, and the work was slow – we were having to traverse, which required us to be methodical, especially when applying different technical rope skills to our descent. We pulled and lifted, the pair of us struggling under the weight of our semi-conscious casualty.

Shortly after starting our rescue, I realised another climber was coming towards us on the line, but he was heading up rather than down. *Was it help?* Whoever it was seemed to be working alone and looked seriously ill-equipped for the effort – every movement was laboured and simply clinging on to the line appeared to be an incredible strain. Then I recognised the summit suit. *It was Rodrigo!* He was still moving towards the top and I experienced a sensation of dread. Because it was mid-afternoon, there was no way he'd be able to make it to the peak of Kanchenjunga and descend to safety all alone in the darkness.

As he moved closer, I grabbed at him again. 'Look, brother, you need to go down now. It's nearly two o'clock.'

But Rodrigo was still unwilling to listen. His body might have been failing, but his determination seemed unbreakable.

'No, the summit is very important for me,' he shouted.

'Yeah, brother, but if you leave, you can come and summit next year. You are very, very slow, you'll be dead soon if you don't turn around.'

Rodrigo tried to push past me on the line. I recognised the tell-tale indicators of summit fever, a disorientating condition where an individual becomes so obsessed with making it to the top of whichever 8,000-er they're climbing that they forget the importance of executing the second part of the mission: getting home. I reckoned Rodrigo had also been spun out by altitude. Without oxygen, his brain was probably unable to process any important information as readily as a climber working lower down the mountain.

In some instances, when the end of a project is in sight, an unflinching desire to finish the job is essential. During the London Marathon, it's common to see runners collapsing two hundred metres short of the finishing line. Some of them give up, but the majority find a way to get their medal – they stagger, crawl, or lean on another runner for assistance. At sea level an exhausted individual can make that final push; they won't die. But above 8,000 metres, to press for the finishing line without thinking is incredibly dangerous, because in marathon terms to reach the summit is like running 13.1 miles. *There's still another 13.1 to go.* The peak is only the halfway point, and it's very difficult to seek help if trouble arrives. Rodrigo had made that choice, either through altitude sickness, or with a clear mind – only he would have known – and Kanchenjunga's summit was his death-or-glory moment.

I shouted out to him as he moved ahead. 'Look, brother, I cannot force you to get down from here now. Please be very, very careful – it's your life.'

Then I grabbed the radio and called down to Camp 4, where I knew Rodrigo's expedition operators and camp support were waiting. This was their responsibility, not mine. I'd twice tried my best to talk him out of what was sure to be a suicide mission. Now it was their turn.

13

In Times of Chaos

There was no time to wait out. With Biplab so close to death, we descended from the summit ridge as quickly as we could. Every now and then our casualty groaned faintly. This was good news: at least Biplab was still alive. The bad: we'd been forced into hefting him through the peak's rocky field where the work was roughest, and our casualty was taking a number of bruising hits. But there was no other way to transport him effectively.

During my military career, I'd performed a series of CASEVAC drills where I'd learned that speed was of the utmost importance. When transporting a seriously injured soldier to lifesaving medical treatment, a few extra cuts and bruises in transit were considered collateral damage, because the alternative was to take extra time and care, during which the injured operator might bleed out. Biplab was in much the same situation and there was no time for subtlety or tender bedside manners. There were also the elements to worry about and as the temperature dropped with the sun, the mountain would slowly take our soul.*

* Here's the science. When it comes to CASEVACs in war, medics have what is called a 'golden hour' – the timeframe in which to get an injured soldier away from the battlefield and to a hospital. Extracting them in that time gives

Weird things stick with a person during chaotic events. I remember the perfect visibility on Kanchenjunga that day and there was a bright blue sky around us. Whenever I took a second to check my surroundings, or the line below, the views resembled a picture postcard, or one of those aerial photos from *National Geographic* magazine. An hour had passed already, our route home was clearly laid out below, with Camp 4 visible in the distance, but taking into account our current speed I estimated we were approximately six hours away. I prayed Biplab could hold on for that long, but he was only one component in a rapidly deteriorating situation.

How was Gesman holding up? At what point would Mingma feel the effects of altitude sickness? Where was the help?

At around 8,400 metres, as I game-planned our descent, looking out hopefully for our reinforcements and those promised oxygen cylinders, I noticed another climber had slumped in the snow ahead of us. From a distance he seemed OK, his eyes were fixed on the mountains ahead. *Maybe he was taking in the scene?* But as I got closer, I recognised the same awful expression of fixed terror I'd seen in Biplab an hour or so earlier.

I shook the man's shoulder. 'Hey, are you OK?'

'Yeah, I'm OK,' he said, introducing himself as Kuntal, as if it was simply another afternoon on the mountain. But Kuntal's eyes wouldn't meet mine; he seemed hypnotised by the

---

the wounded a greater chance of survival, though, of course, those odds change according to the severity of the bullet wound, or injury. When it comes to altitude, time is important, but altitude is vital: as soon as you start bringing the casualty down, more air hits their body, and the blood flow, breath and heart rate begin to normalise, helping the vital organs. It's not only oxygen that is helpful for survival. Increasing the barometric pressure – the atmosphere's weight – is imperative too and like air it decreases at altitude. This is why some climbers have died at high camps, even when they're given oxygen.

landscape. Then I registered the awful reality. *Fucking hell, I think he's snow blind.*

'Why are you staying here?' I said, checking over his situation. When I looked at Kuntal's oxygen cylinder, it was empty.

'I can't get down. My guide has left me. My team have left me, too.' He seemed resigned to the end. His voice was eerily calm. 'I think I'm gonna die.'

I looked at Mingma and Gesman sadly. *Was this really happening again?* Whatever expedition team was responsible for Kuntal had seemingly decided his climbing days were over and that he couldn't be saved. They must have gone down without him and now we were forced into making a heavy, morally loaded decision.

Should we leave Kuntal to die, too? Or do we risk the lives of our casualties further by adding another person to the risky-as-fuck rescue operation?

As far as I was concerned, there was very little room for debate: on missions I'd been encouraged to leave no operator behind. The rules were certainly very different during high-altitude expeditions, but my attitude had been hardwired, plus it was the reason I used oxygen in the first place.

'Let's get this dude down as well,' I said.

I unclipped my mask and placed it around Kuntal's face, thankful for the promise I'd made to myself after the rescue of Seema on Everest in 2016. Though I'd been working with bottled air throughout our ascent's final stages, my vital organs weren't jolted by the sudden lack of oxygen. It didn't whoosh from my lungs; my heart rate hardly soared with the physiological reality of Death Zone climbing. Instead I knew my deterioration at high altitude would be slow, but I trusted my body to weather the storm for the next few hours, by which point the rescue team from below might have arrived.

I steadied myself further by remembering I'd previously

survived on Everest for several hours with HAPE, so I knew it was in me to survive. The fact I'd then recovered quickly enough to climb again a week or so later gave me hope, but my ever-decreasing chances of survival on Kanchenjunga felt unsettling. When I'd saved Seema on Everest, it had only taken me around an hour to get from her original position to Camp 4, but that was because I'd had oxygen.

Six people were attempting to escape Kanchenjunga; three were incapacitated, and the others, while being physically mobile, had given their oxygen to the casualties within the group. Our descent to Camp 4 was now going to take us a hell of a lot longer. I reckoned that if help didn't arrive soon, there was every chance that at least one of us would die.

And where were those climbers that were supposed to be helping?

I called down for assistance again. A voice told me not to worry, reassuring me that help was on its way and everything was still cool. *Was it the same person?* Through the scratch of radio interference, I couldn't be sure. But when I looked down to Camp 4 in the fading light, there was still no sign of activity. Perhaps our rescue team was gathering together in a tent to plan their mission. If so, they'd have to move fast, because our resources were dwindling away at an alarming rate and we were taking hit after hit after hit.

An hour on from resuming our snail's pace evacuation, Gesman's strength had faded. He'd already developed frostbite in his toes during the rescue of Dr Chin on Annapurna three weeks previously and his feet were prickling and tingling again – a sure sign the cold was taking another gnaw at his flesh. For one moment I became worried by his behaviour, too. When I turned around to check on the group, I noticed that Gesman had yanked away Kuntal's goggles and was jabbing a finger towards his eyes.

Had Kuntal died? Or did Gesman have HACE?

'Brother! What the fuck?'

'He's lying,' shouted Gesman, furiously. 'The guy can see. Look!'

He pulled a hand back, as if preparing to smack the casualty across the face. Kuntal flinched. Then he flinched again. Apparently Gesman had noticed Kuntal reacting to one or two moments of danger – *but how could a blind man hesitate before making a risky step he couldn't see?* When I then leant over Kuntal and repeated the same test, he cowered with every poke and prod.

Gesman was right!

I groaned. Had Kuntal admitted the truth about his snow blindness, we could have moved at a much faster pace and covered more ground. Instead, fear had caused him to lie. Kuntal wanted us to do the hard work for him, because he'd been too scared to do it for himself. Now he was helpless; he certainly wasn't thinking straight and my temper broke. I grabbed Kuntal by the hood of his summit suit and pulled him close.

'What the fuck, man?' I shouted. 'Listen, we three are risking our lives for you, carrying you like a dead body. And you're pretending to be snow blind. Why?'

But Kuntal was too weak to answer. Despondently, Gesman grabbed at his shoulders, lifting him up and we continued walking into the dark, heavy shadows now falling across the mountain. I didn't have the energy to waste on rage, not with the lives of so many people on the line. My anger passed quickly.

* * *

It was as if we'd been abandoned. Nobody seemed to be coming.

I must have radioed down to Camp 4, or Base Camp, over one hundred times and with each communication I became increasingly disheartened. But despite my rising frustration, I still worked hard to maintain a sense of calm, convincing myself that assistance *was* on the way. Oxygen *was* coming.

I knew at least fifty people were sleeping in the tents below. Nearly all of them had summited Kanchenjunga that same day and it would only take a rescue party around two hours to reach our position. Among their numbers were experienced alpinists and solo climbers. There were people I knew to talk to, or to party with at Base Camp, and there were other dudes whose reputations at extreme altitude were beyond question.

Surely out of all those climbers, a small group will feel inclined to help?

With every radio call, the unease increased. Hours passed, our situation became increasingly desperate, and yet the same response was delivered over the radio every time.

'Someone is on their way to help, Nims.'

'They're coming, bro.'

'Not long now . . .'

But from what I could tell, that someone hadn't even left Camp 4, unless they were stupid enough to climb without a head torch. No tell-tale lights were approaching from below.

It was around 8 p.m. Judging by my watch, we'd been working through the rescue mission for several hours. The weather was fairly calm, thank God, and there was very little wind, but it was still bitterly cold. Between Gesman, Mingma and myself, we had the skills to survive, but the worrying news was that the oxygen we'd given to our casualties had run low and due to the lack of support from below, morale was fading.

Kuntal, withering under the stress of altitude sickness, seemed unable to communicate; Biplab was deteriorating, too. Then, not fifteen minutes later, as we resumed our slow trudge to safety, I noticed something different about his body as we lowered him down, foot by foot, over the rock and ice. His pained groans had stopped; the instinctive, muscular spasms that braced against our every movement were gone.

Biplab was dead.

Desperately I checked his vitals. 'Please don't let all this work have been for nothing,' I sighed.

But there was no pulse, Biplab wasn't breathing. I even poked him in the eyes, the one action that usually triggered a response in a seriously injured person, but there was no reaction. When I glanced down at his oxygen cylinder, I realised the awful truth. Biplab's air had finally run out and his body had failed immediately. Because of the rapid physical decline, my guess was that he hadn't been acclimatised properly as he'd moved up and down Kanchenjunga's lower camps in the weeks leading up to his summit push.

'I'm sorry, brother, we did everything we could,' I said sadly, pulling his hood down around his eyes.

I looked angrily at the lights of Camp 4. The suggestion that help was on the way had been bullshit and every request for assistance had been ignored – *but why?* I felt betrayed.

'People are nasty, man,' I thought.

The mountain had shown me the truth about who, and what, I really was – on both the climb up, and on the way down, as I'd worked to keep our small unit alive. I could hold my head up high. But a painful reality regarding some of the individuals I'd once respected within the community had also been revealed – the mountaineers sleeping in their tents, as a man had died on the line above them. The people who had claimed, over and over, that help was on its way.

Their truth would be impossible to escape.

＊ ＊ ＊

Gesman looked at me fearfully. His frostbite had become increasingly painful and now it seemed as if he could barely walk. He had to go down. At first he protested, arguing that he wanted to fight with the rest of us, but unless he descended to the lower camps there was every chance Mingma and myself would have another casualty to work with. We couldn't take the risk. Gesman walked off into the darkness as the group said our farewells and apologies to Biplab, leaving him to the mountain. Carrying him for longer would have only slowed down our escape.

Assessing our situation, I reckoned our current position was ordinarily around half an hour from safety, but only if all of us were in a condition to walk fairly quickly. With only two incapacitated individuals to care for now, the journey was likely to take a painful couple of hours, maybe more, but there was no choice, other than to put in the effort. Having descended away from the Death Zone, nearly a thousand metres in altitude, Biplab's Sherpa was now able to move more freely. Together, Mingma and I pulled and dragged Kuntal; I cajoled the guide during breaks from our heavy lifting, but Mingma was beginning to struggle, too. He was showing the first signs of altitude sickness and when we next stopped to catch our breath, I could tell something was up.

'Brother, I can't feel anything in my legs, my face, my jaw,' he said. 'I think I need to go down. It's probably HACE. You'll have another body to worry about if I stay here for too much longer.'

Mingma was the strongest Sherpa guide I'd ever known. He wasn't the type to make excuses, or to look for an easy way out. But he was also experienced enough to realise when his limits had been met, and to push past them at that point would have meant certain death. Though I'd be alone on the mountain with a seriously injured climber and a Sherpa, I couldn't stand the thought of losing a team member to the mission.

To make matters worse, word then came through on the radio that another climber had been reported missing on the mountain. 'If you see him, make sure to bring him down,' crackled the voice from Base. I stared angrily at the lights flickering in the distance at Camp 4. Still nobody was moving towards us. Hugging Mingma, I sent him on his way.

'And tell the others down there what's happening,' I shouted after him.

What was I doing? Was I really in the best position to conduct this rescue? For starters, I was without oxygen. Having been on the mountain for over twenty-four hours, I was also physically destroyed, especially after those five gruelling days on Dhaulagiri, with barely any rest – I estimated I'd had a total of nine hours sleep in that time. Every muscle begged me to stop. I dragged at Kuntal's weight for another two hours, the Sherpa stepping in to help from time to time, until eventually I arrived at the physical crossroads that sometimes takes place during a rescue operation.

Option one was for me to stay with the rescue party, all the while hoping that help and oxygen might arrive soon, though seeing as nobody had stirred from the tents below, the likeliest endgame was that we'd all die from the cold and a lack of air. The second option was to leave Kuntal where he was, moving quickly down to Camp 4, in a journey that would take me fifteen minutes, where I could beg for a rescue party to save him. I knew that enough people would have been well rested by the time I made it down; several climbers were certainly powerful enough to execute the mission, even despite topping Kanchenjunga during the morning. If I could rouse them into action, there was every chance Kuntal and the guide might be saved. I was taking option two.

'Listen, this oxygen is about to run low,' I said. 'If Kuntal's anything like Biplab, we'll lose him soon after. But there are people in Camp 4 that I think will listen to me – they'll come to his rescue. Either you can stay here with him, or you can come with me. It's your call.'

Once I'd started my descent, the Sherpa tailed me all the way down, the pair of us confident of saving Kuntal's life, when a weird scene emerged in front of me. Not fifty yards ahead was an old dude, wandering aimlessly around in the snow. He looked ragged, manic; his beard was matted with ice and he was dressed in a reflective summit suit that pinged away the light from our torches like laser beams.

At first, I wondered if the altitude had finally warped my thinking. *Was HACE kicking in?* No, I quickly realised that what I was seeing was the other missing climber, who I later discovered was called Ramesh Ray, and behind him was a reassuring sight. Finally, after hours of waiting, headlamps were flickering below us in the distance. A rescue party had been mobilised. We rushed down to the lost mountaineer, holding him up until the glowing blobs became people, and the people turned into shouting voices.

'This guy needs to go down,' I said as we gathered together. 'You're in a better place to take him than me. And the other guy, Kuntal is over there.'

I pointed to where we'd left our casualty with a small oxygen supply. 'He's not too far away. Take him some air and go and rescue him.'

The mission was done. Biplab might have been lost to the mountain, but at least his guide, and Kuntal, would soon be safe. Hopefully the other climber was OK as well. Climbing down into camp around one a.m., I found Mingma and Gesman's tent and crawled inside, pulling the sleeping bag around me for warmth, but resting felt impossible. I was so angry at how our calls for help had been ignored. *Why were we lied to, over and over, on the radio comms?*

The thought of hanging around for too long with those people felt demoralising and I knew I'd find it impossible to look any of them in the eye when they woke. I brewed a tea and sat silently until it was time to leave the mountain.

* * *

I rummaged through my bag for a pair of fresh socks and packed my kit. I was going to wake Gesman and Mingma, and then I was going to descend to Base Camp, ignoring the waves from passing climbers, avoiding the gaze of anyone who approached me. But first I was going to call Suchi.

Biplab's death had broken me.

I patched a call through to our home in England. Straightaway, she knew something was wrong, because I rarely called her from the mountains. 'Nims, what's up?' she said. I could hear the fear in her voice.

'I've failed,' I said, fighting back tears. 'I've failed.'

I retold the story, my sadness twisting into anger. 'The climbers up here were thinking only of themselves. They say they're badasses, they boast about how they can climb this mountain and that mountain . . . but where are they now? If one of them had just brought up some air, we would have been fine. This dude would have lived.'

Suchi tried to soothe my distress, but I was too fired up to listen and my mood was to darken even more once I'd woken Mingma and Gesman. Apparently, Rodrigo was dead, too.

During the rescue, stuck between the summit and Camp 4, I was unable to see Kanchenjunga's peak, but word had reached Mingma that, from a little lower down, the Chilean's head torch had been visible. It had flickered at the top all night, unmoving, until eventually the battery burned out. His body was now a frozen reminder of a bleak twenty-four hours on the mountain.

At least Kuntal had been rescued and was on his way to a hospital in Kathmandu – or so I believed. While climbing down through Kanchenjunga's camps, a helicopter had passed overhead. It was flying towards a suitable pick-up point higher up the mountain, and I figured Kuntal would be on board.

I felt relieved, happy that our work hadn't been for nothing; I'd been so determined to keep everybody alive. But when I arrived at the bottom of the mountain, I was told that the chopper had only collected Ramesh Ray. From what we could tell from the people around us, Kuntal had been left where we'd positioned him, even though the rescue party had been so close and they could have reached him quite easily.

I felt sick, realising the poor bloke was probably still on the mountain and there was no way he would have survived, not without oxygen. I raged at Mingma and Gesman.

'These people! They take the glory on social media, but they wouldn't do the job on the ground. They disgust me. When the shit hit the fan, where were they? I'll tell you: hiding in their tents!'

War had taught me two things about handling mortality. I understood that soldiers died in battles because they were fighting for a cause. (In much the same way, mountaineers died at high altitude because they were testing their levels of endurance in an unforgiving environment.) But sometimes death happened in stupid or preventable incidents, and men and women working in a warzone were killed by friendly fire.

In the mountains, distressed climbers died because they, or the people around them, were ill-equipped to work effectively in deteriorating circumstances. Those situations, to a degree, were painful but understandable – they were usually caused by human error or accidents. But the deaths of Biplab and Kuntal felt totally unacceptable, because their endings had been settled by choice. Somebody could have made an effort to help us. *They could have been saved.*

And I still have no idea of why the rescue never came.

As far as I was concerned, there were no excuses. In the cases of both Indian climbers, some of the guys sleeping below our position could have moved into action if they really wanted to. After summiting, those expeditions had managed to grab some rest for a few hours. They'd also moved slowly up the mountain, camp by camp, over a few days, so they were better rested, whereas I'd barely slept for five straight nights and had then climbed Kanchenjunga in one push. Yet, I'd been the one doing the rescuing.

I also knew from my experience of running guided expeditions that it was imperative to put the lives of paying clients first, no matter how determined they might have been to reach the summit. In those situations, it was my job to bring them back to reality, or haul them to safety. But it wasn't like that for others, and the high-altitude mountaineering world, as I was learning the hard way, was cruel and crazy.

As we flew to Everest Base Camp for what would be the last three peaks in Phase One – Everest, Lhotse and Makalu – refocusing on the job at hand became my priority. Yes, three men were dead, but my primary mission was still in place.

I had to leave the ghosts of Kanchenjunga far behind.

14

Summit Fever

Finally, the jokes and sarcastic comments about my ambitions were beginning to quieten a little. My expeditions were gathering more and more attention on Facebook, Twitter and Instagram, while an increasing number of potential investors were coming forward, but I couldn't afford to let my guard down. Though Everest, Lhotse and Makalu felt like home territory because of my world-record climb a year previously, none of them were to be taken lightly. Every 8,000-er was a challenge and it annoyed me that people had recently become a little dismissive of the world's tallest mountain.

No, Everest wasn't as dangerous as Annapurna, Kanchenjunga or K2. And yes, a number of not-so-skilled climbers had made it to the top, thanks to the work of the excellent Sherpas assisting them on the way, but it wasn't an easy ride. If the weather was clear and calm, then it was possible to reach the peak without too much stress, but if conditions deteriorated at the higher camps and the shit hit the fan? Well, then the chances of survival were slashed dramatically. People died.

The mountain was a death trap, right from the very beginning. Expedition parties had been ripped apart at Base Camp as they rested in their tents and avalanches often roared down

183

the mountain, devastating everything along the way, as those tragedies in 2014 and 2015 had proved. Once the climbing started, the Khumbu Icefall, which divided Base Camp from Camp 1, was equally treacherous and had become notorious for its fracturing seracs that twitched and moved as the glacier shifted by three or four feet a day.

It was beautiful in there, like an alien planet from a sci-fi film, but its shimmering terrain was deceptive. A number of climbers had been killed or seriously injured having stood in the path of an ice chunk as it sheared away from the mountain, and though I loved the risk of climbing through it, the Icefall was a sketchy place to be in – it was impossible not to feel a little exposed. And that's before a mountaineer had negotiated the challenges associated with the peak, such as the Hillary Step, and then the exhausting climb back down to safety. Everest was no joke.

Yet, despite these obvious risks, the mountain was still getting a bad reputation. By the time I attempted it again during Project Possible, people had long been complaining that it was nothing more than a playground for super-rich climbers with very little experience of operating on the high mountains. The old guard of mountaineers, those people that had scaled Everest thirty or forty years ago, argued that many individuals leant too heavily on their guides and Sherpas, and were undeserving of making it to the top.

Other critics pointed to the Nepalese government and moaned about the charges associated with climbing Everest. Mountain permits were too low, they said, and anyone was able buy their way in, regardless of skill; although the cost of gaining access was still beyond the reach of most people. A permit to climb the mountain was priced at around $10,000 in 2019 and that was before a mountaineer had bought any kit and provisions, booked flights and accommodation, or hired their guide for the expedition.

Regardless of the expenses involved, Everest had become overcrowded. The ledge leading up to the Hillary Step could sometimes resemble a city crossing as dozens and dozens of people hovered on the fixed lines, either waiting for their moment of glory on the highest point on earth, or attempting another step down as they tried to descend safely. This had become a frustrating experience for everyone. By waiting for other climbers to finish ahead of them, some mountaineers were being denied their shot at reaching the summit. Or worse, they were being delayed for so long that their descent felt increasingly precarious as the daylight faded. With all the toing and froing, a volatile mood at the peak was not uncommon.

My attitude towards the mountaineering politics swirling around Everest was to tune out any negativity as best I could. As far as I was concerned, it was still the highest point on the planet and needed to be respected, though some of the grumblings were legitimate. Overcrowding was definitely a big problem, but there were ways around it. If the line towards the summit was congested a badass climber could always pick another plan of attack, and there were plenty of old routes to be explored or reopened.

I'd noticed that whenever people failed, if they were unable to top the summit or were forced back by fatigue or altitude sickness, they had a tendency to train their excuses upon the other people climbing in that window – their guides, fellow mountaineers, or even the individuals responsible for managing Everest. That drove me crazy. In life I was always encouraged to admit to a mistake. If ever I fucked up on a military operation, I would mention it to my teammates. By shining a light on my failings, I was able to improve upon them and I would never use the excuse that a mountain was impossible to climb because of traffic. I'd plan and find another route to the top.

A bigger issue, as far as I was concerned, was the Himalayas' deteriorating environmental health. In 2015, the head of Nepal's mountaineering association, Ang Tshering, announced that the human waste being left behind by expeditions had the potential to become a major health hazard; given the mountain had become so popular, the spreading of disease was a serious concern. Just as worrying were the impacts of climate change, which had become increasingly obvious and unsettling. Nepal was a third-world country and while it was developing, it was happening slowly, so it was still without a lot of the resources enjoyed by far wealthier countries.

The Himalayas were its greatest asset. They brought in huge amounts of money in tourist revenue. The spirit within its people, who are humble and kind, certainly added to its appeal as well, but as a community they were suffering from the effects of global warming. It didn't take a meteorologist to spot the considerably lower levels of snowfall. The mountains now thawed much earlier in the season too, and the increased melt caused floods and mudslides throughout the region.

When I summited Ama Dablam in 2014 – it was possible to scoop up the snow from Camp 1, before melting it down for drinking and cooking. Bottled water wasn't necessary. But when I returned in 2018, the snow was nowhere to be seen and we were forced to carry gallons and gallons to the higher camps, adding kilos to the weight on our backs. I also noticed similar changes when climbing Dhaulagiri in 2019, and when I looked to the peak, the glacier had almost faded away. The sight was heartbreaking.

A year on, as I readied myself for the final three mountains of Phase One, I realised Project Possible now presented me with the platform to speak out on climate change, a position I'd hoped to reach when I first announced my idea. People were now watching my progress. I needed to alert them about the damage that was being inflicted around the world by posting one or two comments on social media, each one outlining my fears.

At that point, though, it was as if I'd been screaming into the dark. While my social media numbers were growing and I'd gathered followers in the tens of thousands, they weren't yet astronomical numbers – the hundreds of thousands that would show up during the mission's latter stages were a few months off. Despite these figures, however, I was still proving that with a little imagination and some serious effort, people were capable of taking on tasks the world had deemed beyond imaginable.

I'd climbed my first mountain in 2012 and not seven years later, I was on my way to working through all fourteen 8,000-ers in seven months. I'd proven to everybody that it was never too late to make a massive change in life. And if I could pull off such a project and show the world that a positive mindset was all that was required for far-reaching results, what would that say about the potential for environmental efforts around the planet? As people responded to my comments on climate change, I felt humbled, but I also became emboldened.

Among the voices I was interacting with online were kids, teenagers, and young adults on the verge of making their first big life decisions, such as who to vote for, or what career choices to make. Some of them were individuals considering their first mountain climb – the type of people emotionally invested in the future of the Himalayas and the environment. I wanted to show them exactly what was happening to the world at high altitude, the good and the bad.

I'd already decided that my efforts should begin close to home. I insisted on our missions being as environmentally friendly as possible; I was the expedition leader, so I had it in my power to instigate change. Everything we took to the mountain, we brought back down with us, including oxygen cylinders, which seemed to litter peaks across the Himalayas. When it came to briefing my clients before climbs, I always made my position very clear.

'Yeah, you come here for the love of the nature, but if you don't respect it, you've got no place in my expedition,' I told them. 'If you don't follow the rules, you can take your money and you can leave.' Overall, most people on my climbs turned up with a passion for the environment. Getting them to follow my protocols wasn't too tricky.

The impact of climate change, as I often told people, was universal. For too long we've all been guilty of regarding our houses as the only home we have, but that's simply not true. We weren't built for hiding indoors; we're outdoor animals, and the wider environment around our towns and cities is where we should be investing our money and attention, because when the force of nature hits, nothing can stop it. I've seen Nepalese villages ripped apart by mudslides and flooding. From a distance, the carnage looked like the aftermath of a bombing raid.

Throughout 2018, California was ravaged by a series of wildfires that scorched nearly two million acres of land; the same environmental catastrophe struck Australia a year later. *What was it going to take for people to pay attention?* The biggest problem facing humanity at this moment in history is our inability to think long-term. Ours is an overcrowded planet, and we worry about the days, weeks and months ahead, but when it comes to the contemplation of our environmental health in twenty or thirty years' time, we tend to switch off. Maybe the process is too scary to contemplate; it is certainly sobering.

I realised that the best way to draw attention to our global health throughout Project Possible was to shout about it from the mountaintops. And then an opportunity to highlight some of the conflicts between nature and man arrived much sooner than expected.

* * *

I was keen to break my speed world record for climbing Everest, Lhotse and Makalu. In 2017, I'd gone from the peak of Everest to Lhotse in ten hours and fifteen minutes. By the end of my trip with the G200E team, all three mountains had been climbed in five days. But on my way to Everest Base Camp for the Project Possible expedition, I decided that it was probably within my capabilities to cut that time by 50 per cent. I believed in my mental and physical strengths and while those mountains were beasts, they were ones I'd become fairly familiar with, though I respected their dangers.

Accompanied by Lakpa Dendi – one of the guides that had helped out the Gurkhas during the G200E in 2017 – I pushed off a little later on Everest than some of the other expeditions climbing on 22 May. As we moved over the Hillary Step, dawn cracking the sky above us, I noticed the flash of cameras going off and the flicker of head torches ahead. There were a few groups in front and they were moving slowly, tired with the effort of having climbed so far, but we soon stepped past them to hit the summit. The view, when we got there after three hours of climbing from Camp 4, was mindbending.

The morning sun was rising above the Himalayas and as one or two other climbers joined us on the top, everybody seemed energised again; the guys who had looked spent on the line up only moments earlier were immediately full of life. It was as if the new sun had delivered us all a fresh burst of purpose and optimism, even in the freezing cold. *If only I could soak up the light all day*. Then I felt somebody tugging at my summit suit. It was Lakpa.

'Brother, we should go,' he said. 'If you want to break that record, we need to turn around now.'

I nodded, grabbing a few photographs before stepping off the peak, but a few metres on, I was greeted with a chaotic scene. A long line was snaking around the thin crest that led away from the Hillary Step and at first there looked to be a few dozen people edging towards us. Then I realised the crowd was bigger, much bigger, and there were probably around one hundred and fifty climbers squeezed onto the fixed line, with the group moving slowly in both directions. We tried to edge down the rope carefully, checking in with each person we passed, but I quickly sensed a growing mood of panic.

Some people, I could see, were angry. They had invested a lot of money, time and effort to scale Everest and their progress had been stopped dead, like traffic behind a motorway pile-up. I feared that some climbers were taking serious risks with their lives, plus the safety of those around them, by not making the call to descend before their oxygen had become perilously low.

Others were worried at what was fast becoming a danger-ous situation: I overheard one bloke complaining that his toes and fingers were starting to become frostbitten, and the ledge leading away from the Hillary Step was an intimidating place for any expedition party to cling on to, especially if they were being exposed to the kind of high winds that often whipped across the mountain above the high camps. Anyone moving along the ridge was presented with dangers on either side: there was a 2,400-metre drop to the left and a 3,000-metre drop to the right. A climber falling from that height wasn't coming back.

The people I worried for the most were those climbers lost in the chaos; they were in fear and emotionally spiralling. I'd often thought that anxiety at high altitude wasn't too dissimilar to a drowning event. In the middle of the ocean, somebody who thinks they're about to go under will grab at anything, or anyone, for buoyancy, even their loved ones. They thrash and panic, often yanking the nearest person down with them in a desperate attempt to survive. Mental freak-outs above 8,000 metres weren't that dissimilar, and people flapped and made reckless decisions, which often impacted the safety of the climbers around them.

With summit fever and anxiety growing among the different groups, I felt the mood on Everest was approaching boiling point. People were arguing around me; somebody was about to freak out, or act recklessly. Because several lives had been lost on Everest already that year, I recognised something drastic needed to happen if the body count wasn't to increase further.

I climbed to a small rock ledge that overlooked the queue. The scene below me was ugly and when I made some early stabs at guiding people as they moved up and down the line, very few people in the scrum seemed to be listening. Both lanes of traffic had claimed right of way and neither side wanted to give ground. Collisions were taking place every couple of minutes; a succession of frantic overtaking manoeuvres threatened to wobble somebody from the safety rope at any moment. Every now and then, the quicker climbers that were descending shouted aggressively at the slower individuals ahead.

'It takes you half an hour to cover five metres,' one climber yelled to a dude ahead of him who was clearly struggling at the top of the line. 'If you let us pass, everything will be clear.' I noticed a Sherpa, conscious of the anarchy, begging his clients to turn around, fearful for their health. Some agreed reluctantly. Others ignored him. Everything was madness.

I had to present authority.

With nobody else stepping up to help, I started organising the congestion, though the biggest problem with adopting such a bold position was the mountain-climbing community: it was packed with alpha males and females, exactly the type of people that turned up in the Special Forces. I'd learned during service that the best way to work with personalities of that kind was to pretend to be bigger and better than all of them. But I also knew that in life-or-death situations, where the management of interconnected groups and individuals was the key to success, the people involved tended to listen if control was exerted. *Nobody wanted to die.*

At first, I ushered through the climbers that had been waiting the longest. In many ways, my role wasn't too dissimilar to that of a traffic policeman, but instead of cars I was waving through mountaineers. Some of them were so fatigued, they seemed to have forgotten the basic skills required for high-altitude climbing. Altitude sickness had them gripped. On other occasions, I'd check in with the Sherpas who were guiding clients that were visibly struggling, to see if they could continue. If they couldn't, I suggested the guides should send them down.

In the end, I remained below the Hillary Step for close to two hours. With every assessment, I knew any chance of breaking my own world record was diminishing, but once the logjam had cleared, around 90 per cent of the crowd had either summited with enough time to turn around, or were already winding their way along the ridge and down to Camp 4. It was time to make the same move and heading across to Lhotse was now my primary objective.

If I wanted to break my world record for climbing Everest and Lhotse, I estimated I was at least three hours behind schedule and yet I wasn't overly concerned. If I could shave an hour or so off my previous time, I'd still have fulfilled my promise, though fatigue would undoubtedly come into play. Lhotse was a steep incline and pulling myself along the fixed line was a challenge – for long periods my quads and calves burned as I put one foot in front of the other. To prevent my muscles from burning out, I switched techniques, sidestepping up the mountain, like a crab, so that my efforts were focused on the iliotibial bands in my legs.

The climb across Lhotse was lined by both beauty and brutality. The couloir, a narrow gully that led to the peak, was lined with black rocks that sparkled in the sunlight. Ahead was the massive presence of Everest, standing tall, dressed in cloud, a line of people still visible as they descended towards Camp 4. But there were also a number of unpleasant reminders that life at high altitude could be harsh and unforgiving. I passed at least three corpses along the way, the most unsettling being a dude in a bright yellow summit suit, his jaw set askew in a rictus grin. Apparently, he'd been stuck there for years.

When I topped out and turned around in a time of ten hours and fifteen minutes, matching my time from 2017, I used the image as a cue to switch on. *That might be you if you don't take care, brother.* There was still plenty of hard work to be done.

I was able to climb Makalu quickly, helicoptering to Base Camp and then resting up for a few hours before moving to the peak with Geljen. The lines had been fixed, the snow covering was shallow and we moved fast and light, in eighteen hours, reaching the summit on 24 May. Phase One of the mission had been executed as promised. And I'd broken one of the two promised world records: I'd climbed from the summit of Everest to the summits of Lhotse and then Makalu in forty-eight hours and thirty minutes, smashing my time from 2017.

Annoyingly, my hold-up on Everest had stopped me from improving upon the time taken from the summit of Everest to the summit of Lhotse. But the bigger objective was still in play. Phase One of Project Possible had been smashed in thirty-one days and I buzzed at the effort.

Could anybody doubt me now?

15

The Politics of a Mountain

The scene under the Hillary Step was still weighing on me. It had been crazy up there, close to catastrophic. *Did people understand what it really took to climb Everest these days?* Twenty-four hours earlier, I'd scrolled back to the photo of those waiting climbers. Then I logged into Facebook and Instagram and uploaded the images, not for one second picturing the political headache to come.

Before long, my shot of one hundred and fifty climbers, clustered along the thin ridge below the Hillary Step was pinging around the world. On social media I received click after click, like after like, and while a lot of the attention was focused upon the chaos of that morning, the image's quality had helped too.

As any high-altitude mountaineer will testify, it's tough to take a half-decent picture above 8,000 metres. Because of the detrimental effects that altitude can have on the body and brain, the simple act of taking off the gloves, rummaging around in a pocket for a camera, and then pointing and shooting can be bloody knackering. If someone wants a portrait, lifting the camera to take a selfie can be challenging in itself, and not a lot of Sherpas were qualified photographers. Unless the climber is fortunate, a lot of shots that come back from Death Zone expeditions are blurry or out of focus. *But I'd got lucky.*

While waiting to leave Makalu's base camp, with Phase One of Project Possible smashed, I scrolled through my laptop, emailing potential investors and sponsors, reminding them I was well on track to completing my mission. Then a friend, who was a professional photographer, messaged me with an idea. *What if I sold the Everest picture?* So many people were commenting on it; plenty of others were sharing it with their mates, and one or two climbers had even asked for a copy. *Could this be a clever way to drum up some extra funding?*

I advertised the print online, offering to sign a limited number of copies and slapped on a price tag of three hundred quid. I wasn't entirely sure of how much money I could expect to make, but I was keen to make up the shortfall in financing for Phase Two. I needed all the help I could get.

One of the things that I'd learned by living in Nepal was that Everest makes money – a lot of money. Where there's money, there's politics. And whenever politics arrives, trouble is sure to follow. Apparently, a number of people had registered complaints with the Nepalese government about my posting the image from the Hillary Step on social media and were accusing me of working to give the country a bad name, which was bullshit – the truth was that well over one hundred people had approached the mountain at once, all of them hoping to top out during what was a very short weather window of three days.

(Interestingly, some of the complaints came from people that were either directly or indirectly connected to guiding companies that were rivals to Elite Himalayan Adventures. Some of them even asked the government to ban me from climbing in the Himalayas, which would have prevented me from finishing Project Possible.)

When the authorities learned that I was hoping to make a little extra cash from the same photograph, they called me in for a meeting, but the cat was very much out of the bag by then. After leaving Base Camp, the picture had gathered 4,000 comments on Instagram and was being splashed across newspapers and websites, but an incorrect version of what had taken place underneath the Hillary Step was circulating and, in many people's minds, my photo was being misconstrued as a daily event. Suddenly the public were calling for a cap on the number of climbers allowed onto the mountain.

The backlash was fierce. Certain social media voices seemed sceptical about its authenticity. They claimed I'd created the image to draw attention to the politics surrounding the mountain, the environment, or to hype up my mission, but they hadn't heard my side of the story. Figures in the mountaineering community were reacting angrily, too.

In the *Nepali Times*, a climber and a good friend of mine, Karma Tenzing – who had summited Everest a week prior to my summit push – was explaining how the mountain had been quiet during his ascent. He'd also posted a photo of the empty ridgeline arguing, rightly, that my experience had been a once-in-a-season occurrence. (Though once-in-a-season was surely too much, when the risks were so high.)

'It has been portrayed around the world as an everyday event at the summit,' he complained, in an article entitled, 'Most Days It's Not So Crowded on Mt Everest'.

But Karma's anger wasn't being aimed at me; he seemed frustrated at the kneejerk reaction to my viral photo that claimed the annual number of people climbing Everest should be capped. He later argued on Twitter against restricting access:

> Weird seeing non-mountaineers voice opinions about the rush to summit of #Everest. No, don't cap the number of climbers! These are 'real' climbers who've paid their dues & are qualified & remain. With only 3–4 clear window days to summit, this will happen every darn year. I feel you should voice yourself only if you've been in the mountains and climbed the deadly Khumbu Icefall trying to avoid any killer falling ice, climbed to Camp 3 with brute jumar strength pulling yourself up for hours and hours and then to Camp 4 where the air has hardly any oxygen. Finally making it to the summit, dead tired after 12 hours of intense climbing (with 3 days of no sleep & non-stop walking) only chocolate bars for nutrition. After that, making it down to Base Camp walking for 2 days calculating every step in case you slip & fall. Only then, I'll hear your opinion. PS: Even with very little climbers on the 15th and 16th, folks perished in Camp 4 and above. In the end, the climb to the summit ain't a catwalk or easy as in photos. #Stupidity.

I couldn't argue with his position. When I eventually returned to Kathmandu, I was invited to meet with several concerned politicians, including representatives from the Department for Tourism. They wanted to know what I'd experienced and why I'd decided to sell my photograph. That annoyed me. The previous day, I scanned through Google Images, checking for evidence that other people had taken a similar picture, either from that summit push, or any other year. There were dozens and dozens. By the time of my appointment, I was feeling a little slighted. *Why the fuck are they picking on me?* I arrived with a PowerPoint presentation on my laptop and a gallery of old images detailing the queues on Everest.

'Is it because I'm trying to do something different?' I asked, when we settled down to talk. 'So far I've been nailing these mountains in the way I said I would. I'm putting the focus back on to the Sherpas with our work, too. So why are you treating me as the enemy? I'm not the first one to take this kind of picture. It just so happened it was my picture that captured a lot of attention.'

I registered one or two nods of understanding around the table. Someone pointed out that a number of complaints had been raised regarding the fact I was selling my photo online, and it was their job to get to the bottom of what was happening on Everest.

'Yes, fine,' I said, 'but let's get to the point: the queue is there. If you're saying it's a bad situation, why don't we do something about it? Are you just going to hide it? Or, now that everybody knows about it, are you going to fix it? This situation can cost peoples' lives. It's been like this for years, but it doesn't have to be so crazy. Maybe the time to make a change is now.'

I worried that their first suggestion when looking to correct the issue of congestion on Everest might involve a financial adjustment. A number of people online had proposed that the overcrowding problem was solvable by simply increasing permit costs. If the price point became much higher, they argued, fewer people would feel inclined to visit Everest. Meanwhile, the government could still make the same yearly profits from those adventurers with the cash and determination to climb. But it pissed me off that certain people in Nepal, and beyond, wanted to reduce Everest to a luxury available only to the very rich.

'Whatever you decide, can you please not increase the cost of climbing Everest?' I said. 'A price shouldn't be placed on nature. The mountains are there to be enjoyed by all.'

I then explained that, sure, there was an argument for introducing certain restrictions on who could climb and when, but they had to be fair. For example, the problem was easily fixed by creating a qualification system. As with Gurkha Selection, the process would be designed to weed out those that could, from those that couldn't.

For example, if a mountaineer was able to prove that they'd successfully topped out on an 8,000-er, such as Manaslu or Cho Oyu, only then could they apply for a permit to climb Everest. (Or perhaps they could climb a series of 6,000- and 7,000-metre peaks in Nepal, which would generate more money for the local community.) Adjusting the Everest climbing calendar might help in the future, too.

The problems I'd encountered in 2019 were down to the fact that the lines on Everest had been fixed very late in the mountaineering season, and that had created a backlog of climbers waiting to make their summit push. Once the ropes were set, everybody made their ascent from Base Camp at the same time, creating the traffic jam I'd witnessed under the Hillary Step. Resolving that logistical issue would also help to ease congestion.

'How about we fix the lines on Everest a month earlier, in April, when the season starts? So, when people arrive they can have a full month to pick and choose when they'd like to summit.'

The people at the table nodded and told me my suggestions would be taken under consideration. The pressure upon them was rising. Eleven mountaineers had died on Everest that year already and a number of new rules would be set in motion by

2019's end. The Department of Tourism would ultimately ask climbers to prove they had already scaled at least one 6,500-metre peak in Nepal, which was not quite as challenging as my idea, but was a start at least.

Elsewhere, any Sherpas working on the mountain would need to prove their experience if they were to guide on Everest, and every climber had to validate their good health. Of course, there were some downsides to all of these proposals. Almost every Sherpa would qualify under the new criteria, and health certificates were easily forgeable, but again, they were a step in the right direction.

After all the tragedy I'd experienced in the Himalayas during Phase One, these efforts, while not being perfect, were better than nothing.

* * *

Mum wasn't getting any better. Her heart condition was worsening.

As she rested in hospital, regular updates on Project Possible were given to her by Binesh, a friend of the family. He had first come into our orbit when I joined the Gurkhas in 2003, and at that time Mum and Dad were on their own, after all the kids had left home, but I hadn't known they were struggling with the stresses of day-to-day life in Chitwan. The realisation only dawned on me while visiting them on leave.

One afternoon I took the local bus with Mum, but when it rumbled into view, I noticed that the carriage was jam-packed, a commuter trip from hell. During busy times, the drivers accepted passengers only if they were travelling for longer distances; it was a way of charging more money. Because our destination that afternoon was only around six kilometres away, our chances of getting on were slim, and we'd probably have to wait a while for the next bus.

Sure enough, the driver tried to wave us off. 'I can't take you,' he said.

Mum, undeterred, stepped up to get on, but then a bus conductor quickly shoved her away and slammed the door shut. I couldn't believe it; I lost my temper as the bastards drove off and in a fury I ran home to get my motorbike, bombing through the streets until I'd caught up with the bus. Pulling in front, I got on board and beasted the conductor.

'Never, ever do that to anyone!' I shouted as he cowered in a seat. 'Especially not to elderly women.' The guy looked terrified.

'I'm not having you do this any more, Mum,' I said, when I finally got back to her. 'I'm going to get a car for you, that way you won't ever have to use the bus again.'

There were two downsides to my plan: the first was that Nepal sometimes charged as much as 288 per cent tax on purchased vehicles and I'd have to get a loan from a Kathmandu bank. The second was neither Mum or Dad could drive, and so having bought a car, I employed Binesh to take them grocery shopping whenever they needed food and he often drove them to their friends' houses for get-togethers and dinners. Before long, Binesh was very much a part of our family life and by 2019, eleven years later, he was charged with caring for my parents while the kids were away working.

As I'd moved through the Himalayas in May, Binesh sat by my mother's hospital bed in Kathmandu and read her newspaper stories on my expeditions and world records. He showed her video clips from Facebook and explained how I'd rescued Dr Chin; Binesh even told Mum about the tragedy on Kanchenjunga.

Once my meeting with the Department for Tourism was done, I visited her in hospital as much as I could, holding her hand while I retold my stories. After a while, she looked at me and smiled. 'It sounds like my son is unstoppable,' she said.

Mum knew how important Project Possible was to me, and she'd come to accept my passion, even though some of the risks I'd been taking clearly worried her. Mum also knew that I was going to do everything in my power to get her and Dad into an apartment together, once my work was done. But seeing her in a hospital bed, attached to wires and bleeping machines, was very upsetting. Tears streaked her cheeks as we spoke. Mum was everything to me; she'd made me the man I was, and I hated the thought of leaving her behind. There was a moment of doubt.

With Mum's poor health, was Project Possible still justifiable?

If I couldn't finish this, what would happen to Suchi and me?

And what would become of my reputation if I didn't deliver on my ambitions?

Mum seemed to sense I was worried. 'Nims, you've started this mission now,' she said. 'So complete it. Our blessings are with you.'

I squeezed her hand and promised to return home safely again as soon as I could. And then I remembered.

Quitting was not in the blood.

* * *

As I moved into Phase Two of Project Possible at the end of June 2019, which would take me to Nanga Parbat, Gasherbrum I and II, K2 and Broad Peak, the conversation surrounding my goals had shifted within the extreme mountaineering community, but only slightly. Yes, a number of people were making encouraging noises about the speed at which I'd climbed all six mountains in the first chunk of the mission, but there were plenty of others casting shade upon me, too.

The most common complaint was that Nepal was my home turf; people argued I'd probably understood the local culture and terrain better than climbers from another country and it had given me an advantage. That was fair enough, I suppose, though it conveniently overlooked the fact I'd been climbing for only seven years. Other figures even claimed that Project Possible was only successful because I'd travelled between some base camps by helicopter, whereas in Pakistan, the infrastructure for that type of mobility wasn't available.

'Yeah, stand by, guys', I thought, feeling a little annoyed. 'You don't even know . . .'

On the other hand, I understood that Pakistan presented a different challenge entirely. It was certainly a more unpredictable region in which to climb. The weather was known for being vicious on K2; across Gasherbrum I and II, huge storms could blow in out of nowhere, bringing whiteout conditions to an otherwise sunny day. The logistical support at base camps across the Karakoram mountain range, such as communications and accommodation, was also less sophisticated than in Nepal, so I would have to trek between base camps rather than taking a helicopter.

Overall, though, my biggest stress when climbing in Pakistan was the threat of my team being wiped out in a terrorist hit on Nanga Parbat. My experience with the people of Pakistan had always been fantastic, they were lovely, but an attack from Taliban forces was considered a very real concern during the months building up to Project Possible.

The backstory to this issue began on 22 June 2013, when sixteen Taliban fighters, dressed in paramilitary uniform and wielding AK-47s and knives, moved into Base Camp, dragging twelve climbers from their tents and tying them up with rope. Everyone's passports were confiscated; photos were taken of each captured climber, and their smart phones and laptops were smashed with rocks. Eventually, the group was led to a field outside the camp and executed. Only one man escaped, a Chinese mountaineer called Zhang Jingchuan, who was lucky enough to free himself from his binds as the shooting began.

With rounds ricocheting around him as he fled, Zhang escaped into the dark barefoot. The poor bloke was dressed in only his thermal underwear, but he hid behind a rock, turning hypothermic, until he felt safe enough to crawl back to his tent, rummaging around for a satellite phone and some warm clothes. Around him, eleven people, friends and colleagues, had been massacred. Knowing the terrorists might still be nearby, he moved fast, calling the authorities for help. Later that morning, a military helicopter was hovering above Base Camp and Zhang was rescued.

I heard about the story while scrapping with the Special Forces and the atrocity had made our fight seem all the more relevant. But when Project Possible rolled around several years later, the very real threat of a Taliban attack during the mission felt unnerving, especially as I'd be operating on their turf in Pakistan. For starters, any fighters could arrive quite quickly, because it took only a day to trek to the Diamer District of the Gilgit-Baltistan region (where Nanga Parbat could be found) from the nearest towns, whereas the Karakoram range, which was where the likes of K2 and Gasherbrum I and II were located, was ten days away and there were a number of military checkpoints to pass through. I would also be unarmed and unable to defend myself if life got noisy as we waited in Base Camp.

This was not only about me; I also had several other dudes in the team to consider and none of them possessed any military experience. The other concern was the profile that I'd generated while organising Project Possible. I'd talked openly about my ambitions in order to push for funding, and my social media presence had grown as a result. All of which made me a high-level target for any terrorists looking to make a name for themselves. Knowing that my background in the military was hardly a secret, anyone with an axe to grind about my involvement in the War on Terror would find me exposed and vulnerable on Nanga Parbat. I would have to work carefully.

There was some good news on the funding drive at least. While planning my climbs in Pakistan, I'd become painfully aware of what was still needed to get the mission completed on schedule. Everything I'd earned so far had gone into Phase One and I needed a huge cash injection. But there was a lifeline.

A number of my mates in the Special Forces had worked alongside Bremont, a British watch company. Following an introduction through a mutual friend, they had previously offered to give me fourteen watch faces as I prepared to leave London for the Himalayas and Phase One. The idea was to take every one to the summits during Project Possible and they would be turned into a unique watch. All the watches would then be auctioned off, with most of the money feeding back into my expedition costs. Then came the upswing. By the time I'd completed Phase One, Bremont wanted to increase their involvement.

'We want to sponsor and promote Project Possible and advance you £200,000, interest free,' they announced.

I was delighted. There was no other funding offer on the table at that time and without financial support, the completion of the project looked unlikely. But with the backing of Bremont, who would also provide publicity for the mission – now to be called Bremont Project Possible – a large chunk of my expeditions in Pakistan could be paid for. With some more guiding expeditions and another injection of cash from my GoFundMe page, drawing together the required numbers for the second phase was within my reach. But there was a major catch.

'We'd love to be named as your sponsors before you climb Nanga Parbat,' said Bremont.

I paused. Their input was invaluable and announcing Bremont's involvement was something I was delighted to do, but only after I'd safely climbed Nanga Parbat. I needed to stay off radar from the Taliban until then.

'Look, because of my military background, I can't take a single risk,' I explained. 'It only takes one bad dude to say, "OK, this guy's going, here's $200 to brass him up." Someone will take that offer up in a heartbeat.'

Bremont understood. The last thing anybody wanted was for Project Possible to end in a bloodbath. As it was, Nanga Parbat had its own plans for finishing me off.

16

Quitting's Not in the Blood

I worked hard to bombproof the Nanga Parbat mission.

To confuse any potential terrorist attackers, I booked three different flights into Pakistan throughout July, hoping to cover my tracks. Another couple of grand was added to the total bill as a consequence, but that was preferable to being on the wrong end of an ambush or kidnap. I also wasn't publicising any of my movements on social media until I'd made it away in one piece from the Diamer District.

As a final precaution, I separated myself from our private client, an accomplished mountaineer who had paid to top Nanga Parbat alongside the team. I decided it was probably safer if she rendezvoused with us at Base Camp. If something kicked off, I didn't want anybody else to suffer in the blowback.

Even my teammates were forced into a procedural change or two, which included an adjustment to our relaxed attitude in the mountains. During treks, we liked to smash back the booze and play loud music, and we often brought a raucous atmosphere to most base camps where there was very little to do, other than to sleep, eat and chat. With a small Bluetooth speaker, the Project Possible team was able to transform any dining tent into a club after dark, banging out Nepalese pop hits and loud rock music into the early hours of the morning, as we passed around bottles of beer and whisky.

The drinking and dancing had first started in Annapurna, and continued after the vicious Dhaulagiri climb, and together we kicked back and played tunes, having survived a life-or-death expedition. As far as team-building exercises went, it was an immediate hit: I noticed that some of the quieter lads opened up about the mission after a few beers. Others found the confidence to talk about their fears at high altitude, or their ambitions once the fourteen mountains had been climbed. By partying together, everybody felt more included in the project, we were able to communicate and connect, which created a sense of cohesion, and among the crew there was an understanding that, yeah, we were there to work hard, but there was room to mess around, too. Getting sloppy wasn't an option, though. Whenever we partied through the night I made sure to wake up earlier than everyone else. I meant business, I demanded excellence and it was important everybody around me knew it.

At first, that rowdy spirit extended into our arrival in Pakistan. When a van arrived to take us from Islamabad towards Nanga Parbat, the driver's radio was playing. We turned the volume up even louder, singing and shouting as we started our journey into the mountains, but almost immediately I received a sobering reminder of what we were taking on when the renowned Pakistani mountaineer, Muhammad Ali Sadpara, called.

Ali had climbed Nanga Parbat a number of times already. He was more than familiar with the region, and I'd asked him to operate as our base camp manager. But hearing the music and singing in the background as we spoke, Ali delivered a stern reminder of our need to be unseen and unheard during the coming week.

'Nims, I've been told about your reputation,' he said. 'I know you like to party through the night. You drink; you play loud music. But in Pakistan that won't happen. This is not Nepal. No messing around!'

His warning freaked me out a little bit, though he was right: because of my situation, it was wise to keep a low profile whenever possible. Staying alert was key, too, and as we later started our trek to Nanga Parbat, the team trudged silently through villages at night and past trekking lodges, ever focused. Once installed at Base Camp, I drew upon the defensive skills gathered from my military training as the sun went down, remaining switched on, checking in with the tents and the guys, who were chatting quietly.

The vibe was eerie. Every now and then I'd watch the horizon for approaching lights, or some sign of any unusual activity, but my sentry patrol was only half the job. Having realised that my position could be compromised by a tweet or Instagram post from one of the other expedition parties waiting at Nanga Parbat, I called together their different team leaders, briefing them about the importance of discretion, especially when tagging people on social media. I couldn't take the risk that a terrorist group in Pakistan might pick up on the info and strike at us.

'The reason I'm working covertly is because of the security issue,' I said. 'What happened here in 2013 was brutal and it's not a hundred per cent safe, even now.'

Someone argued that I was overreacting, but I wasn't having it.

'A terrorist cell hoping to reach Base Camp could probably get here in twenty-four hours. And if they come, they won't end it with me. So, don't let people know I'm here – *please*.'

I was very much erring on the side of caution, but it seemed best not to take the risk, especially when there were plenty of other dangers to stress about. I'd rather have died in an avalanche than an execution.

* * *

A few expedition parties had taken up residence on Nanga Parbat before our arrival, including climbers from Jordan, Russia, France, and Italy. One or two of them had been busy, and the Jordanians were claiming in Base Camp to have fixed the lines leading from Camp 2 to Camp 3. Elsewhere, an international team had apparently fixed the lines from Camp 1 to Camp 2, and their climbers had later gone on Twitter, boasting of how the ropes were fully secured. Among the expedition parties, this was widely considered as legit intel and we planned accordingly. (Given we wouldn't have to fix any lines early on, we could perform a load carry of equipment on our way up, with rucksacks weighing around thirty kilos.)

Everybody was accustomed to trusting the other climbers on the mountain, and as soon as we'd settled, I led an acclimatisation rotation from Base Camp towards Camp 1, with the view of scaling the Kinshofer Wall to Camp 2 – an intimidating, sheer face of ice and rock that was negotiated with ice axes. But having started our ascent, a heavy weather system soon closed in around us. The mountain was blanketed by a snowstorm and our luck worsened further once we pushed past Camp 1. The lines set by the international team were nowhere to be found.

The fear that the line had not been fully secured started to nag at me. But hoping the efforts of the international team might have been cloaked in the whiteout, we dug furiously through the growing drifts. The digging and pacing made for heavy work. Meanwhile, the terrain around us was so steep that any gathering snow had the potential to flood, unloading from above and rushing through the rocks like a lava flow.

It wasn't long before I recognised an all-too-familiar whooshing sound: a huge swell of powder was pouring in from overhead and was soon smashing everybody sideways. At the time I'd had my eyes on Mingma. He was reaching around for some sign of a buried rope. The white swallowed him up in an instant.

I panicked. *Was I about to lose him?*

Gathering my senses, I crawled through the billowing fog and powder around us, hoping for some indication that he'd survived until, thankfully, his frame came into view. Mingma had saved himself from a fatal drop off a nearby ledge by forcing his arms into the drifts around him, but his position was precarious. In the chaos, his legs had twisted, and his grip on the snow was barely strong enough to hold his weight in place. One wrong move might collapse the powder around him, releasing him for at least a few hundred metres.

Given the slope, it was unlikely Mingma would die in the fall, but he'd definitely experience a serious injury if he collided with one of the nearby rocks on his way down. Slowly we worked our way towards him. By fixing a couple of ice axes into the snow as makeshift handholds, we were able to give Mingma a firm grip, and he untangled his limbs before climbing his way to safety. Bloody hell, he was lucky to be unhurt.

I'd had enough, the lines weren't there, so grabbing our kit together we abandoned our plans to move up the Kinshofer Wall. As the team descended to Base Camp, I became determined to deal with the international crew for having misled me on Twitter. I was furious, sick and tired of people lying to me on the mountain, especially after Kanchenjunga, and this time the bullshit had thrust my team firmly into the line of fire. I was also annoyed with myself – I'd been too trusting. When I found some of the international climbers, my anger at their phantom lines and Mingma's near-death event intensified. I stormed into their tent.

'Why did you fucking lie?' I shouted. 'Why did you say you'd fixed the lines when you hadn't? I nearly lost my most capable guy because of you.'

To my surprise, they made no attempt to bluff their way out of it.

'Nims, we're sorry,' said one of the group. 'The lines are *partly* fixed. We put the word up on Twitter, but maybe it wasn't detailed enough. We didn't expect you guys to be looking at it too.'

'Yeah, but it caused me to plan differently. I'd have gone light rather than carrying a super-heavy load.'

I shook my head. It all sounded so confusing. By the sounds of it, they had made the post to impress their sponsors and followers on social media, and it was a worrying realisation. At that point I realised that the only trustworthy people on Nanga Parbat were the guys from Project Possible. But I also understood our summit push wasn't going to be made any easier if I started brawling with everyone else in Base Camp.

I checked myself; it was the right moment to simmer down. I knew there was no point looking for a scrap when the option of diplomacy remained on the table.

'Listen, brothers, we have to be on the level here,' I said, lowering my voice. 'From now on we'll only deal with accurate information. To climb this mountain, we need to have a bomb-proof plan.'

Somebody pulled out a bottle of vodka and some canned tuna. A truce was called. As a compromise, I suggested the line-fixing workload should be shared between the different teams during our summit push, which was scheduled for the

The conditions were so bad on Dhaulagiri the snow seemed to strike us like bullets.

Mingma, Gesman and myself attempt to rescue Biplab from Kanchenjunga.

With one photo I captured the chaos that sometimes kicks off on Everest.

Making it to the peak of Lhotse on May 22nd, 2019, shortly after summiting Everest.

Geljen works his way towards the end of the French Couloir on Makalu.

Hope is God: at the summit of Makalu.

By strength and guile I made it to the top of
Nanga Parbat, despite a near-death fall.

Trailblazing like a badass.

This picture was taken at the shared base camp of Gasherbrum I and Gasherbrum II. You can clearly see the tattoo on my back. The ink is mixed with my family's DNA.

Working my way to the top of Gasherbrum II. The views in the Death Zone can be mind-bending.

The expedition brothers having completed the line fixing effort on K2, with Dawa, K2 basecamp manager, also included. From left: Lakpa Dendi Sherpa, Mingma David Sherpa, Geljen Sherpa, Nims, Dawa Sherpa, Halung Dorchi Sherpa, and Gesman Tamang.

Just 200 metres short of K2's summit, I was about to complete a task many people had believed was beyond me.

Lifting my knees through the powder
on the Broad Peak summit push.

With Mum, my
inspiration. Following
the completion of the
mission, she met me at
the Nepal-Tibet border.

Opening up the
route to Cho
Oyu's peak.

Manaslu Base Camp.

was leading a team of clients to the top while climbing one of the final mountains of the mission. Guiding has become my passion.

On Shishapangma I opened up a new line to the summit:
The Project Possible Route.

Job done. The team descends Shishapangma, having climbed the fourteen
Death Zone peaks in six months and six days.

following week, on 3 July, when the weather conditions were forecast to improve.

Seeing that some ropes had been partly set between Camps 1 and 2, I suggested that the Project Possible team conduct the trailblazing effort through the freshly laid snow while fixing lines where necessary, before resting overnight at Camp 2. Later, if the Jordanians' old rope was still in place from last year, the different teams could share the workload as we climbed to Camp 3. From then on, I was happy for the Project Possible team to set the rope to Camp 4 for everybody to use and then trailblaze to the top.

The international team nodded in agreement. *We had a plan.* Word was spread to the rest of the teams resting in Base Camp. The misbehaviour had been nipped in the bud – for now.

When the climbing began for real, the Project Possible team trailblazed across the mountain towards Camp 2 the following morning, digging out any submerged rope before resting up in our tents for the night. We were thankful for the limited sleep. Handily, the Jordanians proved to be a powerful unit and unafraid of sharing the heavy workload as they led the way to Camp 3 the following morning. Some sections of their lines from last year were easy to find, but some of it had been buried under a layer of snow. To climb it we needed to pull the line free, but the powder wasn't too deep, so it made for fairly easy work.

But with our work underway, a couple of the expedition parties seemed unable to stop themselves from bickering and bitching. Some people moaned that certain climbers weren't putting in the required effort, or were just following slowly on the line. At least two teams were planning to ski off Nanga Parbat once they'd summited, and they sounded very keen to outdo one another. (A French climber had already summited ahead of us, alpine-style, and performed the same feat.)

The breaking point, as far as I was concerned, arrived when one experienced mountaineer refused to help with the rope-fixing effort. His excuse? That it was more important to concentrate on flying the drone he'd brought along for a film he was making. I felt pissed off again. Everybody wanted to fly drones and capture exciting film footage. I knew I did. But on expeditions where a series of climbing parties had opted to work together, it was considered bad form to shirk from any responsibility. Teamwork and the overall mission took priority over personal agendas.

Though we weren't directly involved, the squabbling was distracting. Throughout my career, I'd never been interested in individual recognition or glory hunting; personal fame or recognition wasn't my thing as a soldier and I enjoyed working in a team. It was the same for everyone around me, which meant that all of us in the squadron were able to trust one another implicitly. In the military elite I understood my priorities: the mission and the group came first, and nobody was going to step over me, or take unnecessary risks that might jeopardise the life of my teammates, least of all for personal success.

Sadly, Nanga Parbat was re-emphasising some of the harder lessons I'd learned on Kanchenjunga. Some people were only out for themselves.

My frustrations with the other teams turned up a notch the following morning after we'd stayed overnight at Camp 3 and trailblazed across a steep incline to Camp 4, where the snow was deep, and the line-fixing effort proved physically intense. To prepare for our summit push, the expedition parties decided to rest at Camp 4 for a few hours, though there was very little chance to sleep. Six people were crammed into one tent, because we'd decided to travel across the mountain with as little kit as possible.

When the time to depart arrived, I could hear chattering outside the tent. The other teams had gathered together and were waiting for us to lead yet again, when they could have easily taken the initiative instead. They were relying on us, they wanted the Project Possible team to trailblaze for them, and for a little while we stayed inside, wondering if any of them might take on the job, but nobody moved an inch. Once more it was down to us to lead the way. I was annoyed, but my frustrations increased even further when the intel I'd been given about our final push to the summit turned out to be a little off the mark.

Some sections of Nanga Parbat, between the lower camps, comprised stretches of hard ice that required a climber to bite into the terrain with their crampons while working cautiously along the line, if one had been fixed, that is. Without one, there was every chance a mountaineer might slip and fall, skidding across the mountain like a puck on an ice-hockey rink. If they were lucky, a self-arrest might stop them from picking up too much speed. But on compacted snow and ice, there was every chance that gravity would launch an individual to his, or her death.

For that reason, tackling ice of that kind without a fixed line was considered less than ideal. And yet, here we were, approaching the peak of Nanga Parbat, stepping gently across a slippery spur coated in the stuff, without a rope, because the information I'd gathered while researching our expedition had told me a line wasn't needed from Camp 4 to the summit. That might have been true for one or two previous expeditions, but not for ours.

A few days earlier, I'd been stung by those claims regarding the international team's fixed lines. Now I was being stung again and the slope we were traversing was pitched at a steep angle of around fifty degrees. I should have triple-checked my intelligence. And then triple-checked once more.

When I looked down, the exposure was intense and Base Camp was visible through the clouds. My heart pounded. My hands felt sweaty. As a group we decided to sidestep across the icy incline and it seemed as if one misstep might hurtle me past the other teams climbing beneath me, exploding my body on the rock below. I looked at the others; they seemed to be moving fairly steadily. Then I called out to Geljen. He had taken on most of the trailblazing between Camps 3 and 4 and when we'd awoken for the summit push that morning, he looked like a dead man – the effort had been that intense. Geljen's face had been pale; he seemed broken.

Surely he was now feeling the fear too?

'Hey bro, is this not a bit sketchy?' I shouted.

Geljen laughed. 'Fuck, yeah! It's crazy, Nimsdai. Let's be super-careful.'

Knowing it wasn't just me, I puffed away a sigh of relief. But that one tingle of fear caused me to re-evaluate our situation. I switched on, kicking my crampons into the mountain, the metal teeth shredding chunks of ice away until a deep foothold appeared. I then gouged out another with my ice axe. And another.

'Guys, kick out a path for the others!' I shouted. 'Otherwise someone might take a lethal fall up here.'

We carved our way to the very top, and having dug out a visible trail, the team eventually topped out around 10 a.m. on 3 July. Some way below us, the arguments and angry confrontations were still playing out, but teamwork and shared focus had pushed Project Possible to the top of our first Pakistan 8,000-er.

* * *

I switched off. Only for a second or two, but it was enough to nearly kill me.

I'd been keen to get to the Base Camp quickly, resting overnight at Camp 4 before descending early in the morning. Having moved away from the Kinshofer Wall, and into the soft powder that had nearly sucked Mingma away a few days previously, I stepped down carefully, holding onto the line on a pretty steep slope of around sixty or seventy degrees – a gradient that should have caused me to take greater care.

Why I became distracted, I don't know. But when a climber from below shouted that I should get off the line, I unclipped my carabiner and stepped back, and then down, without thinking. I guess the dude hadn't wanted any extra tension on the rope, which was unreasonable, but I was happy to give way seeing as he was caught up in what seemed like a minor meltdown. It was so nearly a fatal move.

The analogy for focus that I've used previously talks about being able to remain fairly alert and functional without being 100 per cent switched on, in the same way that someone is able to drive and talk at the same time. But when unclipping from the line and stepping back, I relaxed momentarily, and my concentration levels dropped. It was a sloppy move and, in essence, I was texting from behind the wheel at 90 miles per hour. I skidded backwards, landing on my back and banging my head before spinning and sliding down the mountain at a rapidly increasing speed. Metre after metre passed by in a blur as I started falling away quicker and quicker.

I'd been in sketchy falls before, but I hadn't panicked. During a parachute-training jump with the military, I once pulled at my release cord, only to watch as the chute sailed away. Rather than panicking as I hurtled through the sky, I followed my training and released my reserve. The second canopy had thankfully billowed open around me.

This was much the same experience and every second

counted. I yanked at the leash holding my ice axe in place, burying the pick into the snow, hoping to slow my speed in a self-arrest. Once I'd come to a stop, it would be possible to walk back to the rope, but the axe wouldn't hold. *I'd had a malfunction.* It was time to reach for the reserve. I stabbed with the axe again, but the surface was too fluffy and I couldn't pump the brakes.

Now was the time to panic, I was in free fall, and it was only once I'd spotted a brief glimpse of the rope alongside me that I realised there was a fighting chance of survival. Reaching out, I grabbed hard, pulling myself to a stop. Somehow, miraculously, I hadn't been killed. The route I'd been taking was bound to launch me off Nanga Parbat, which would have made for a messy end, and all because I'd taken my eyes off the ball for the briefest of moments. As I clipped myself back onto the line, my legs wobbling a little, I made a promise to myself – *I'll always concentrate; I'll always get down safely.* As far as mottos to live by went, it was as good as any. I crept down the mountain slowly, repeating the words over and over.

There was no time for celebration. We moved away from Nanga Parbat without too much fanfare.

I was lucky to be alive.

17

Through the Storm

Project Possible was teaching me lesson after lesson, on and off the mountain. At sea level, I was developing my skills as a fundraiser, one-man PR machine, environmental campaigner and political mover. Above 8,000 metres, I'd learned more about my true capabilities under pressure, where I could lead and stay calm while managing potential disasters such as severe altitude sickness, avalanches and rescue operations. When moments of near-death crept into my peripheral vision, such as my fall on Nanga Parbat, I didn't shy away; I tackled the issue head on.

At no point did I moan when the going got tough. Instead I followed the principles of war and led by example, maintaining team morale through hard effort and positive thinking. That style of work often translated easily into civilian life, as elemental dangers rarely came into play, but on a mountain where an ever-changing weather system could mean the difference between survival and dying, those leadership qualities were thrown into sharp relief.

There would be occasions when one of the advance team was setting up our tents at Base Camp as a nasty weather system was blowing in. A panicked radio call would come over on the radio: 'Nimsdai, it's snowing heavily on the mountain. It's going to be a rough climb!' Rather than wallowing in negativity, I'd make a smart-arse comment to lift the mood. 'Come on, bro, what do you think we're getting on a mountain? A bloody heatwave?' I revelled in the challenge of leading my team into battle, across testing terrains where the weather conditions were often grim. The hard graft felt both rewarding and inspirational.

During those moments where the burden of leadership seemed too much to handle and fatigue crept in, I checked my reputation as a Gurkha, a Special Forces operator, and a world-record-breaking climber. That was usually enough to shake away any flashes of negativity. Reminding myself of the motivations that had first kick-started the project helped me to power through any episodes of extreme tiredness, too. But most of all I had belief. When operating at sea level, I often felt as if I didn't belong, it wasn't my place. But in the big mountains, I seemed unbreakable.

I told myself, '*You* are the champion. *You* can do this.' I remembered the stories I'd heard about Muhammad Ali and how, even in his senior years as a fighter, he never considered defeat. Likewise Usain Bolt during his Olympic gold-winning races. At the base camp of every mountain, I tried to think in the same way, never once imagining that the summit above me might be out of reach. Instead, I told myself it was there to be taken.

'You are going to make this happen,' I would say. 'You're the man here.'

To some people that attitude might have sounded egotistical, or overly ambitious, perhaps even dangerous, but it was never about ego – the mission was bigger than that. I wasn't being nonchalant, or dismissive of the mountain's prowess. Rather, I possessed a supreme level of self-belief in my ability and what I was about to do – and that was the most powerful rocket fuel of all. Now Gasherbrum I and Gasherbrum II, the eleventh- and thirteenth-highest mountains in the world, were the next peaks on the Phase Two schedule. There was no time to ease up.

Despite the funding problems that had dogged my mission from the off, I was able to stay focused; Mum and her health concerns in Kathmandu were stresses I had to manage as best I could, as was the extreme fatigue I was experiencing. But there were some issues that were beyond my control. The journey from Nanga Parbat to Skardu, and then the shared base camp of GI and GII, was supposed to take eight days and we were set to travel through a couple of areas that were known to be patrolled by Taliban fighters. It was important that everybody remained on high alert until we reached the Karakoram range. (To cover our tracks further, we camped away from the trek-king lodges on the road.)

There was no time to rest and we drove non-stop for twenty-four hours for the first part of the journey, the entire team and our kit jammed into a mini-van. When a landslide on the road threatened to slow us down, we unloaded our rucksacks and equipment and then packed them into another vehicle on the other side. I knew that to rest unnecessarily when a hostile force was in pursuit could be a suicidal move.

Before the walking started, we hired mules and porters to carry most of our equipment the rest of the way, but I worried they might move too slowly along the trails. That would hold us back and before we set off, I told the porters to double up the number of mules we would be using to transport our equip-ment. Time was against us, the mountain season was coming to a close, and following Nanga Parbat, I'd decided that I didn't merely want to break the world record for climbing the region's five 8,000-ers, which was set at two years, I wanted to destroy it. There was a fire in my belly. My stated ambition was to climb the five tallest mountains in the world in eighty days, but my team was being held back.

'Look, we can't go at the normal speed,' I said. 'Let's double up the mules and porters, guys. If we can get to GI in three days, I'll still pay you for the full eight.'

The porter wasn't having it. 'Nims, it doesn't matter whether the mules carry thirty kilos or forty kilos. They always travel at the same speed.'

'Give it a go,' I said. 'You get one chance. I don't want it to affect the mission.'

My request fell on deaf ears. The following morning, as we were about to depart from Askole – the start point for most treks throughout the Karakoram region – the porter arrived with the same number of mules, adamant that reinforcements were pointless. On the first night, we waited for four or five hours for our porters to catch up with us as we camped. The same thing happened the following evening. And on the third, I became wound up.

'Fuck this,' I snapped. 'You know what? You guys are too happy to work in your comfort zones. We need to move faster.'

I checked in with Mingma, Geljen, Gesman, and the others. 'If we can carry our climbing kit by ourselves, we'll be so much quicker. Are you willing?'

The team nodded; everyone was in agreement. We left our camp at 4 a.m. and arrived at the bottom of GI around 5 p.m., covering fifty-four kilometres in thirteen hours, while carrying a lot more than thirty-five kilos per person. All of us were exhausted, but unbroken.

Despite the huge effort it had taken to get there, I felt ready for the Karakoram stretch of the mission, confident we could tackle the tests ahead, but respectful of what I was about to take on. Gasherbrum I, while not carrying the ominous, headline status of K2 or Annapurna, was still a worrying adversary and had killed more than thirty climbers since 1977. It wasn't a mountain to be taken lightly, especially after I'd been so nearly wiped out on Nanga Parbat.

I had a funny relationship with fear. The running joke was that Gurkha soldiers never experienced terror or anxiety, but the reality was very different. Being scared was human nature; we had only figured out how to manage its debilitating effects. Rather than allowing negative emotions to paralyse us, we transformed fear into an inspirational energy, a motivator. On other occasions, I'd used it as a reminder of the primary mission's overall importance and the value of staying calm. 'I'm scared because this means something,' I'd tell myself.

In war, for example, one role of the Special Forces was Deliberate Detention: arresting a wanted and dangerous individual. During those situations, my life was secondary to the operation; capturing the target was our goal. Meanwhile the pride I felt for the institutions I'd been representing was way bigger than any concerns I might have held for my health or mortality. That attitude silenced any negative thoughts regarding what might happen if someone was to open fire on me, or whether or not I'd lose a limb or two in an IED detonation. The same psychology rang true on the mountain.

I often acknowledged that the odds I might die were quite short during an expedition, and there was a chance I could seriously hurt myself, but that's as far as I ever went. I never contemplated how it might happen, or the pain I might experience during my final moments. Instead I focused on my reputation as a hard-core mountaineer; I recalled the importance of being brave and acting with integrity. Strength and guile could take me anywhere and with the courage of ten men I would prevail. If the weather turned bad, or the mountain looked primed to avalanche, I used my nerves to focus, mainly by treating the environmental dangers around me in the same way a military unit would work to outwit an enemy. I looked over my resources and assessed the hostiles ahead, then I figured out the best tactics to neutralise them.

Having settled in at Gasherbrum I and Gasherbrum II's shared base camp, I focused on how to overcome any traps the mountains might have laid for me. Then I put aside the bad thoughts regarding my tumble on Nanga Parbat and in doing so, another dialogue with the mountains had begun.

So, come on then, motherfucker. This is you versus me.

Clouds gathered at the peak and a storm seemed to be growing, but it was of little bother. I understood that my team had the assets to overcome any looming dangers. After all, extreme altitude climbing was a mind game as well as a physical endeavour.

This is yours, Nims. This is where you come alive.

I wasn't being disrespectful. After Kanchenjunga, I'd deliberately adopted a neutral attitude to the peaks I was about climb. Meanwhile, over-confidence was a dangerous position to take – it led to corner-cutting and laziness, and I'd received a little warning about intelligence-gathering and trust on Nanga Parbat. Trepidation was also sketchy – it caused an individual to overthink when they needed to be in a flow state. So my default setting before any climb was pitched somewhere in the middle, neither fearful or overly relaxed, but my aim was always to be aggressive: *Whenever I attack a mountain, I attack at 100 per cent.*

I knew more than anyone that nature didn't care for reputation, age, gender, or background. It was equally indifferent to personality: the mountain couldn't give a shit if the people exploring it were morally nasty or nice. All I could do was to place myself into the right frame of mind. Then I'd be able to tackle the challenges above.

Deep powder? *I will trailblaze like one hundred men.*

Avalanches? *I can mitigate.*

Crazy whiteouts? *Bring it on.*

I needed to make myself a solid force on every mountain, capable of smashing through any obstacle. Then it was go-time.

* * *

The American writer Mark Twain once wrote that if a person's job was to eat a frog, then it was best to take care of business first thing in the morning. But if the work involved eating two frogs, it was best to eat the bigger one first. In other words: *Get the hardest job out of the way.* As we waited in Base Camp, a battle plan was set. GII was very much the smaller frog and we intended to take it at a relatively leisurely pace, resting in some of the lower camps as we climbed. But GI was the bigger, uglier test, so I wanted to take it first with Mingma and Geljen, hopefully in one hit.

The work was gruelling. Nobody had dropped any air off for us in advance and so the team needed to load up with oxygen cylinders, full mountain kit, equipment and supplies. But having set off following two days of rest, it didn't take long to figure out we were still knackered following our trek from Nanga Parbat. We wandered through a crevasse-scarred gully on the mountain's lower stages, a longer, but less impressive version of the Khumbu Icefall, our energy levels depleting quickly. Thankfully, fixed lines would take us all the way up and I was fairly hopeful of finishing GI in pretty good time.

I'd previously topped Makalu, the world's fifth-highest mountain, in eighteen hours after climbing through Everest and Lhotse while barely sleeping for four or five days. Kanchenjunga, the world's third-highest had been scaled in similar circumstances, having come through a rough expedition on Dhaulagiri. At 8,080 metres, I reckoned we had it in us to do the northwest face of Gasherbrum I in one push. By my estimation, we'd reach the summit at around midday.

One of the challenges was the Japanese Couloir, a steep, seventy-degree ridge that divided Camp 2 from the higher camps. Once we'd climbed above it, our job was to pull ourselves to the top, the final stages of which involved a traverse across another sharp incline. The work was bloody tough; it took us much longer than expected and by the time we'd negotiated the Japanese Couloir and reached Camp 3, the sun had fallen. There was no way to press on and we were forced to rethink our plans.

I knew that to forge ahead in the dark was potentially suicidal; we weren't entirely sure of where the summit was, there wasn't a route marker in sight, and we would almost certainly become disorientated when figuring out the exact route up, even with our GPS tech. There was every chance the mission on GI would end in tragedy: one of us could become confused and fall into a crevasse, or off a cliff edge.

The more pressing issue was our lack of equipment. Because the plan had been to push towards the summit in one go and we'd failed, our operation now felt exposed. In order to complete the expedition in time, we'd need to stay at Camp 3, where there was at least an old, broken tent for us to crawl into. Once in shelter, we could rest up for a few hours until the time came for our summit push in the morning, but because the team had travelled light, apart from those oxygen cylinders, there was no food between us and we had only our summit suits for warmth, plus one sleeping bag.

Our only respite from the biting cold was to huddle together, our body heat saving us from the plummeting temperatures, until at 3 a.m., too cold to sleep, we roused ourselves for the summit push. It took ninety minutes for everyone to get the kit together. We were exhausted.

The climb to the top was a slog. We moved up the slope without ropes, perpetually confused as to which way to turn in the early morning light. *Was the peak to the left or the right?* I couldn't tell, but I had to know for sure that we were heading in the right direction. There were too many horror stories of climbers scaling one summit, only to be told they'd reached a false peak after making it back to Base Camp. I didn't want to suffer as a result of a navigational error and exhaustion was threatening to overwhelm me with every step, so I called down to Base Camp and was patched through to a climber who had made it to the top a couple of weeks previously.

Following his directions, we found our way to the summit, taking in the sight of GII and Broad Peak in the distance, the three of us trudging, exhausted, to a razor-thin edge of rock that marked our turnaround point, the reality of GI dawning on us. *This was a challenging mountain and despite my promise to be neutral when considering the tests ahead, I'd underestimated it a little.*

My first summit pushes at high altitude, such as Dhaulagiri and Everest, were strange experiences where the importance of timing had been cruelly revealed. Occasionally, I'd pushed myself too hard as I climbed and then suffered from exhaustion and altitude sickness in the fallout, as had happened on Everest in 2016. I had watched with horror as climbers from other expeditions made their summit pushes too slowly, or too late, and then were unable to descend due to fatigue and poor judgement. Sometimes those miscalculations were fatal; on other occasions the climbers were rescued.

During my early expeditions, I was keen not to repeat those same mistakes and I rushed down from the tops of Dhaulagiri and Everest, hoping not to land myself in trouble above the high camps, rather than soaking in the views and enjoying the moment. In a way, I didn't understand my true strengths back then. A climber needed to have confidence in their ability. It was everything on the mountains and mine was not then fully formed.

That all changed with experience. Having climbed Everest with the Gurkhas in 2017, I stayed at the top for two hours. During the mission, once I'd reached the peaks of an Annapurna or a Makalu, I made sure to hang around for an hour or so, acknowledging my latest achievements and celebrating with the rest of the team. I took pictures and made videos; I hung flags and credited the people at home who were helping me along the way. I was able to make time for myself, because I knew it was in me to travel all the way down to Base Camp quickly, maybe in a few hours or so if the conditions were OK.

For a lot of people, that same trip might have taken eight to ten hours and the journey would have been wracked with fear and anxiety. The work was never easy, though. We often climbed down in extreme weather conditions, where the wind threatened to tear us from the mountain and whiteouts dizzied us on precarious inclines, but the team rarely crawled home. Experience changed my attitude: I came to understand the importance of resolution on every mountain. Most of all, though, I made sure to take in the view.

Nature at that altitude could be both beautiful and violent, and seeing the Himalayas stretching out before me on GI somehow jolted me back to my first-ever moment on Everest's summit. I remembered standing there with Pasang, feeling relief at first. I'd overcome a sketchy brush with HAPE and my fingers and toes seemed close to snapping in the metallic cold, but the first glimmer of sunlight through the peaks had changed everything. Everest's energy shifted from dark to light, death to life, and I knew I'd make it home.

That same mood swing was happening now on GI and our struggles felt distant, from another lifetime. Especially now, with the mountaintops glowing; the gloopy clouds around them burning away. A new day was kicking off; everything was going to be cool again.

Then gravity kicked me out of my comfort zone.

The fear struck me as soon as we turned around for our descent. I looked down. The ground seemed to rush up at me as the memory of my tumble on Nanga Parbat flashed back for a split second. Without a safety line, I suddenly felt vulnerable and very exposed. I watched nervously as Geljen and Mingma turned around and began digging their ice axes into the slope, stepping down backwards, as if it was just another routine descent. *But was it?* I wasn't so sure. My legs were wobbling, the adrenaline was racing, and for the first time in the mission I feared for my mortality. Self-doubt hit me like shrapnel.

It would be quite easy to slip here. *Would I die?*

We weren't tethered together. *Why didn't I bring any rope?*

If I lost my balance, I'd go into free fall. *Would a self-arrest fail me again?*

These emotions were a shock, but I'd been exposed because I'd forgotten one of my most important rules: I had underestimated the mountain. The realisation felt like a slap across the mouth. Another unfamiliar reality was even scarier: my self-confidence was unexpectedly in ribbons. I turned around and drove my crampons into the ice, moving down slowly, cautiously, step-by-step, my heart rate banging through the roof. Once we'd made it to flatter ground, I felt more at ease and walked confidently to Camp 3, praying the loss of self-belief had been a one-off.

Then I remembered the sporting greats I loved: the mark of a true champion was usually found in the way a person reacted to a fall or defeat. Muhammad Ali was knocked down in fights before going on to win. Usain Bolt had false-started, or been beaten in smaller championships, before taking gold at the Olympic Games. My tumble a week previously could be regarded as an equally minor setback; it was a one-off and definitely unsettling, but with time and work I could put it behind me, especially if I recalled the Gurkha attitude to fear. For now, though, I needed to dust myself down and get back in the game.

* * *

There was always room for more drama.

As we moved down to Camp 2, checking in with Base Camp, a message from another expedition pinged up on my satellite phone.

'Nimsdai! There's a climber called Mathias stuck at Camp 2. Can you call out to him and bring him down?'

I sighed. The time was around 3 p.m. and seeing as we were presumably within touching distance, there was no reason not to help. Having located the stranded individual, the three of us waited patiently as Mathias gathered his stuff together. Five minutes passed. Then ten. At one point, Mathias announced that he would be ready in 'just a few' and so Geljen pressed on down to the next camp, assuming that we'd catch him up fairly quickly. Once a quarter of an hour had slipped by, we were thankfully on the move again. I was freezing cold and exhausted, and the delay had cost us dearly.

From nowhere, a heavy weather system swept in and within minutes we were swaddled in cloud as the heavens dumped a blanket of snow on us. Our visibility was reduced to nothing and in the confusion, I heard a cry. *Mingma!* He'd taken a misstep and been sucked into an unseen crevasse. I crawled across to find him, fearing the worst, careful not to plunge into another hidden maw; but when I peered into the body-sized hole, Mingma was peering back at me. By some sheer fluke, his bag had snagged on the edge, fixing his body in place. With some careful wriggling, Mingma was able to free his arms, grabbing a hold on the ice as we lifted him away from trouble. That was two near-death scrapes he'd endured in as many mountains.

Between my fall on Nanga Parbat and now Mingma's accident on Gasherbrum I, it was as if the mountain gods were trying to swallow us whole. *And if Mingma could slip into an unseen crevasse, would Geljen be OK?* Without a clear view to Camp 1 in the clouds, there was every chance he might step away from the line and disappear into the mountain, as Mingma had. I grabbed my radio and attempted to call him back, but there was no answer. Then I heard a faint beep and a crackle of static in my rucksack. Oh, no. *Geljen had left his comms behind!*

I took a quick moment to check on our situation: there was no way up, the route was shrouded in mist. We didn't have much of a chance when climbing down either, the snow was too heavy to see through. At first, the three of us set about digging a hole into the snow with our ice axes. If we could create enough of a breaker from the growing wind and white-out conditions, there was a hope we might stay warm enough by cuddling up close, but as we hacked and chipped away, there didn't seem to be enough room to protect us all. I knew that if we hung around for too much longer, there was every chance we might die. The time had come to take an even riskier step.

'Fuck, we're going to have to get back up to Camp 2,' I said.

I looked at Mathias. 'Is there enough room for us to get into your tent up there?'

He nodded. We'd been presented with a shot of survival at least, but it was a risky one – if Mingma's experience was anything to go by, there was every chance one of us might fall into another crevasse. Cautiously, we moved back up to Camp 2. Every now and then I'd radio down to the expeditions below, hopeful that Geljen might have made it down to Camp 1, but nobody had laid eyes on him.

Fucking hell, was Geljen still alive?

I was beginning to fear the worst. It was only once we'd made it through the cloud, beyond the freezing squalls, and squeezed into a small two-man tent for shelter, that I felt safe. Then my radio beeped and coughed with static.

'Nimsdai! I'm home!'

It was Geljen. He was in one piece and had borrowed a radio from another climber. For a brief moment, we had room to breathe.

18

The Savage Mountain

We saw out the night, shivering in the freezing conditions for several hours. As we climbed down the next morning, my confidence seemed to return gradually; I felt stronger and more comfortable when dealing with extreme exposure. By the time we made it back to Base Camp, the worst of the wobbles I'd experienced at the top of GI were behind me, or so I hoped, although I guessed I wasn't yet back to 100 per cent. My plan was to work hard on bomb-proofing my emotions through Gasherbrum II, because I would need every ounce of emotional resilience to survive the more challenging terrain of K2. For now, I had to focus on the primary mission, by leaning into an age-old military adage.

Prepare for the worst, hope for the best.

When I looked up at GII from Camp 1, a peak that was considered to be fairly calm, I readied myself for a challenge, though I was excited at the realisation that I could move like a regular mountain climber at least. We weren't planning on climbing all 8,034 metres of it in one hit. Instead, the team would rest at Camps 2 and 3, and as we worked our way up the mountain, GII's moods felt calm. We summited on 18 July, and at the top I felt awe and excitement. In the distance was K2, and it looked picturesque. The sharp peak curved towards the skyline like a shark's tooth; it was glowing pink with the sunrise.

I'm going to be on top of that. And I'm going to show the world how it's done.

Not everyone shared my optimism. As I made my way down GII, I learned that K2 had been in a fairly unforgiving mood. A number of experienced climbers were waiting at Base Camp and several expedition parties were holding out there for a suitable weather window – some of them had been hanging around for months. Around two hundred climbing permits (including Sherpas) had been issued by the Pakistani authorities that year, but around 95 per cent of those hoping to climb K2 had packed up and gone home. The other five had hung around, hoping I might lead them to the top.

I passed several teams that were trekking away from the mountain as I arrived, many of them stopping to tell us their K2 horror stories. At least two summit attempts had taken place, but on both occasions, the line-fixing teams brave enough to attack the peak had been beaten back by some horrendous conditions. They had only made it past Camp 4 and onto a section called the Bottleneck, a thin couloir positioned below the peak at 8,200 metres above sea level. Meanwhile, a number of ridges along the way were apparently primed to explode with avalanches. Even the Sherpas were in fear of what might happen up there.

When I joined up with the others at Base Camp, I was pulled aside by Mingma Sherpa, a friend of mine with serious expertise on the big mountains. He had twice set the lines on K2 in recent years and was regarded as a fearsome climber within the guiding community. This time, though, Mingma Sherpa had been spooked by the mountain.

'Nimsdai, it's so, *so* dangerous to climb,' he said, pulling out his phone to play several minutes of video footage captured from his attempt at the summit a few days earlier. 'Take a look . . .'

The clip made for sobering viewing. The snow was chest-deep in some sections, which wasn't going to be a physical issue for me, or my team, but every step was loaded with risk. At one point, according to Mingma Sherpa, the lead climber in the fixing team had been swept away by an avalanche. Luckily, he'd survived, but the video certainly had me worried.

I gathered my team around me. 'Right, tonight we drink,' I said, patting Mingma Sherpa on the back and sparking up a cigarette. 'We party hard. And tomorrow we plan.'

It was time to prepare for the worst.

* * *

My mission was in jeopardy.

As I met with the various expedition parties at Base Camp and figured out how best to tackle K2, an update arrived regarding my permit request for Shishapangma – the world's four-teenth-highest mountain and the final peak on the project schedule. So far, the problem in reaching it had been geo-polit-ical. Located in Tibet, it was up to the Chinese government to rule upon who could climb it and who couldn't, and for the entire mountaineering season of 2019, it had been decided that nobody was being granted access to the peak.

I'd hoped they might make some exception, given the scale of my mission, but the news wasn't great. The Chinese Mountaineering Association (CMA) had turned me down flat, citing a number of safety concerns, and Shishapangma was to remain closed, no exceptions. The chances of my climbing the final mountain of Phase Three seemed increasingly unlikely.

It was hard not to feel a little disheartened. So far, I had scaled every peak on the schedule in the time and the style I'd promised from the outset. The team had proven self-sufficient and effective, and we'd worked with speed. Now bureaucracy was about to crush my ambitions, but I wasn't going to let it derail me: there would be some way of finishing off the job. *There had to be.* For now, though, it was important to absorb the latest intelligence on Tibet and the Chinese permit issues, before boxing it away emotionally. With K2 to deal with, shutting the door on any negative thought became important. The politics and paperwork could wait.

With hindsight, this was the best position to adopt. When climbing K2, I knew that the work often became a test of both psychological and physical resilience – and there was little room for distractions. Yes, it was a tough mountain to top and the conditions were often unforgiving, but I had faith that my team had the psychological minerals to manage the workload, though I feared the news about Shishapangma might knock them off course. It felt important to maintain a positive mood, and despite the increasing levels of fatigue, everyone within the expedition party seemed to be fired up and incentivised.

So far, my tactics for the big peaks had been to lead experienced Nepalese climbers to the top of mountains they were yet to scale; by doing that, they would have the credentials to work there in the future, and as a result the demand for their services would increase. (When a climber tackles an 8,000er for the first time, they will always prefer a guide who has climbed it previously because they know the route and its dangers.) It was my way of setting them up as legitimate guides with Elite Himalayan Adventures, while preserving their energy for the good of the overall mission. Once the project was finished, they could expect to be held in high esteem.

I also had to consider how best to tackle K2. Before showing up at Base Camp, I'd been toying with the idea of taking on Broad Peak first – a small expedition party had climbed it a few days previously, and all the trailblazing and line-fixing had been completed. But when I spoke to the other climbers at K2, I realised they'd been waiting on me to arrive. They wanted to see if my team were able to finish the rope-fixing job, before deciding on whether to pack up and go home themselves. That increased the pressure weighing on us for sure, but I liked the idea of helping those climbers to their dream of scaling one of the most dangerous peaks on earth.

I needed all the experience and manpower I could get. On K2, the weather was set to be horrendous and high winds were predicted for the next few days; it would be painfully cold, too. I understood that failure on K2 would mean I'd have to make a second attempt at it, or more, before climbing Broad Peak, and by that point the Pakistan climbing season would be over.

Time was bloody tight and I mission-planned accordingly: it was down to us to fix the last of the lines on the mountain above Camp 4. Meanwhile, I hoped to climb K2 with Gesman and Lakpa Dendi Sherpa, but the mountain's unforgiving nature and the sketchy conditions around the peak required me to plan with a near military precision.

'Look, guys, this is a risky climb,' I said. 'The work is going to be rough. My plan is to assess the situation from Camp 4. Gesman and Lakpa Dendi, you're coming with me. If it's too dangerous up there, we'll come down and I'll swap you out. Mingma and Geljen, you'll then fall in behind and we'll go again. I'm going to rotate two guys every time so you can rest, but I'm going to lead this thing from the front. And I'm only giving up when we've made at least six, seven attempts at the top.'

There was another pressing issue to deal with, too. Many of the climbers waiting nervously at Base Camp were rattled by fear, and some of them appeared beaten already. They had learned that the South African-born Swiss, Mike Horn – an explorer known for climbing Gasherbrum I and II, plus Broad Peak and Makalu without oxygen – had been held back by the dangerous weather.

The understanding that some other big-time mountaineers were unable to scale K2 was unsettling the expedition parties still in attendance. A number of individuals even wanted to bail out and go home, and it didn't help that several people were noticeably freaked out, having watched a line-fixer being swept away by an avalanche ahead of them as they climbed. The incident had left some mental scars.

One afternoon, Clara – a woman from the Czech Republic, whom I'd known to be a very strong climber – came to my tent. She was scared.

'Look, Nims, I don't think I can do this. It's too much.'

The morale at Base Camp was clearly broken and it was down to me to fix it. When I gathered everybody together for a group briefing, I outlined my plan, detailing to the expedition parties how I intended to use my guides to help forge a path to the top, and how everyone could follow in behind me. Then I tried to lift the group's self-belief. I preferred not to prepare or operate when surrounded by bad energy and pessimism. On K2, I sensed that the battle was being lost in the mind, but the climb was within everybody's grasp if they showed enough heart. Positivity was needed.

A lot of people might wonder why I cared so much about how confident the other climbers were feeling about their expeditions. The truth is that it would have been quite easy for me to behave selfishly. I could have moved over to Broad Peak, climbed there first and returned to K2 a little later, once the other parties had left the area. Instead, I wanted to show them that the impossible was within reach.

'You've already been up to Camp 4,' I said. 'But you only turned back because there were no fixed lines beyond that, and the conditions were bad. Since then, you've had time to rest. You're strong.'

'But it's so tough up there,' said one climber.

'Look brother, don't talk yourself out of it. I've just climbed back-to-back mountains without sleep. In Nepal I made rescue attempts and then climbed again the next day. You guys haven't had to do that. You're in a much stronger position than I was on Everest, or Dhaulagiri, or Kanchenjunga. We'll lead the way and a day later, you'll summit.'

I told them about the UK Special Forces Selection process. How around 200 people put themselves through it every year, knowing that sometimes only around five or six people would qualify. 'Yeah, there's always a high risk of failure,' I said, 'but those two hundred people all started out from a point of positivity. They didn't quit before the very first day.'

I reminded them that with positive thought, courage and discipline they would survive, but approaching K2 with a negative mind was the fastest route to failure, or death.

'You can rest in the jungle when you're tired and still survive. You can give up in a desert without food or water for a few days and still be rescued – you won't die instantly. But death happens fast on the mountain and to give up, or to be half-hearted, will only cause you to stop. And to stop is to freeze and die.'

I knew the climb would still prove hard going, regardless of my enthusiasm for adventure. Beyond the hair-trigger avalanches and screaming gales on the famous Abruzzi Spur route of the mountain – the most popular line to the top – K2 had another booby trap in its armoury: the Bottleneck.

At that point on the route I'd have to lean on my oxygen supply, though that wasn't going to help me to negotiate the more pressing dangers. The Bottleneck bristled with seracs and was set at around fifty-five degrees, so its steep, overhanging face couldn't be climbed using rope and ice axes. Instead the only way up was to traverse cautiously around it, all the while keeping a watchful eye on the precarious seracs above.

It was an unnerving approach, but there was no alternative line. The Bottleneck was the fastest route to the top, although according to some stats, a worrying percentage of K2's fatalities had happened there – in 2008, eleven climbers were killed during the worst single incident on the mountain; a number of them having died as a result of an ice avalanche in that stretch of the climb.

Timing was also an issue. With the conditions, it was important to hit the Bottleneck at around 1 a.m. during a summit push. In the middle of the night, the terrain was colder and the snow tended to harden, so it would be possible to trailblaze through it without slipping and sliding around. Any later and most climbers hitting the Bottleneck found that the surfaces were softer and trickier to negotiate. Climbing at that time also presented me with a psychological advantage. In the dark, it wouldn't be possible to look up at the intimidating seracs above.

We took our time, rolling up the mountain, fixing any anchors that were damaged, while still working out our route to the top. The climb was marked by a series of physical and emotional tests. Our backs were weighed down by rope, anchors, and oxygen, and between Camps 1 and 2 we had to negotiate the House Chimney, a 100-foot-tall wall of rock, so called because of a 'chimney' crack that ran through the middle of it, and also due to the fact that American mountaineer, Bill House, was the first to climb it in 1938. Luckily, we were able to scale it fairly easily, making the most of some fixed ropes that dangled from the top.

Later, beyond Camp 2, was the infamous Black Pyramid section of the mountain, an imposing, triangular rock buttress that stretched up for 365 metres and required us to scramble over a tricky stretch of rock and ice. We worked slowly, taking our time so as not to suffer a disastrous slip, but my body was feeling weird. I'd started out strong, but as we approached the Shoulder, a glacial hump that was manageable without the use of a fixed rope, there was a worrying gurgle in my guts. Then another. My bowels were cramping and knotting, and I recognised the first onset of explosive diarrhoea. I prayed that the sensation was a one-off.

By the time we arrived at Camp 4 at 3 p.m., my stomach had settled a little, but I knew the situation would be doubly tricky, as we were fixing the lines in tough conditions. Above us sat the Bottleneck and the summit of K2. On a good day, we might expect to take around six hours to reach the end. The Bottleneck was followed by a short but challenging ice ridge, which eventually led to the peak, and there were stories of several climbers being fatally buffeted by high winds around the summit. Unable to hold their footing, they were then blown off the side of K2, where they tumbled to their deaths.

I decided it was best to stress over those issues as and when they happened. For now, my biggest concern was how best to manage the lurching in my stomach, because on troublesome expeditions there were always events that could not be planned for, no matter the moods of the mountain.

I decided to adjust my thinking, pulling out my camera and

grabbing several reconnaissance photos, zooming into the image to pick out the best route around the Bottleneck. I wanted to figure out an alternative line should the well-travelled route prove trickier than expected. My team had gathered around me. We were fully geared up with ice axes, crampons, snow bars, ropes and ice screws. We were ready. The time had arrived to deliver my war briefing.

'Guys, we are the best climbers from Nepal,' I said. 'It is time to show the world what we are capable of. Let's get this done.'

We pulled on our heavy packs and oxygen masks. Then we started our climb to the top, moving with the energy of one hundred men.

19

A Mountain Mind

We made our summit push at 9 p.m., eventually reaching the Bottleneck at one in the morning. The adrenaline pulsed through me. I knew the seracs were hanging over us like a toothy jawline. It needed only one to crack and crash down the incline for all of us to die in a grisly collision, or for a chunk of falling ice to shred through our rope, pulling the team down the mountain with a violent yank. Moving slowly around the intimidating terrain, I focused my thoughts, ignoring the occasional attack of stomach cramps as we later advanced up the summit ridge to reach the peak.

My heart was full as I braced myself against the winds, but the buzz of success was strangely fleeting. Having topped out at one of the world's deadliest mountains on the morning of 24 July – a climb that was steeper and riskier than the world's highest – I was reluctant to take in the clear blue skies for too long, or enjoy the now.

I wanted to get down as soon as possible, because (1) my stomach had been feeling weird for a few days and I guessed that climbing down might prove as uncomfortable as climbing up. (2) I wanted to hit Broad Peak as quickly as possible on the next expedition. And (3) the sooner I completed the Pakistan phase, the sooner I could deal with the pressing issue of gaining the permits for Shishapangma. There was no room for reflection or emotion this time.

On occasions, my attitude towards climbing a mountain was not dissimilar to the psychological position I'd adopted for military operations. In both circumstances I was never sure if I was going to come back alive, and once a mission was finished, it was often the best course of action to leave safely and efficiently. Of course, I was always supported by information: before military jobs we worked from the gathered intelligence regarding the enemy, their location and their capabilities. On climbing expeditions, we relied heavily on our knowledge of the mountain, weather reports, and our equipment; but some factors were forever beyond our determination in both scenarios.

In war, unexpected hostiles might be lurking nearby. During climbs, a rock fall might explode from nowhere. Once a team stepped into action, the unpredictable became a dangerous opponent. The best approach to neutralising it was to work steadily and methodically, without emotion.

I wasn't a robot, though. There were some moments when my work on the mountains felt overwhelming. On some occasions during the mission I even prayed for death (though I never worried about it, or feared it), in moments when the very thought of putting one foot in front of the other felt too draining to contemplate.

These events, though rare, usually happened during trailblazing or line-fixing efforts, where I'd become so exhausted after climbing for twenty hours or more, that to close my eyes, even for a second or two, caused me to slip into sleep. As my body dropped to the ground, my brain would often jolt, shocking me awake like one of those falling dreams that kick in whenever a person drifts off too quickly, their muscles having relaxed all at once; triggering a hypnagogic jerk, where the brain imagines the body as tumbling from bed, or tripping over a step. On some peaks, fighting off the urge to snooze fitfully became a never-ending battle.

Sometimes the elements seemed capable of overwhelming me, too. Climbing through extreme weather conditions with sudden drops in temperature caused my bones and extremities to burn. Hurricane winds whipped up spindrifts; they ricocheted off my summit suit, and weirdly, banner-day conditions were sometimes equally demoralising. On Kanchenjunga, under clear, still skies, every muscle in my body had trembled with pain as I struggled to bring those casualties to safety.

Each step had felt torturous as I heaved their weight towards Camp 4, and every now and then I briefly imagined the sweet release of an avalanche collapsing above me. Picturing my fall in the whiteout, I felt the eruption sucking me down deeper, a rock or chunk of ice knocking me unconscious. Out cold, I'd suffocate quickly, blissfully free of pain; the suffering would come to an end. Thankfully, those thoughts were only ever fleeting.

I've never been someone that grumbles about pain in front of others, or opens up about any emotional hurt I might be experiencing – not too much anyway. I feel weirdly exposed even writing these ideas down: it's a vulnerable process. But a lot of that strength had to do with being a soldier, where an alpha-male culture encouraged individuals working within it to suffer silently.

The lads I served with rarely grumbled about discomfort, or discussed any psychological hurdles they might be overcoming, and I followed suit, managing my issues alone during Selection.

Sometimes Suchi would ask me what it had been like and I'd mumble some vague and limited description. I suppose to admit that pain was part of my job would be to accept its reality, and to do that would increase my chances of becoming crushed by it. What the UK Special Forces required were people that could grin and bear it. I sucked up the agony thrown my way and laughed as much as I could.

My combat mentality later helped me to overcome the turbulence of the Death Zone. For one, I was able to use discomfort in positive ways by turning it into a motivational fuel. During rare moments of weakness, where I'd briefly envision turning around, I'd think: *Yeah, but what happens if I give up now?* Sure, quitting would have brought some much-needed respite, but the relief would prove temporary – the longer-lasting pain of giving up would be bloody miserable.

My biggest concern throughout the mission was not finishing, either through weakness or dying, so I used the potential consequences of failure as a way of *not quitting*. I pictured the disappointed people who had once looked to my project for inspiration, or the joking doubters that would inevitably make comments in interviews and call me out online. Their faces fired me up. Most of all it felt important that I complete the fourteen expeditions in one piece. I needed my story to be told truthfully and in full because my success was not a coincidence.

Then I remembered the financial risks I'd taken. I visualised my parents living together in the not-too-distant future, once my mission was completed, and the love I had for them was enough to inspire positive action. My heart and intentions were pure. I didn't want failure to sully them, so at my lowest ebbs, such as in the middle of a day-long trailblaze, I forgot about the aching muscles in my legs and back simply by imagining the burn of humiliation. I was soon able to make another step through the heavy snow, or along the rope, until one step became two, two steps became ten, ten steps became a hundred.

No way was I allowing myself to quit, so I also recalled my undefeated record. *I have reached all my objectives, from the Gurkhas to the Special Forces and then at high altitude. Now is not the time to break down.*

In many ways, this was the echo of an old mind trick I had used in war. When trying to negotiate pain, I often worked to create a bigger, more controllable hurt, one that would shut out the first – *replacing an agony that was beyond my control*. If my Bergen felt too heavy, I'd run harder. Any backache I'd been experiencing was soon overshadowed by the jabbing pain in my knees. On K2, I moved faster to forget the cramps in my bowels, but I also once climbed with a grinding, pounding toothache, the result of a condition called barodontalgia, where the barometric pressure trapped inside a cavity or filling changes with the high altitude. (Some people have complained of fillings popping out during a mountain expedition.)

On that occasion there was no option to turn around; I had a group of clients to lead, so instead I worked towards locating a second, more uncomfortable pain, one that I could turn off if necessary. That day, I climbed non-stop, working for a full twenty-four hours at a speed that left me fighting for breath. My lungs were tight, my whole body was in turmoil, but by the time I reached the summit, the throbbing in my gums had been forgotten.

Suffering sometimes created a weird sense of satisfaction for me. The psychological power of always giving 100 per cent, where simply *knowing* I was delivering my all, was enough to drive me on a little bit further: it created a sense of pride when seeing a job through to the end.

I remember there were times throughout Phases One and Two of the mission when the thought of leaving my warm sleeping bag filled me with dread. I knew the temperatures outside would be painfully cold, and the climbing would be hard, but to stay cocooned in relative comfort would have slowed down the mission – I wouldn't be giving 100 per cent. The best option was to move quickly and purposefully. Simply unzipping the door and pulling on my crampons helped to motivate me for the next push.

Though a physically small step, this was a huge psychological gesture during an expedition because it showed desire. In much the same way that making the bed first thing in the morning was a mental cue that a new day was beginning, so the arduous effort required to pull on my boots and crampons was a trigger for the work to come. Self-discipline was my biggest strength during the mission. I was always the first to get up, even when it felt horrendous to do so, and there were times when I wished someone could encourage *me*. Instead I had to motivate myself at all times to step away from the relative comfort of my shelter.

Once I was outside, it was far easier to plan for the conditions; to hang back and rely solely on computers or radio communications for an indication of what was going on with the weather, felt like a shortcut, and taking any shortcuts during the expeditions would have suggested to everyone around me that I wasn't fully committed. In turn, that one half-hearted effort might have led to countless other half-hearted efforts on the climb.

The knowledge that I was giving 100 per cent also served as a motivational factor during the fund-raising drive for the mission. I contacted a number of people who, on paper, were never going to help in a million years. One example was the successful entrepreneur and billionaire Sir Richard Branson: I sent him a handwritten note before the mission started that explained who I was, what I was doing and why I was doing it. The letter was posted with the assumption that Sir Richard probably receives hundreds of similar requests every week, and that mine was another one to lob at the bin. I even sealed the envelope with wax and stamped an 'N' into it with an embosser I'd picked up from a stationery shop. There was no donation in the end, but knowing that I'd explored all possibilities allowed me to sleep comfortably at night. I was leaving everything on the table, it was important to have zero regrets.

There needed to be balance, though, and I made it my job to practise patience at all times. Because of my desire to achieve so much in so little time, restlessness was an easy trap to fall into – for all of us. The group had been climbing for three months. It was highly unlikely we'd make it into the final phase before autumn, and that was only if Shishapangma was open for us to climb. In the meantime, we had to remain calm. There was no point in rushing at high altitude, or making rash decisions, seeing as we were waiting on events that were out of our control, such as those permit applications. Every moment on the mountain was a next-level test, where restlessness might prove fatal.

New challenges were thrown at us every day. I had been going from mountain to mountain in quick succession, so it was important to assess my team, my expedition and myself constantly. *Were we ready? When is the best time for our summit push? Are our bodies too exhausted to climb?*

I didn't waste a second. If I was pinned to a position by the weather, I rarely sat back and relaxed. While stuck at a base camp, for example, I worked on figuring out the best ways to tackle the incoming conditions, or I worked on the funding of the mission. I also used those moments to train or to calm my mind by taking in the environment and the scenery. As a result, I often felt at peace while working at high altitude.

Most of all, I learned how to function effectively in unpleasant conditions. Throughout my military life I was trained to survive and succeed in almost any environment going, so I found it easy to work through the mountains. But that same mindset was available to every climber. It was possible for a novice to become accustomed to the harsh realities of life in base camps very quickly; after a few days or a few weeks, surviving even higher up the mountain becomes a habit for a lot of people, especially if they have positivity.

It helped that war had given me a low baseline in terms of personal comfort. As I told Suchi when financing the early stages of the project: I could live in nothing more than a tent for months and still find a way to earn money for the family. I'd previously lived in jungle, mountain and desert environments for work. Anything else felt like a luxury. I was primed to function effectively at high altitude. As we moved down K2 and readied ourselves for Broad Peak, my mind felt strong. Ten peaks had been ticked off the list. Discomfort was fuel.

* * *

As the second phase came to a close, the fantasy of dying pulled on me once more. Having rested at K2's base camp for three hours, and met with Mingma and Halung we then pressed on to Broad Peak, the twelfth-highest mountain in the world at 8,051 metres above sea level. The pressure upon me was building. I'd hoped to top out on Phase Two's final mountain in one day, but more and more challenges seemed to be stacking up. We were knackered, both physically and emotionally, and I was still feeling sick. Worse, my kit had been soaked through on

K2. As we prepared at Base, I made sure to air out the equipment as best I could, but there was no way of drying my heavy summit suit in such a short period of time.

When we started out for Camp 1, my trousers and coat felt like a sodden, squelchy bear hug. At a much higher altitude that unpleasant sensation could become potentially dangerous, particularly if the moisture inside my suit turned to ice. I would freeze quickly, so at Camp 1, I took advantage of the high sun and dried out my kit as best I could. The importance of nailing Broad Peak as speedily as possible was becoming increasingly evident to everyone. But the mountain gods had made other plans.

Broad Peak was smothered; a heavy snowfall had landed shortly before our arrival, burying the fixed lines, and while a light path had been marked by a couple of climbers who had made it to around Camp 4 a couple of days earlier, a lot of their footfalls had been filled in. We'd have to trailblaze a path to the very top. The burden of heavy work was upon Mingma, Halung Dorchi Sherpa, and myself, and as we charged through the powder, my body seemed unable to cope with the workload. Not only was the rope to the summit buried, requiring us to yank it up through a few feet of snow, but we were having to lift our knees high, over and over, for any forward momentum.

My breathing was laboured. The energy levels I'd once carried in reserve were depleted and my guts still rumbled like a blocked drain. Every now and then, I'd steady myself against the stomach cramps until I couldn't ignore them any more. Nature was finally taking its course.

'Oh, fuck, no', I thought, looking around desperately for somewhere to unload my bowels. But my current position was too sketchy and taking a dump at high altitude was no joke. Perching on a steep slope, with or without rope, while fumbling around with the zippers and Velcro of a summit suit in sub-zero temperatures was an awkward situation. I'd find myself exposed and likely to fall in the most undesirable circumstances, so I pushed ahead in agony, until I noticed the mountain levelling off above me, around 200 metres in the distance.

'This is my chance,' I thought, as I charged ahead, my lungs burning.

The climb seemed to be never-ending, but the pain in my legs and chest overwhelmed the churning in my guts, until, finally, I was able to locate a spot where I could hold myself without too much effort. I unzipped my suit and dealt with a very unpleasant level of personal admin.

Physically I seemed near to failure. Realising that a record-breaking time for finishing the Pakistan 8,000-ers was within reach, I leant heavily into the mountain mind. Stubbornly, I worked even harder. I closed down the pain in my cramping stomach by striding forcefully to the top, stage by stage. By the time we'd made it to 7,850 metres, the effort had finally taken its toll, and my back and legs were buckling. While the discomfort in my guts was fading away, I felt exhausted. Slumped in the snow, an extreme pain flooded my muscles and bones.

Whenever I coughed, the taste of blood seemed to cling to my tongue, a sign the high altitude was impacting on my body. Broad Peak had worn me down, but with our morale in a precarious state, it felt wise to outline a clear plan of action; not explaining the situation, as obvious as it might seem, could sometimes give a team a misjudged set of priorities or expectations. The bottom line was this: the route to the top of Broad Peak was a beast and it needed us to climb a steep couloir towards the ridgeline. From there we could work our way over to the true peak, hitting the very top at sunrise.

'Guys, we're all pretty fucked,' I said. 'The conditions up here are tough, so we should rest a bit, regroup, and then work really hard to the top.'

In my condition, this was set to be one of the more gruelling events of the mission's second phase, but we were on the move again a few hours later, oxygen masks strapped across our faces. But having climbed to around 8,000 metres, my breathing felt increasingly laboured, and when I checked in with Mingma and Halung, they confirmed that, yeah, the workload seemed even more challenging than usual; Halung had trailed behind us for some time and had been unable to help with our efforts as we climbed.

At first, I put our combined slump down to the physical fallout from K2, but the decline in energy was still alarming and when I clocked our oxygen cylinders, the awful truth about our slowing pace was revealed. *Fuck, we were out of air!* Even worse, the fixed lines had finished, so we would need to traverse the last fifty metres or so to Broad Peak's summit as quickly as we could, alpine-style. I'd been presented with one of those life-or-death decisions that were so common during combat, where evaluation and decision making would prove key.

Option one: retreat by returning to Camp 3, where we could gather some extra oxygen and push for the summit a day later, though a system of bad weather was due to rush in.

Option two: get the job done, without a visible route to follow while relying on our GPS system to steer us onwards, while keeping us clear from a nasty fall off the mountain.

Option two it was, then.

We walked around the mountain's ridgeline, bombproofing our steps, working towards what looked like Broad Peak's highest point, but once we arrived, another, higher promontory emerged through the clouds ahead. And another. Managing the emotional highs and lows under intense exhaustion was challenging enough, but operating with our GPS soon became impossible.

Though the worst of the weather wasn't upon us yet, it was still bitterly cold and windy; the visibility was poor, we were shrouded in thick cloud, and barely able to see in front of our faces. Considering that none of us had climbed Broad Peak before, we weren't entirely sure which way to go. (And it was for exactly these reasons that mountain climbers liked to work with experienced guides.) Only by communicating with our radio contacts in Base Camp, Kathmandu and London, all of whom were linked up to another GPS to track our location, were we able to get a steer on our exact position. Voices in the clouds told us to move left, right, or forward.

The work rarely eased up; we were at our limits. Extreme fatigue gripped us all, and as we became increasingly disorientated, our lives were very much on the line. There was every chance that one of us might take a fatal misstep or make a stupid decision. Like those confused climbers I'd heard about, prone to hallucinations or delirium in the Death Zone, we'd been exposed. At one point, I looked down and realised that we'd been climbing alpine style for some time having forgotten to connect ourselves to a safety rope* – a high-altitude health and safety priority.

---

* When climbing in this way, if one of us had slipped and fallen, the other dudes on the line would have to hit the ground, digging their ice axes into the snow and ice. That action was designed to stop anyone from stacking it off the mountain.

Disconnected from one another, I knew that if Mingma, Halung or myself slipped, there would be no chance of arresting the fall – a horrific slide from the mountain, into a sheer drop below, would surely follow; but if we were all linked, the combined weight and effort of the group might help to slam on the brakes. Our oversight had been a result of extreme tiredness. I pulled out a length of line and lashed everybody together.

While I liked to carry the bare minimum of equipment and supplies during a summit push, Mingma often travelled with one or two luxuries. During a short rest, I noticed him rummaging through his rucksack until he pulled out a packet of Korean coffee. Tearing it open, he tipped the ground beans into his mouth, gesturing that we all do the same. The powder was bitter and claggy, we coughed on the acrid taste, but a caffeine kick was soon working through our system.

Before long, Broad Peak's summit flag appeared in the distance. We hung around for as little time as we could, laughing bleakly at how the mountain had nearly killed us, and taking only a couple of pictures before descending again. There was very little joy. I couldn't wait to get down and the team had been angered. For a lot of the time it felt as if Broad Peak had defeated us, even though we'd reached the very top in tricky circumstances.

Mingma and Halung decided to sleep at Camp 3 for a few hours, but eager to get home, I carried on down, wandering into a layer of thick cloud. *Big mistake*. I was soon confused, unable to locate the fixed line that would see me all the way to the bottom of Broad Peak. At one point, I even found myself perilously close to the edge of a sheer drop, which fell away by several hundred feet. I cursed my luck and poor judgement. 'Why the fuck do you do these things?' I thought. My damp summit suit was freezing; I was cold and unable to focus on the terrain ahead, and what I really wanted to do was sleep. Suddenly, surrendering seemed like a viable option.

If I died here, then all of this pain would end.

It had happened again. I was being overwhelmed by the effort, but I wasn't beaten. Before any military operation, a sure sign of approaching failure was to enter into it believing that a defeat was on the cards. The only way to succeed was through positive thought.

I need to kick-start my revival.

Turning my thinking around, I found fuel: I saw myself a year down the line, fuming at my inability to pull through at the end. I thought of the people that had put their faith in me, the friends I had made along the way – and most of all I considered Suchi and the family. *They needed me to get back.* Finally, I envisioned the finishing line, my ascent on Shishapangma and the reception in Kathmandu as the world learned of my successes. The fug of despair was lifting.

Just make it happen. You can't give up here.

With the sun rising higher, it didn't take long to figure out that somehow I'd moved away from our earlier route in the confusion. Our ascent had taken place mainly in cloud and at night, and we'd followed the fixed lines up to Camp 4 for much of it; we'd only found ourselves in trouble after hitting the ridgeline, and when the satellite technology proved too problematic, our radio comms had then helped us to the top.

Thinking that I'd be able make it down by sight alone, especially in such thick cloud, while exhausted, was an error. I needed to reconnect with the ridgeline somehow – by doing so, I could hopefully locate the fixed line, and from there I'd be able to switch into autopilot. I had only to look out for some visual cue. I scanned the horizon for footfalls in the snow, and there, a hundred or so metres above me, was a barely visible path, gouged into the powder by our earlier trailblaze, the prints shadowing a length of rope.

I turned around, using all of my strength to go up, then to go down again, all the way visualising the spoils of success and the fury of failure.

20

The People's Project

As I worked my way back from Broad Peak to home in Nepal, the obstacles in my path seemed to grow in size and stature, and I decided to knock them down one by one. My most pressing issue was Shishapangma. The paperwork required to climb it was still being held back by the Chinese and Tibetan authorities, which left the mission schedule in chaos. Finding a solution required me to hustle, but despite my reluctance to admit defeat, it was also time to consider a Plan B, some fall-back option that might replicate the effort and endeavour required to see out a fourteenth peak.

Considering the scale of what was being attempted, I thought about climbing one of the other 8,000-ers again – maybe Everest, Annapurna or K2. In the end, I decided that if the worst came to the worst, I should repeat Dhaulagiri. The climb was gnarly; it had also been my first 8,000-metre expedition, and I also pencilled in Everest as a bonus mission. Fifteen Death Zone peaks in seven months wasn't quite the original objective, but it might help to silence any trolls throwing shade on my achievements in the weeks and months to come.

More world records had been broken: I'd finished the Pakistan 8,000-ers in 23 days; the world's five tallest mountains

(Everest, K2, Kanchenjunga, Lhotse, Makalu) had been climbed in seventy days (when I initially planned to do it in eighty); but I understood that failure to complete the ultimate mission would result in some level of pushback.

My other plan for climbing Shishapangma was to find an alternative route into Tibet. If sneaking across the border via some backdoor route were viable, it might be possible to scale Shishapangma without alerting the authorities. I checked the map. Accessing Shishapangma by trekking from the Nepali side into Tibet was certainly an option, but the plan was loaded with risk.

Firstly, the authorities were sure to be trailing my activities on social media. Also, my project had become a highly publicised endeavour where everyone was acutely aware of the limited timeframe available to me. Border patrol soldiers would be ready for my arrival and I wasn't so keen on being taken down, nor did I fancy causing a diplomatic incident. A captured, ex-Special Forces operator was likely to receive some interesting questions having trespassed into Chinese territory. Meanwhile, the risk to my teammates would be just as high; I didn't want their safety jeopardised for my cause. Inserting into Shishapangma was a job I needed to do alone.

In the end, I temporarily shelved the idea. My best hope was to find some way of convincing the Chinese and Tibetan authorities to reverse their decision. If I could apply a little political pressure, there was a chance I might score a permit, but I knew it was pointless to use the UK's diplomatic channels – the relationship between both nations was, at best, frosty. I was better off approaching the authorities via a Nepalese conduit; Nepal bordered on China and the two countries enjoyed a friendlier understanding.

Besides, my mission wasn't about representing one nation, or a single entity. I hadn't been climbing the 8,000-ers to boost the achievements of Great Britain or Nepal. Nor was I trying to enhance the profile of the UK Special Forces or the Gurkha regiment. (Though there was undeniably a knock-on effect to be had.) My goals went way beyond culture or caste, regiment or country. I was representing the efforts of the human race.

I called friends in Nepal and pulled strings; I contacted everyone I knew with the influence to arrange a meeting between any individuals with the power to help. To my relief, appointments were made with a number of government ministers, including the Home Secretary, the Minister for Tourism, the Tourism Board, the Nepalese Mountaineering Association and the Ministry of Defence, until, eventually, I was granted an audience with the former Nepalese prime minister, Madhav Kumar Nepal – a politician with considerable links to the Chinese government. *This was my chance.*

When I was ushered into his office, I didn't feel phased or overawed by his stature. My previous career had taught me about the protocols of meeting people in authority; I understood the finer details of respect, the importance of civility and cultural integration. I also appreciated the value of people's time. Mr Kumar was a busy man and there was a limited window in which to present my motivations for completing the project. I sensed he didn't have much room for small talk or niceties – but then neither did I.

I briefly summarised my motives behind the fourteen expeditions, first telling Mr Kumar about my work in enhancing the reputation of the Nepalese climbing community.

'I've wanted to put them back on the map,' I said.

Then I explained my attempts to raise awareness of some of the environmental issues affecting the 8,000-metre peaks.

'Isn't this an expedition the Nepali people can unite behind?'

Mr Kumar nodded silently. *Was this going well, or badly?* I couldn't tell.

'But I also want this to be an inspiring story for generations of people, no matter where they come from. This endeavour is for mankind. That's why I'm working so hard, every day, to push the story out. Mr Kumar, I want to prove the power of imagination. People have laughed at me, and made jokes, but I'm still going strong. If I can get that Chinese permit, nothing will stop me from finishing what I've started.'

Mr Kumar was smiling now. 'Nims, let me make some phone calls,' he said. 'I can't promise the Chinese will issue you with the paperwork, but I'll see what I can do.'

We shook hands; I felt positive. I had a hunch that if a figure with the profile of a former Nepali prime minister was to back my cause, then the Tibetan and Chinese authorities might soften their attitude. I needed all the positive PR I could get. At that time, very few people outside of the mountain-climbing community, or my social media bubble, were paying too much attention to what I'd achieved so far; in terms of newspapers and magazines, radio or TV shows, my efforts had passed by with very little fanfare, which was frustrating.

It's highly likely that if I'd been a climber from America, Great Britain, or France, then every outlet in the world would have noticed the effort. I was also a realist. Those media companies with the biggest global outreach were mainly owned by Western investors. The story of a climber from Chitwan and his attempts to scale the world's tallest mountains in record-breaking time didn't carry the same impact as a mountaineer working towards a similar goal from New York, Manchester, or Paris. Even though I was technically a British citizen, my nationality had positioned me under the radar of almost everyone.

On a lower level, though, the mission was still gathering momentum. My social media profile increased day by day, and more people were commenting on my photos and video clips, particularly once my dramatic picture of the Hillary Step went viral in May. (Though annoyingly, a lot of the media outlets that were ignoring my attempts to scale the fourteen 8,000-ers had conveniently forgotten to credit my work when using the photograph.)

Having left the military with nothing in the way of public relations experience, I'd somehow developed a knack for gathering hundreds of thousands of followers, which was mind-blowing on a personal level, but wasn't enough to translate into huge expedition funds. The messages I received were still inspirational: kids mailed me to say they'd written a story on the successful expeditions so far and drew pictures of my team in action. Others commented on my photos, or promised to organise an environmental awareness programme at school. One or two more donations had trickled in, too.

My project was fast becoming the people's project.

* * *

Time was on my side at least. I had all of August in which to fund the final phase and I managed to secure a branding deal with Osprey, a company that specialises in mountain-climbing and hiking equipment, and the IT company Silxo. Between them, they were able to cover nearly 75 per cent of Phase Three's logistical costs, and a little extra money was raised by a visit to the Nepali Mela UK, during an awareness drive for my work. This was a big deal. A mela was a festival attended by the Nepalese community living in the UK, and the 2019 event was being held at Kempton Park in August.

But my heart sank when an appearance was first suggested. Working at the mela required me to move from stall to stall, each one celebrating a different aspect of Nepali culture, while being introduced to various people of influence. Then I'd have to ask for money. The embarrassment was huge: I'd never begged for anything in my life and the idea dented my pride. I was an elite soldier and going from person to person, appealing for support and donations, felt like a step too far.

'This is not for me', I thought sadly.

But what other option did I have? The very idea of my expedition had been alien and unfamiliar from the outset. It made perfect sense that the funding process would seem alien and unfamiliar, too. I turned my attitude around.

Yeah, Nims, you're embarrassed. But that's your ego talking, which is nothing. Think of the endgame here. This isn't about how you feel. It's for the human race.

I moved through the stalls, shaking hands, making contacts and taking donations of £5, £10, and £15 until I was exhausted. My pride was dented, but there was also a relief in knowing I'd given 100 per cent, as I had done with those letters to Sir Richard Branson and a list of other business types, even though nobody had responded.

The strain upon me was building, though. For much of the year I had managed the project while dealing with booking agencies and mountain-climbing associations, but throughout the summer of 2019, I also had the Chinese and Tibetan authorities to worry about. Planning the logistical schedule for the three final climbs – Manaslu, Cho Oyu and Shishapangma – was a highly testing experience for me. Though Suchi helped with some of the administrative details, I was very much working alone. At times, the paperwork and planning felt as stressful as my summit push on Broad Peak, or a night spent rescuing those individuals on Kanchenjunga. I was emotionally drained.

Then Mum fell sick again.

Her condition was worsening. Throughout the mission, I'd used her spirit as inspiration; it had urged me on in turbulent moments and I was determined to see out the fourteen mountains with her in my heart. But I was placed in an impossible position. After climbing the fourteen 8,000-ers, I'd be free to work on other money-making projects with which to bring my parents together in Kathmandu. Now time was against me; that was becoming more obvious by the week. Mum had been hospitalised yet again, and according to the doctor, her chances of making it through another heart operation were slim.

'Ninety-nine per cent of people who have had this procedure at her age have died,' said the surgeon.

She was then placed on a ventilator, and fearing the worst, I called my family to Nepal. At that point, my brothers were living in England; my sister Anita flew all the way from Australia. There was a very real chance that we might have to say goodbye to Mum.

Although we hadn't always seen eye-to-eye on the issue of my personal ambitions, my family was everything to me, and before starting out on the first mission phase, I'd had a tattoo of all fourteen 8,000-ers etched into my back. Beginning at the top of my spine, the promontories of each mountain were spread out across my shoulder blades in an epic tapestry. The tattoo was a statement of everything I hoped to achieve and during its painful creation, the DNA of my parents and siblings, and Suchi, was mixed in with the inks. I wanted to carry everybody along with me for the journey, to places they would never have been able to experience for themselves ordinarily.

My parents were both in their seventies and immobile – there was no chance that either of them were going to see the entire Himalaya range spreading out beneath them from the top of Mount Everest, nor were they going to experience the Dutch Rib on Annapurna, or K2's Bottleneck. Neither Suchi or my siblings had shown any desire to climb with me either, but I wanted to take them to some of the world's most beautiful and inhospitable places, spiritually at least. They were joining me on a journey of the soul.

There was another reason for having their DNA enmeshed with my own: it acted as a sobering reminder, a voice of reason. The margins between making the right and wrong call in the mountains are fractional. I might take a risk and injure myself, or a member of my team. At times, summit fever could cause me to push myself too hard, breaking the thin line between bravery and stupidity. By having my family on my back, I was constantly reminded of the people I was fighting for.

So far, the gesture had kept me humble and safe, when I could quite easily have been reckless. If ever I felt like taking a chance, I remembered Mum and Dad: they needed me to care for them when my work was done. I recalled how my brothers had sent me to boarding school with their Gurkha wages. I owed my family everything; all that I'd achieved so far was for them.

Mum understood that she was my inspiration. She seemed to be hanging on to life, knowing her death would shatter the dream of completing the fourteen mountains. In Hinduism, when a parent dies, the family embark on thirteen days of grieving during which they mourn alone. Emotions are expressed freely, so that those left behind can get on with their lives and heal the huge sense of loss; the energy of mourning is turned into something productive.

If Mum passed, I'd have to lock myself away from everyone else to process, eating only once a day, and even then I would only be allowed to eat a few vegetables. While I wasn't a religious person, Mum was. I'd have happily performed the ritual for her memory, even though it would have meant closing down the last three expeditions of the year. But she was much stronger than we expected. Having undergone an invasive heart operation, she pulled through.

As I sat by Mum's bedside, holding her hand, I explained my plans for the coming month.

'I have only the three mountains to climb,' I said. 'Let me go do this.'

There was a nod and a smile. But she didn't have to say anything – I knew Mum was on my side. She always had been.

21

Epic

Finally, progress.

After a full month of paperwork and politicking, the right move was to press ahead with Phase Three as best I could, first by climbing Manaslu, and then by bouncing into Tibet shortly afterwards for Cho Oyu. Meanwhile, the Chinese and Tibetan authorities were apparently warming to the idea of granting me an all-important Shishapangma permit.

Seeing that nothing had been fully confirmed, I was hesitant to put too much faith in the news, so rather than taking my foot off the gas, I maintained a small campaign of public pressure, encouraging friends and social media followers to bombard both governments with emails and letters that pleaded with them to open the mountain. Until that moment arrived, I focused my attention on Manaslu, where I would need to take extra care given I was leading a party of clients. A Nepalese 8,000-er with a heavy kill rate, it was ranked highly on the world's deadliest list.

Stressing about alarming statistics of that kind wasn't my job, but once the first rotation cycles up to Camp 2 had started, it became hard not to feel a little overwhelmed, emotionally at least. I was so close to finishing the mission, but at the same time everything seemed off-kilter.

I'd become weighed down by the realities of Mum's health. The strain of completing the last mountains in the time and style I'd promised was a burden, too. And then there were the financial implications of my career choices – no immediate pension, no security. Not that I was going to let on to anyone about the true depth of my hurt. Whenever the other climbers at Manaslu asked about the workload, or mentioned some of the adventures I'd experienced so far, I held back from discussing the mental obstacles. Once again, I chose not to acknowledge my pain.

That attitude, while undeniably pressurised, would stand me in good stead. After a week or so of being at Manaslu, a rumour moved through the Base Camp: apparently Cho Oyu was closing down for the season earlier than expected and, for some reason, the Chinese authorities had decided everybody should evacuate the mountain by 1 October. I checked my calendar. *Shit!* There were only two weeks remaining in September and I was being left with very little choice but to interrupt my Manaslu expedition.

I did some calculations. It was probably within my timeframe to climb Cho Oyu and then return to Manaslu for the summit window with my clients. There was no way I wanted to let them down – I'd given them my word that I'd be climbing with them and I wasn't going to break the promise. The effort would be bloody huge, though; it increased the pressure and I had very little margin for error, so accompanied by Gesman, I packed up and travelled to Tibet, via helicopter and road. After a series of border checks, I was allowed in for what had suddenly become a panicked expedition.

On the ground, I worked tirelessly. My first job was to figure out how to make it to the top of Cho Oyu as quickly as possible, and I learned that the line-fixing team had reached only as high as Camp 2. Offering to chip in with setting the ropes at the higher camps, we then performed a load carry to Camp 1, dragging our oxygen cylinders, tent and rope with us, before returning to base where the real work could begin.

Because of the short window in which to climb Cho Oyu, a number of expeditions were gathering at the mountain and among them was my friend Mingma Sherpa, a mountaineer with fantastic connections, who was planning to visit the Base Camp with several high-ranking officials from the China Tibet Mountaineering Association (CTMA). He was also planning to climb Cho Oyu around the same time that we were. I guessed he might be able to grease the wheels for my permit application on Shishapangma, and between meetings on weather systems, trailblazing efforts and workloads, I moved between tents, trying to find him, only to discover that the news of his arrival had been a little off. I eventually learned that Mingma Sherpa hadn't yet arrived, but I left a message anyway, hoping to talk if he became available.

Elsewhere I sensed a weird mood gathering among some of the mountaineers. Jealousy was an emotion that occasionally built between expedition guiding companies. The market was quite small and competition for clients was fierce and cut-throat, especially on some of the tougher, more remote mountains. When a new presence joined the scene, their arrival sometimes created resentment among the existing organisations, especially if they were considered to be a serious player, with experienced personnel.

Thanks to my mission, Elite Himalayan Adventures – and with it the likes of Mingma, Gesman, Geljen, Dawa and the others – had begun to flash upon everyone's radar. Our reputation was set to increase even further if I managed to climb the final three 8,000-ers on my list. We were on the verge of becoming one of the scene's top dogs for sure, but not everyone was happy about our achievements. As I prepared myself for the summit push one afternoon, a friend from another guiding company arrived at my tent with some troubling gossip.

'Nims, the Nepalese climbing community is so proud of what you are achieving,' he said. 'Your name is out there and it's beautiful you're highlighting our capabilities . . .'

I knew the guy well, he was a nice bloke, but he didn't have to flatter me. *Something bad was coming.* I could tell.

My mate carried on. 'But be careful, because some people are very envious of what is happening. They talk. And it takes only one push for you to disappear from the mountain for good.'

That was it. *The warning.*

Somebody had made a comment, either as a joke, or as part of a more sinister plan to end me, and my friend was relaying the information. I wouldn't describe myself as a paranoid person, but I wasn't naive either. People had fatal accidents at high altitude all the time, even highly experienced mountaineers. If a stranger or two from the line-fixing party, rival guides, wanted to push Gesman and myself from the mountain while we weren't looking, what was to stop them from saying we'd slipped and fallen? The alibi was perfectly plausible. There would be very little evidence to support any suspicions it had been deliberate. The conspiracy was particularly watertight if a group working together executed the plan, rather than a couple of rogue individuals.

Emotionally, the news didn't dent me. So, a couple of people had become jealous and were shooting their mouths off around the camp. *Who really cared?* But it was a hard reminder that not everyone could be trusted. In situations where faith between climbers was vital – such as a crew fixing lines in sketchy conditions – that was troubling. I asked my friend to act as an extra pair of eyes and ears for me during the expedition and when our work later began from Camp 2, I scooped up a long loop of rope and trailblazed for four hundred metres in one push.

Boom! Boom! Boom! I strode forward. I wasn't hoping to prove a point or wear the others out. But if people were feeling a little sore about the successes of Elite Himalayan Adventures, it felt important to show them why our reputation was strengthening. With Gesman, I headed to the top on 23 September. Our hard graft and speed would do the talking for us.

* * *

Having ticked Cho Oyu off the list unscathed, there was no time to celebrate. Returning to Manaslu as quickly as possible was imperative. My weather window was closing and so I packed up and left. If the mission as a whole was a marathon, I'd found myself at the tricky 22-mile mark, where the remaining distance seemed as daunting as anything that had gone before, but only because the diplomatic hurdles were so huge. I knew that once I'd climbed Manaslu, around four days after scaling Cho Oyu, I'd have ticked off thirteen of the fourteen 8,000-ers, but Shishapangma still seemed so out of reach, despite my lobbying efforts.

Could I finish what I'd started?

So many people were watching now. Many of them had initially dismissed my chances of making it this far. A lot of expert climbers had doubted I'd even last through Pakistan, so my efforts throughout 2019, even without Shishapangma, could still be regarded as considerable. The work of the

Nepalese climbers alongside me had also gathered plenty of attention, so in that respect, the work had already been a success. I had to do only three things from then on.

The first required me to finish Manaslu and the final mountain, hopefully Shishapangma, possibly Dhaulagiri and Everest, before bringing Mum and Dad together under the same roof once more as the second. The third was to make the world pay attention to some of the damage we'd been inflicting upon the environment. And with the eyes of the climbing community upon me, I decided that Manaslu wasn't simply a peak to be crossed off the list; it felt like a platform.

I climbed to the very top and made my point.

'Today is the 27th of September,' I said, as Gesman filmed me. 'Here I am on the summit of Manaslu. We're not going to talk about Project Possible, but what I am going to talk about from the summit [is the environment]. For the last decade, it's pretty obvious there has been a huge, significant change in terms of global warming. There is a huge change in the melting of the ice. The Khumbu Icefall on Everest: every day the glacier is melting, it's getting thinner, and smaller and smaller. The earth is our home. We should be more serious about it, more cautious, more focused about how we look after our planet. At the end of the day, if this one doesn't exist, we don't exist.'

Nothing about my speech was really considered in advance. The words came from the heart, but they were the purest reflection of what I felt for the world. As far as I was concerned, the biggest challenge faced by humankind in the coming decade or two had to be the problem of climate change, but fixing it required a course correction of massive proportions. All of us were insignificant specks on a huge planet, but in truth, the actions of an individual carried the potential to overcome the most insurmountable of problems.

If I could climb the Death Zone mountains in seven months – give or take the final peak – then what was to stop another individual from finding, and climbing, their personal Everest in the field of environmental science, alternative energy, or climate action? My efforts had proved that everyone had the potential to go way beyond what was considered humanly achievable. It was meant to stand as a glimmer of hope. Now I wanted others to use it for their own challenges and projects in a show of positive action. If my work created a spark for change, however small, I'd be happy.

* * *

And then Shishapangma was on.

The why and when of how it came to be were a dizzying blur of phone calls, emails and meetings, which are tricky to recall in full, but in the end it took just one effort to tip the balance in my favour. *Mingma Sherpa*. The man I'd so nearly liaised with at Cho Oyu's base camp had learned of my efforts and was impressed by my keenness to explore every available avenue to the final peak. In Tibet and Nepal, humility went a long way.

Seeing as I'd previously been rejected by the mountain-climbing authorities such as the Chinese Mountaineering Association (CMA), and they were yet to officially backtrack on their decision, it would have been in my rights to sulk and complain. Instead, I'd sought to reconnect with them via Mingma Sherpa, in a humble way, because I was a firm believer in the equality of friendship: I reckoned that everyone should be treated the same unless they behaved in a manner that suggested otherwise. When people took the piss out of me, I put them back in their shoes; if somebody showed kindness, I returned the gesture and everybody had the chance for redemption. Holding grudges against figures of authority because of a group decision didn't fit with my ideals.

The news of my approved permit first filtered back to me having returned to Manaslu's base camp. A well-connected climber claimed to have heard that my application to climb Shishapangma was in the bag. 'Nimsdai, it's happening,' he said, excitedly. The other lads from the team began talking about a celebration beer, but I struggled to share in their enthusiasm. I couldn't shake the fear that this was a false dawn.

'I need to see the paperwork before I get too excited,' I thought.

I didn't have to wait too long. The CTMA got in touch; they wanted to chat and the conversation was positive. Having taken into account the scale of my ambitious project, it was decided to open up Shishapangma for a brief time so I could finish the mission. I puffed out a sigh of relief. After all the stressing, a finish line was in sight.

There was one catch, however. Mingma Sherpa explained that in order to access the mountain, he would have to travel with me to Base Camp – it was a condition from the CTMA. At first, I felt unsure. I worried it might be an attempt to muscle in on my hard work, or perhaps a way for the CTMA to grab a slice of the limelight for themselves. In the end, I parked my concerns and remembered the potentially positive impact of a successfully executed mission.

If Mingma Sherpa coming with us to Base Camp was the difference between completing the fourteen mountains and missing out at the very end, then I was happy to have an extra body in the camp. He would, at the very least, provide some additional manpower for the team, though in hindsight, I needn't have fretted too much about his involvement. Mingma

Sherpa quickly proved himself an asset. He acted as a drinking buddy, an expedition resource, and a fixer for some of the more complicated aspects of the project. It turned out that Mingma Sherpa was about the most connected individual in Tibet.

Despite his arrival, pressure still arrived from all angles. Sponsors called, wanting to know why I hadn't posted more photographs to my social media accounts, or attached a certain hashtag. My wisdom tooth was pounding yet again. But the most pressing issue seemed to be the mountain's officious liaison manager. As we checked the weather and figured out the best date to climb, he stepped in with an ominous warning.

'The mountain is too dangerous,' he said. 'The weather is so bad.'

He was right; the snow was coming down hard, but I'd climbed in worse conditions. At first, I tried to make a joke. 'No worries, brother,' I said, clapping him on the shoulder. 'I am the guru of risk assessment!'

The liaison manager shook his head. 'Sorry, but no,' he said. 'If anything happens to you, it will be my responsibility. And there's an avalanche problem.'

'Wow,' I thought. 'This dude is proving to be hard work.'

In the end, I bent him with sheer force. I explained how I'd fixed the lines at K2 when nobody else had been willing to climb. There was a mention of my efforts for the G200E in 2017, when the entire project had hung in the balance. Added to that, I had conducted nineteen successful 8,000-metre expeditions in total; thirteen of them had been undertaken in 2019 and nobody had died on the mountain under my leadership, let alone lost any fingers or toes.

As I explained my position, it felt hard to keep my

frustrations under control, but I knew that to shout was to lose, and to relinquish control of my emotions at such a pivotal time might prove costly further down the line. Eventually, the liaison officer backed down; the final hurdle was in sight. On the eve of the summit push, I sat at the foot of Shishapangma and gathered my thoughts.

'Nims, take it easy,' I said to myself. 'You are here now; you only have to stay alive. Don't take any unnecessary risks unless you have to. Control everything. Stay calm; stay cool. The mission isn't done unless you come back home alive.'

I looked to Shishapangma's peak. Cloud had swept in, an ominous rumble of thunder was echoing through the valley below, and as I watched, it was impossible not to be awed by the size and scale of what lay ahead. No matter the weather raging around it, a mountain like Shishapangma always stayed solid. It never buckled or broke, and instead seemed impervious to the harsh elements swirling around its mass. *I wanted to be like that.*

I knew it was useless to judge Shishapangma's strengths and weaknesses at that point, because the giant peak ahead wasn't going to judge *me*. Instead there was a rush of inspiration. If I could channel the mountain's spirit, becoming bulletproof to pain, stress and fear, then nothing could stop me. Before I rested up for the night, I asked Shishapangma a final question, or two.

OK, will you let me do this?
Can I? Or can I not?
The answer blew in with the snow.

* * *

The weather on the way up was horrific. It was as if the mountain had hoped to deny me the final climb, or at least discover if I was truly worthy of finishing off the job. Winds of 90 kilometres per hour blasted Mingma David, Geljen, and myself as we trudged up the mountain, through the lower camps, fixing the lines and anchors along the way, but nothing could hold me back, though an avalanche came bloody close. We had been working our way to Camp 1 and for a few moments, as the team rested, I took the drone from my rucksack. Climbing Shishapangma was undeniably a big deal. As an ending to the mission it promised to be emotional and I hoped to capture as much of the final expedition on film as possible. When the winds settled down a little, I sent the drone into the air, filming the team as they stepped up the mountain in a short line.

Unexpectedly, the ground seemed to tremble. I was probably around five or ten minutes behind the others, and when I looked up, I saw a slab of snow had cracked below their position on the line. Slowly it was shearing away from the mountain. What had triggered the avalanche was unclear, but as it jolted and began its collapse down Shishapangma's side, I became an accidental passenger. In effect, I was surfing the snow and there was no point in fighting its power.

I looked up, allowing the mountain gods to decide my fate as I glided across the slope, the ground breaking up around me. In an instant, the powder had swallowed my body whole and then puked me up, and as I prepared to be pulled under and smothered for good, the world came to a standstill. I looked down. The avalanche was billowing away below me, dissipating on the rocks and puffing up a white mushroom cloud. But the snow I'd been standing on had somehow come to a stop. The deities had spared my life.

'I can't believe it, brother,' I laughed. 'You've come all this way and nearly died on the last expedition.'

The drone stayed in the bag from then on.

Ever since my fall in Pakistan, my confidence had returned in increments. After wobbling at the top of Gasherbrum I, surviving the night lower down the mountain in grisly conditions had helped. Fixing the last of the lines on K2, when nearly two hundred other climbers had given up on the idea, was a psychological boost too. The pain of scaling Broad Peak while feeling physically destroyed only underlined my fortitude when handling sketchy circumstances.

There was no doubt I'd suffered a mental blow on Nanga Parbat, but I'd managed to heal and grow from it, and as I worked my way back to the line where Mingma and Geljen were waiting, I felt surprised that the emotional aftershocks of yet another near-death experience were not impacting upon me. But by that point, having climbed nearly fourteen 8,000-ers in such a short time, my crampons seemed fused to my body; my ice axe was an extra limb. By that stage in the mission, I often felt a little exposed whenever I was separated from those pieces of kit, as I had done on the very rare occasions I'd been without my weapon in a war.

For the push to Shishapangma's summit, we took a new line to the top, feeling confident enough to climb alpine-style. The gradient was fairly mellow and the weather seemed so much calmer as we moved past Camp 2. When the clouds cleared around us, the winds seemed to die away and everything became peaceful. I was calm, too. The last half of the climb on Shishapangma turned into a slow and steady trek, and though there was little in the way of technical climbing required, emotionally the effort felt heavy as I stepped to the peak. *It was done.*

Everything I had achieved up until that moment started to dawn on me. I'd silenced the doubters by climbing the fourteen highest mountains in the world in six months and six days. I'd shown what was achievable with imagination and a determined spirit, while shining a light on some of the challenges being faced by the planet and its people.

I'd made the impossible possible.

In the distance I could see Everest, the place where it all began, and the feelings I'd bottled up for so long rushed at me at once: pride, happiness and love. I thought of Suchi, and my friends and family. Most of all I thought of Mum and Dad. Tears rolled down my cheeks.

In a way, the mission had been a process of discovery – not only on the mountains I'd been exploring, but personally too. By climbing the fourteen 8,000-ers, I was trying to figure out who the hell I was; I wanted to know how far in the distance my physical and emotional limits had been set.

I'd long known that I possessed an unusual drive. When I was a kid at school, I worked hard to be the best runner in my district. Later, having realised it was regarded as the honourable thing to become a Gurkha soldier, I put everything into joining their ranks. But then came the realisation that simply serving wasn't enough and I had to go even higher. Once I learned about the work carried out by the British Special Forces, and the gruelling effort required when joining their ranks, I didn't rest until I'd been accepted.

Where that desire actually came from, I'm not sure, but it was apparent from an early age. As a small boy in Chitwan, I'd turn over rocks for hours at a time in a stream, in search of crabs and prawns, and I wouldn't quit until I'd peeked under every single one, no matter the time or effort required to finish the job. Fast-forward thirty years and nothing much had changed. My spirit was still the same, only the parameters had altered, and rather than exploring the local river, I was climbing across the Death Zone. With that achievement almost nailed, I was already starting to imagine past it.

I wanted more. *But where could I go next?*

Standing on the peak of Shishapangma, I took in the view, feeling the bitter cold on my face. Then I called home and told Mum of what I'd achieved, and where I planned to go next.

'I've done it!' I shouted into the phone. 'And I'm OK.'

The line was crackling, but I could just make out her laughter.

'Get home safe, son,' she said. 'I love you.'

Epilogue

At the Peak

The enormity of what I'd accomplished didn't hit me for days. The following morning, hung over, I travelled back across the border in Nepal, where a hero's welcome was waiting for myself and the team – *the Special Forces of high-altitude mountaineering*. The word had spread about my record-breaking achievements.

Not only had I managed to climb the world's fourteen highest peaks, shattering the world record by over seven years, but I'd also posted the fastest time for climbing from the summit of Everest to Lhotse and then Makalu. The Pakistan peaks had been nailed in twenty-three days, and I'd climbed the five highest mountains of Everest, K2, Kanchenjunga, Lhotse and Makalu in seventy days, having announced my ambition to do it in eighty. Additionally, I'd climbed the most 8,000 metres peaks in a single season (spring), by topping Annapurna, Dhaulagiri, Kanchenjunga, Everest, Lhotse and Makalu in thirty one days. The mission was an overwhelming success. It had blown minds.

I called up Mum again. A party was being arranged in Kathmandu and despite her condition, the doctors assured me that she was well enough to travel, so I suggested she join me for a celebratory helicopter ride. At first, she wasn't so sure. I told her how important she was to me, and how the mission had been the biggest achievement of my life.

'I want you to be a part of it,' I said.

'Yes, I want to come,' she said, eventually.

When we arrived at the Kathmandu Tribhuvan Airport, the scene was incredible. A marching band was playing, dozens of photographers and journalists had arrived and a huge crowd had circled the airport. I couldn't quite get my head around it. At that point, I think Mum had considered my climbing as a crazy hobby, a risky project that filled me with joy. Not for one minute did she think that my work was being followed by the wider world, not on a big scale anyway, but having seen the crowds and the fanfare surrounding my successes, the penny dropped.

As the rotary blades on the chopper slowed above us, a white Range Rover pulled around with the flags of Great Britain and Nepal fixed to the bonnet. The British ambassador to Nepal, Richard Morris, stepped out and once we'd shaken hands, he thanked me for my efforts.

'We're so proud of you,' he said. 'What you've achieved is unbelievable.'

When we were eventually driven through the city to a reception, the crowds followed us everywhere.

But there was still plenty of work to be done.

In the months after the fourteen mountains had been completed, I did everything in my power to bring Mum and Dad together. A loan was secured with a bank in Nepal and I borrowed money from my family. Elsewhere, Elite Himalayan Adventures ran a number of successful expeditions. Following in the wake of my success at 8,000 metres, these guiding services were in high demand, as were my motivational speaking performances, and with the financial returns I found a nice house in Kathmandu that would work for both my parents.

Excited about them moving in, we completed the paperwork at the start of 2020 and worked towards moving Dad out of the old house in Chitwan and into the new family home. On 25 February, Suchi and I flew to Nepal to bring them together, but when we landed, the phone rang. *We were too late*. Mum had passed away a couple of hours earlier and my heart broke – everything I'd achieved was inspired by her spirit.

Through the hurt of the Hindu mourning ceremony I was able to reflect and grow, and having emerged thirteen days later, I looked towards the positives, turning grief into a powerful energy. Because of the love and support of my family, I'd been able to push myself to the absolute limit, proving to the world that it was possible to surpass any expectations previously set by humankind.

Meanwhile, a lot of people had taken the piss out of my ambitions at the very beginning, but once my mission was executed, I learned that a lot of elite mountaineers were tackling several 8,000-ers a year rather than only one or two. The boundaries for what was considered achievable had expanded and I took a lot of pride from that.

It was great to know that the rep of the Nepalese Sherpa guide had also been amplified. The lads I'd climbed with were being placed on a pedestal. They had come to be regarded as some of the world's best climbers, and rightly so: we worked as a relatively small expedition unit, in teams of three, four or five, but we moved with the power of ten bulls and the heart of one hundred men. They deserved all the spoils awaiting them and as a tribute to the hard work, I gave our new line over Shishapangma a name: The Project Possible Route.

Most of all I realised that smashing the fourteen peaks was a launch pad. I needed more . . . *but what?*

The mountains are there to be scaled; I have only to pick which ones to take on and the style in which I want to do them. There are challenges to be conquered based on speed, style and physical effort – there are no limits to the test I might set myself. The chances I might be killed while trying to attempt those missions are certainly higher than anything I've risked before, but that is the whole point: I have to push my limits to the max. Sitting tight, waiting it out and living in the past, has never been my thing.

I want to be at the world's highest point again, knowing it might slip out from underneath me at any moment.

Because that is the only way to live – and to die.

Appendix One

Lessons from the Death Zone

1. *Leadership isn't always about what* you *want.*

Having made it to Base Camp at Dhaulagiri during phase one of the mission, it was obvious that some of the lads in my team were struggling. Physically they were fucked; their morale was broken. Though I felt absolutely fine, having just climbed Annapurna and conducted a stressful search and rescue mission, I knew it wasn't the smartest move to press on ahead regardless, pushing the others to their limits. Instead, I figured out what was best for the team.

It's easy to work to your own pace in a group setting, especially if you're the fastest or strongest in the pack, but the people around you will soon lose faith. They'll regard you as selfish, overly ambitious and a bit of a dick. The general consensus will be that you don't give a fuck about anyone else and the efforts of the team will fade away. When you need your colleagues to step up again, they won't bother.

Rather than pissing people off in that situation, put yourself in their shoes. Figure out how you can compromise: is it possible to work in a way that benefits everybody? In this case, I took the team for a little rest and recovery. Yeah, we had to work through some terrible conditions a few days later as a consequence, but that one action told the team that the mission wasn't only about me.

As a result, they broke their backs to work for the cause over the next six months.

2. *The little things count most on the big mountains.*

Over the years, I've developed some techniques for lightening my workload when climbing 8,000-ers and one of the most important of these involves my breathing. Whenever I'm at high altitude I wear a buff – it protects my face from the sun and the biting cold – but it's hard to wear one without fogging up my goggles or sunglasses with the condensation from my breath.

To get over that, I changed the way I inhale and exhale. Pursing my lips, I take air in through my nose and then blow down, away from the goggles. The cold air comes in through the buff, warming it slightly, which protects my lungs from failing in the sub-zero temperatures. It might sound like a minor detail, but that one technique saves my body from hypothermia, because the air I'm taking in is not as cold. It also protects my fingers from frostbite, because I don't have to take off my gloves to get to my cleaning cloth. (All of which is bloody exhausting above 8,000 metres, by the way.)

Taking care of the little things feeds into the bigger ambition. For you, that might mean knowing the finer details of a contract so you can succeed in a deal at work, or learning why buying the right running shoes for a 10K race can stop you from getting blisters. Much in the same way that a breathing technique, knowing exactly where my energy gels are, or keeping my ice axe within reach, bombproofs me from stress on an 8,000-er.

3. Never underestimate the challenge ahead.

I first learned about the dangers associated with underestimating a climb in 2015, but those lessons were taken the bloody hard way. As an intermediate mountaineer still cutting my teeth, I climbed Aconcagua in the Argentine stretch of the Andes. The mountain is one of the Seven Summits, a peak with a serious reputation, and while not quite an 8,000-er, it is still a challenging test of high altitude at 6,961 metres.

Mountaineers with ambitions of working in the Death Zone often use Aconcagua as an early test of their mettle, and given it is a trek from bottom to top, and nothing is needed in the way of rope skills when working to the summit, a lot of people figure it to be a fairly benign soul.

That was my attitude anyway. Having flicked through a few climbing guides and magazines, and stared at a tonne of photographs featuring kids and old couples climbing to Aconcagua's peak, my attitude was a little dismissive. *How hard can it be?* Friends I'd made during my expeditions to Dhaulagiri and Louche East figured Aconcagua would be a breeze for me.

'You'll smash it,' said one. 'Trek to Base Camp in a day. Then take a day or two to summit and head back. No dramas.'

I was so convinced of my ability, and Aconcagua's apparently gentle temperament, that I didn't bother packing a summit suit for my expedition. I was travelling during the summer months, at the start of the year when the weather is fairly warm in the southern hemisphere. As far as kit went, I think I packed some hiking trousers, a waterproof coat, and a pair of mountain boots. But once I entered the national park at Penitentes, snow started to fall.

Aconcagua is a remote mountain, it took a trek of eleven hours to reach Base Camp, and given I was travelling solo, I had to use my map and compass to get there, because the paths normally marking the route up were smothered by the heavy drifts. When I eventually arrived at Base Camp and checked in with the other climbers on the mountain, the mood was gloomy. A number of people had made a push for the summit, but had been turned around by the elements.

'It's so dangerous up there,' said a friend from the International Federation of Mountain Guides. 'The avalanche risk is high and the weather is seriously cold.'

I figured I knew better. Having snapped up some boots from another climber, a pair far sturdier than the ones I'd brought along, and also borrowed a down jacket, I pushed to the top, the weather closing in tightly around me. What should have been a fairly straightforward trek became as gruelling as my first-ever climb on an 8,000er, and only 300 metres from the peak, I came close to giving up.

My vision blurred. Having climbed without oxygen, and with altitude sickness quickly kicking in, I felt close to passing out. All my hopes of becoming an elite climber seemed to hang in the balance. *Fucking hell, Nims, if you can't make it to the top here, how can you expect to take on Everest?* I was shaken.

I took a sip from my Thermos flask and opened up a chocolate bar.

You have the speed to climb super quickly. Use it.

Pushing on to the summit, I couldn't wait to turn around, having learned another lesson at high altitude: *Never underestimate the mountain you're about to climb – no matter how easy other people think it might be.*

And another: *Be confident, but show respect.*

From then on, I did my due diligence on every expedition. I readied myself for the challenges ahead and told myself that any mountain had the potential to be my last, if I didn't handle it with care. As a reminder of the pitfalls of what can happen when you let your guard down, I briefly underestimated Gasherbrum I during phase two of the mission and it kicked me in the arse.

Whatever you're doing, treat your challenge with respect. You won't suffer any nasty surprises that way.

4. *Hope is God.*

Brother, you're not going to get to your dream by just fantasising about it. But if you make it your ultimate goal, or god, and give yourself to it entirely, there's a good chance it might come your way.

As a kid, I got so pissed off at being beaten by a runner from another school in the district champs that I started getting up in the middle of the night in secret training sessions. I took that same attitude into the Gurkhas. If we were required to run thirty kilometres in training, I'd tack another twenty kilometres on at the end to push myself even harder, because I knew I wanted to make it into the Special Forces. The job had become my church and I invested all my efforts into it.

So rather than thinking, praying and waiting for your next project or challenge (and not doing it), commit to serious action instead.

5. *A person's true nature shows up*
in life-or-death situations.

A lot of soldiers talk the talk. On the base they act like big heroes, happy to gob off about gunfights that they may, or may not, have been involved in. But the minute it kicks off for real, when bullets start flying and people are getting shot around them, they hide in the corner or panic.

The same attitude can be found on the mountain. At Base Camp, when the weather is sunny and warm, climbers take selfies and mess around, talking about how they're going to conquer the mountain. Once the bad weather whips in, and it becomes important to stay focused and super-disciplined, they freak out. Then their true personality emerges: they act self-ishly, their work rate slacks off, and the safety of others is sometimes disregarded.

It's possible to learn a lot about someone when the chips are down.

6. *Turn a nightmare situation into something positive.*

During my first climbs of Everest, Lhotse and Makalu, my oxygen was stolen on the mountain. I'd asked for cylinders to be left at a number of camps, but as I arrived at each one, it became apparent that the lot of them had been swiped. At first I was furious, which was a very understandable reaction given the circumstances, but it was important to stay calm. Losing it would cause me to waste energy and maybe succumb to HACE in the process. As I explained in Lesson 2, the little things count most on the big mountains. A negative response, like a minor tantrum, would only cost me dearly later in the expedition.

I calmed down and mentally turned the situation around. Rather than stewing in my own anger, I told myself that the air had gone to someone who needed it more than me.

'Maybe someone had severe altitude sickness and needed my cylinders to save themselves,' I told myself, knowing it probably wasn't true. 'In which case, fair enough.'

Yeah, this was a lie in some ways – though it was a very different one to the type discussed in Lesson 8. However, it was a vital self-defence mechanism. If I'd sulked and moaned about the circumstances surrounding my missing air, I would have wasted vital energy, when I should have been concentrating on the mission ahead.

Thinking positively is the only way to survive at 8,000 metres. Nobody cheats death by wallowing in self-pity.

7. *Give 100 per cent to the now . . .*

. . . because it's all you've got.

There were moments on Selection when a programme of gruelling work was laid out ahead of me: weeks of drills, marches and exercises in unpleasant conditions, where I'd have to push myself to breaking point. It would have been easy to feel overwhelmed by the intimidating workload, or stressed that day one's thirty-mile run might burn me out for an even longer run on day two. Instead I gave everything to the job in hand and dealt with tomorrow when tomorrow came around. It was the only way to handle an intimidating challenge.

The same attitude applied to my mission to climb the fourteen Death Zone peaks. While working across a mountain, I tried my best not to think about the following expedition, because I knew I might not make it if I took my eye off the adversary ahead. To be focused on Broad Peak while scaling K2 would cause me to lose focus. And keeping energy in reserve was pointless. I had to give the day my all, because I knew the consequences if I didn't.

Tomorrow might not happen.

8. *Never lie. Never make excuses.*

There were times when I could have cut corners on the mountain. Following the G200E in 2017, when Nishal offered me a helicopter ride from Namche Bazaar to Makalu's Camp 2, I turned him down. With his help I'd have become the first person to climb Everest twice, Lhotse and Makalu in a single climbing season, but it wouldn't have been done properly. Sure, nobody on the planet would have known, apart from Nishal. But I'd have to live with the knowledge for the rest of my life.

It's easy to make excuses. You might be trying to give up smoking or alcohol. A sneaky beer, or a puff on a cigarette, is easy to shrug off as one of those things. *But it's not one of those things.* By lying to yourself, you're only consigning your goals to failure. Lying, or making excuses for your sloppy actions, means you've broken a promise to yourself. Once you do that, you'll fuck up, over and over again.

For example, it would have been quite easy for me to give up on K2, because so many people had tried, and failed to climb. Had I abandoned the project because of a lack of funding, nobody would have blamed me, but there was no way I was going to let myself off the hook with a convenient get-out clause.

If I say that I'm going to run for an hour, I'll run for a full hour. If I plan to do three hundred push-ups in a training session, I won't quit until I've done them all. Because brushing off the effort means letting myself down and I don't want to have to live with that.

And neither should you.

Appendix Two

Fourteen Mountains: The Schedule

COUNTRY	SUMMITED	PHASE	PEAK	HEIGHT (METRES)
Nepal	23/4/2019	I	Annapurna I	8091
Nepal	12/5/2019	I	Dhaulagiri I	8167
Nepal	15/5/2019	I	Kanchenjunga	8586
Nepal	22/5/2019	I	Everest	8848
Nepal	22/5/2019	I	Lhotse	8516
Nepal	24/5/2019	I	Makalu	8485
Pakistan	3/7/2019	2	Nanga Parbat	8125
Pakistan	15/7/2019	2	Gasherbrum I	8080
Pakistan	18/7/2019	2	Gasherbrum II	8034
Pakistan	24/7/2019	2	K2	8611
Pakistan	26/7/2019	2	Broad Peak	8051
Tibet	23/9/2019	3	Cho Oyu	8201
Nepal	27/9/2019	3	Manaslu	8163
Tibet	29/10/2019	3	Shishapangma	8027

Appendix Three
The World Records

Fastest time to climb all fourteen mountains above 8,000 metres.
Six months, six days.

Fastest time from summit of Everest to summit of Lhotse and summit of Makalu.
Forty-eight hours and thirty minutes.

Fastest time to climb the top five highest mountains in the world: Kanchenjunga, Everest, Lhotse, Makalu and K2.
Seventy days.

Fastest time to climb all five 8,000-ers of Pakistan: K2, Nanga Parbat, Broad Peak, GI and GII.
Twenty-three days.

Most 8,000-metre peaks (six) during a single season (spring): Annapurna, Dhaulagiri, Kanchenjunga, Everest, Lhotse and Makalu.
Thirty-one days.

Acknowledgements

When writing a book of this kind, it's hard to remember all the people who helped me to make Project Possible a reality, so I'll do my best here. Hopefully, I won't miss anybody out.

Without the support of my expedition sponsors, Project Possible would never have happened. At the top of the thank you list stands Bremont, who have made a series of Project Possible watches (which is available to buy on their website) and helped me over the financial hurdles that threatened to stop my dream from becoming reality. A salute also goes out to SILXO, Osprey, Ant Middleton, DIGI2AL, Hama Steel, Summit Oxygen, OMNIRISC, The Royal Hotel, Intergage, AD Construction Group, Branding Science, AMTC Group, Everence, Thrudark, Kenya Air, KGH Group, Marriott Kathmandu and Premier Insurance.

Logistical support for the mission was provided by Elite Himalayan Adventures, Seven Summit Treks and Climbalaya. Although the majority of filming above base camp was done by myself and my team, some assistance for the forthcoming movie of my story arrived courtesy of Sagar Gurung, Alit Gurung and Sandro Gromen-Hayes, who also joined me at K2 Base Camp and climbed with me on Manaslu. And I'd like to thank everyone working hard to put the hours of footage together at Noah Media Group, especially Torquil Jones and Barry, and thanks also to Mark Webber for the introduction. But help on the mission also arrived from the SBSA and Ambassador Durga Subedi, and from so many key figures from Nepal: the Nepal Tourism Board, former Prime Minister of Nepal Madhav Kumar Nepal, Deputy Defence Minister of Nepal Ishwar Pokhrel, IGP Sailendra Khanal and Sonam Sherpa of the Yeti Group. A big thanks has to go to Brigadier Dan Reeves for all his help.

In the UK, an administration team helped me to figure out a way of managing my PR, and all the other logistical issues that kick in while climbing to the top of an 8,000er. Most of all this includes my supportive wife Suchi, plus Project Possible's helpers: Wendy Faux, Steve and Tiffany Curran, Luke Hill and Kishore Rana. Thanks also to all the clients that joined me on Annapurna (Hakon Asvang and Rupert Jones-Warner), Nanga Parbat (Stefi Troguet) and Manaslu (Steve Davis, Amy McCulloch, Glenn McCrory, Deeya Pun and Stefi Troguet), plus everyone who donated to the mission on GoFundMe from all over the world, and supported the project by picking up merchandise. There were many organisations that helped me along the way, and I'm extremely appreciative of all of them, but my gratitude goes out to the Nepali climbing community, my Sherpa brothers, and the Gurkha and Nepalese communities: Myagdi Organisation UK, Madat Shamuha, Magar Association UK Friendly Brothers Dana Serophero Community UK, Pun Magar Samaj UK, Pun Magar Society HK, Pelkachour and Chimeki Gaule Samaj UK, Tamu Pye Lhu Sangh UK and the Maidstone Gurkha Nepalese Community.

My team from 2017 world record-breaking climbs of Everest, Lhotse and Makalu also deserve a mention: Lakpa Sherpa,

Acknowledgements

Jangbu Sherpa, Halung Dorchi Sherpa and Mingma Dorchi Sherpa.

Without my family, none of this would have happened. Mum and Dad indulged my adventurous spirit as a kid and allowed me to follow my heart to the mountains after I'd promised to bring them together under one roof. My brothers, Kamal, Jit and Ganga and my sister Anita encouraged me to follow the noble life into the Gurkhas and there's a long list of friends, to name check, in and out of the military: Staz, Louis, Paul Daubner, Gaz Banford, Lewis Phillips, CP Limbu, Chris Sylvan, Ramesh Silwal, Khadka Gurung, Subash Rai, Govinda Rana, Thaneswar Gurangai, Peter Cunningham, Shrinkhala Khatiwada, Dan, Bijay Limbu, Mira Acharya, Stuart Higgins, Phil Macey, Rupert Swallow, Al Mack, Greg Williams, Mingma Sherpa, Danny Rai, Dhan Chand, Shep, Tashi Sherpa, Sobhit Gauchan and Gulam.

Finally this book wouldn't have happened without the hard work of everyone at Hodder & Stoughton, especially Rupert Lancaster, Cameron Myers, Caitriona Horne and Rebecca Mundy. Thanks to my agents at The Blair Partnership, Neil Blair and Rory Scarfe. Finally, I would like to thank my friend and brother, Matt Allen for putting his heart and mind into capturing my story. Without his help (from his heart) the book wasn't possible.

Nirmal Purja, 2020

303

Picture Acknowledgements

The author and publisher would like to thank the following copyright-holders for permission to reproduce images in this book:

Ganga Bahadur Purja: 1, 2 (top left). Unknown photographer: 2 (top right, bottom). Sherpa Porter, name unknown: 3, 5 (bottom). Pasang Sherpa: 4 (top, middle), 5 (middle). Alun Richardson: 4 (bottom), 5 (top). Sherpa G200E fixing team, name unknown: 6. Nirmal Purja: 7 (top). Nirmal Purja/Project Possible: 7 (middle, bottom), 9 (top, middle), 10 (middle), 14 (top), 16 (bottom). Geljen Sherpa/Project Possible: 8 (top), 10 (bottom), 11 (bottom). Gesman Tamang/Project Possible: 8 (bottom), 14 (bottom). Lakpa Dendi Sherpa/Project Possible: 9 (bottom), 13 bottom. Sonam Sherpa/ Project Possible: 10 (top). Mingma David Sherpa/Project Possible: 11 (top), 12, 16 (top). Sandro Gromen-Hayes/Project Possible: 13 (top), 14 (middle), 15.

The author and publisher have made all reasonable efforts to contact copyright-holders for permission and apologise for any omissions or errors in the form of credits given. Corrections may be made to future printings.

An invitation from the publisher

Join us at www.hodder.co.uk, or follow us
on Twitter @hodderbooks to be a part of
our community of people who love the very
best in books and reading.

Whether you want to discover more about a book
or an author, watch trailers and interviews, have the
chance to win early limited editions, or simply browse
our expert readers' selection of the very best books,
we think you'll find what you're looking for.

And if you don't, that's the place to tell us what's missing.

We love what we do, and we'd love you to be a part of it.

www.hodder.co.uk

@hodderbooks

HodderBooks

HodderBooks